"Kudos to Marjorie Lindner Gunnoe f(... cal science and Christian belief. By vie ... through the lens of theology, she illuminates who we are—as embodied, purposeful, moral, accountable children of God. With her lucid prose, informative storytelling, and blend of curiosity and conviction, Gunnoe enlarges our human understanding and informs our faith."

David G. Myers, professor of psychology at Hope College and coauthor of *Psychology* and *Psychology Through the Eyes of Faith*

"Gunnoe adroitly demonstrates how modern psychology can constructively inform Christian reflection on the nature of human life and development. I am especially appreciative of the way that her work gives impetus to reconsidering the dark and often destructive depictions of human nature and original sin rooted in the theology of Saint Augustine and, unfortunately, pervasive in much of evangelical theology today."

Mark H. Mann, professor of theology and director of the Honors Scholars Program at Point Loma Nazarene University

"What does it mean to be and become human? How can we faithfully engage the very different answers to that question offered by influential psychological theories? These questions matter because, as Gunnoe shows, these theories have influenced the broader culture, shaping our parenting, our schools, and the ways we view and speak of one another. Framed by four fundamental questions about personhood, this work deftly leads readers through a nuanced, critical, and constructive exploration of five different approaches to human becoming. By prefacing each theory with a brief biography of its most influential proponents, Gunnoe invites readers into active dialogue, encouraging them to identify their own beliefs about personhood and to take seriously the positive contributions of each approach, while being honest about limitations. Written mainly for Christians studying or teaching introductory or developmental psychology, this book is also illuminating for parents, pastors, schoolteachers, and anyone interested in what it means to be a person."

Heather Looy, professor of psychology at The King's University, Edmonton, Alberta

"Gunnoe's courageous and helpful work illustrates the challenge and promise of integrating psychological frameworks within a theology of personhood. Her book is a welcome port of entry for this important project."

Justin L. Barrett, author of *Thriving with Stone Age Minds: Evolutionary Psychology, Christian Faith, and the Quest for Human Flourishing*

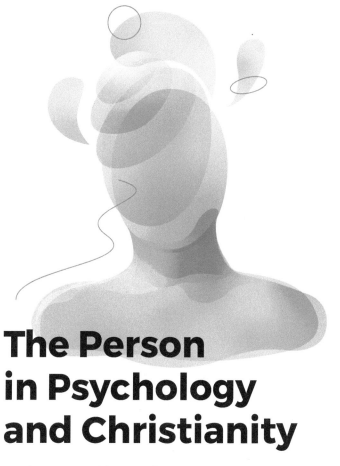

The Person
in Psychology
and Christianity

A Faith-Based Critique of Five Theories of Social Development

MARJORIE LINDNER GUNNOE

ivp
Academic
An imprint of InterVarsity Press
Downers Grove, Illinois

InterVarsity Press
P.O. Box 1400, Downers Grove, IL 60515-1426
ivpress.com
email@ivpress.com

InterVarsity Press® is the book-publishing division of InterVarsity Christian Fellowship/USA®, a movement of students and faculty active on campus at hundreds of universities, colleges, and schools of nursing in the United States of America, and a member movement of the International Fellowship of Evangelical Students. For information about local and regional activities, visit intervarsity.org.

Scripture quotations, unless otherwise noted, are from the New Revised Standard Version Bible, copyright © 1989 National Council of the Churches of Christ in the United States of America. Used by permission. All rights reserved worldwide.

While any stories in this book are true, some names and identifying information may have been changed to protect the privacy of individuals.

Cover design and image composite: David Fassett
Interior design: Daniel van Loon
Image: abstract head illustration © pressureUA / iStock / Getty Images Plus

ISBN 978-0-8308-2872-2 (print)
ISBN 978-0-8308-2873-9 (digital)

Printed in the United States of America ∞

InterVarsity Press is committed to ecological stewardship and to the conservation of natural resources in all our operations. This book was printed using sustainably sourced paper.

Library of Congress Cataloging-in-Publication Data
A catalog record for this book is available from the Library of Congress.

P	25	24	23	22	21	20	19	18	17	16	15	14	13	12	11	10	9	8	7	6	5	4	3	2	1
Y	40	39	38	37	36	35	34	33	32	31	30	29	28	27	26	25	24	23	22

Contents

Acknowledgments

THIS BOOK WAS FACILITATED by the Calvin Center for Christian Studies (CCCS) and a sabbatical from Calvin University. It was commissioned as an article commensurate with a one-course release from the CCCS. (Suffice it to say that we both got more than we bargained for.)

In the past 12 years I have been inspired, directed, redirected, and reined in by many colleagues in psychology, theology, and history. I am grateful to Justin Barrett, Claudia Beversluis, Randy Blacketer, Laura DeHaan, Chad Gunnoe, Dan Harlow, Emily Helder, Doug Howard, Eric Jones, Won Lee, Matt Lundberg, Paul Moes, Neal Plantinga, Blake Riek, Laura Smit, Don Tellinghuisen, Glenn Weaver, and Julie Yonker. These advisers considered only select portions of the book and were not always of the same mind. The final product and any theological missteps should be ascribed to me alone.

I am also grateful to Cathy Parks and Nate LeFebre for administrative assistance par excellence; my IVP editor, Jon Boyd, and an anonymous reviewer for their helpful suggestions; my pastors Elizabeth Vander Haagen and Jay Blankespoor for thought-provoking sermons; my immediate family (Chad, James, Erik, and Katya Gunnoe) and my mom, Char Lindner, for time and support; and both my parents for anchoring my life in an appreciation for Scripture.

Finally, I am grateful to the Calvin students who helped me refine my thinking on the topics discussed herein. After 25 years of grading many fine student papers, I am not always sure what ideas originated with me and what ideas originated with them. Thank you, friends.

PART 1

A Faith-Based Working Model of the Person

CHAPTER ONE

Orientation

THIS BOOK EXAMINES THE INTERSECTION of Christian theology and theories of social development proposed by Erik Erikson, John Bowlby, B. F. Skinner, Albert Bandura, and Evolutionary Psychology. These theories were selected because nine standard developmental textbooks identified them as foundational to the study of social development. In their introductory chapters, all nine summarize psychoanalytic theory (Freud and Erikson). Eight introduce behavioral theory (Skinner) and social cognitive theory (Bandura). One textbook refers to psychoanalytic, behavioral, and social cognitive as the "grand theories" of developmental psychology (Berger, 2017, p. 37).

Attachment theory (Bowlby and Ainsworth) and an evolutionary perspective are also ubiquitous in the textbooks surveyed. Attachment theory is often presented as an ethological theory, but also as a standalone theory, an extension of Freudian theory, and a precursor to evolutionary developmental psychology (EDP). Evolutionary presentations vary a good deal. Four textbooks explicitly distinguish EDP from evolutionary psychology (EP), but five do not. This distinction is important because EP and EDP disagree on some important aspects of personhood (see chap. 9 of this book). For psychologists who study social development, the three grand theories and ethology/evolution are the standard *psychological* "lenses for looking at the lifespan" (Belsky, 2019, p. 12).

Christian developmentalists also look through *theological* lenses, seeking to synthesize the knowledge that God has revealed through the

Bible (often called special revelation) with the knowledge that God has revealed in the patterns of creation (often called general revelation; see Rom 1:20). To do this in a God-honoring way, we must first identify the seeming compatibilities between our faith and our academic discipline. We can then build on these compatibilities and describe development more comprehensively than those looking through only the separate lenses of theology or psychology.

We must also identify seeming incompatibilities. Some incompatibilities require us to reject a psychological claim outright. Other times, a biblical claim that initially seems incompatible with contemporary science may help us distinguish the theological truth God is communicating from the context in which it was first communicated. For example, the author of the book of Joshua claims that the sun stood still, permitting the Israelites to win an important battle (Josh 10). Although Christians in the prescientific world interpreted this claim to mean that the sun revolved around the earth, most contemporary Christians believe that the earth revolves around the sun. Looking through the lenses of both theology and astronomy, we can appreciate both the miracle being reported and the need for the author to report the miracle in a way that made sense to a prescientific audience who assumed a geocentric universe. In a similar way, looking through the lenses of both theology and psychology permits us to refine our descriptions of personhood.

The capacity to articulate compatibilities and incompatibilities across theology and psychology fosters trust in students and clients seeking to construct a psychologically informed, faith-compatible view of self and others. As a professor at a Christian university, I have learned that my (mostly Christian) students enter the classroom with diverse attitudes toward psychology. Some are wary, having been warned not to let psychology supplant their faith. Others are eager to move beyond the compartmentalization of knowledge they practiced in order to retain their faith and succeed in public school science classes. Still others are in the process of abandoning their faith because no one has helped them synthesize what they view as competing worldviews.

During my first decade of teaching, I was ill-prepared to mentor all three groups. Students asked questions about the assumptions and applications of developmental theory that I couldn't answer. Simultaneously, during my first decade of parenting, I asked myself a lot of questions that I couldn't answer. I'd look at a child who had just disobeyed and think, *Should I view that as rebellion or an inherently good but misdirected drive for mastery? Should I be more concerned with punishment or promoting attachment?* As I attempted to answer these questions, I discovered that I needed to expand my psychological knowledge by delving into primary sources and expand my theological knowledge beyond the specific Christian traditions with which I was most familiar.

The result is a broadly ecumenical exploration of the five developmental theories that have been most thought-provoking for me as a professor and a parent. In response to an anonymous reviewer who noted my failure to locate this exploration within a specific confessional orientation, I am guilty as charged. I was born into dispensationalism, educated in a Christian Reformed day school, and married by a nondenominational charismatic minister. In a time of difficulty, I benefited from the counsel of an Episcopal priest. I have always revered Scripture as authoritative while weighing different interpretations of it. At present I consider myself Reformed and still reforming. I am particularly concerned with reforming the very negative view of humankind held by some within the family of Reformed Christianity.

FOUR THEMES

As a developmental psychologist with no formal theological training, I am most qualified to speak on the temporal characteristics of personhood. By *temporal* I mean physical and psychological features overtly manifest in our relationships with other humans and the rest of creation—as opposed to characteristics that are first and foremost spiritual (e.g., our relationship with God, redemption, life eternal). In class discussions, these temporal characteristics tend to converge around four themes that I have used to organize this book. The four themes are as follows:

1. Essence: What characteristics are core or indispensable to personhood? How influential is our morphology (i.e., physical structure)? What indispensable qualities *emerge* from our morphology?

2. Purpose: What are humans supposed to do? What are our primary motivations? Is there a universal, intrinsically motivated, telos-like aim to human development? Is purpose specific to the individual?

3. Moral-ethical tendencies: Are humans more inclined toward good or bad? Are moral-ethical tendencies universal or particular? Are they inherent or learned?

4. Agency/accountability: Is human behavior volitional or determined? To what degree are humans accountable for self and responsible for others?

TWO PARTS

This book is divided into two parts. Part one examines the person through the lens of theology, introducing some of the diverse Christian perspectives on essence and purpose (chap. 2), moral-ethical tendencies (chap. 3), and agency/accountability (chap. 4). My goal for these chapters is *not* to provide a comprehensive treatment of these themes but simply to set up part two by identifying some areas of convergence between Christian theology and developmental theories. To facilitate critique of the five theories, I use part one to construct brief working models for each of the four themes.

Part two looks through the lenses of the five developmental theories. Chapters five through eight each consist of three sections: a biography of the theorist, an overview of the theorist's primary contributions to our understanding of social development, and a delving into the aspects of their theory most relevant to the four organizing themes of the book. The biographies are motivated by a growing awareness that the writings of social and personality theorists are best understood in the context of their own socialization (Demorest, 2005; Martin, 2017). The biographies are written to be appropriate for general academic use (e.g., as part of a course packet at a public university). Chapter nine focuses on a paradigm rather than a single theorist but is organized to approximate the structure of chapters five through eight. My goal for chapters five through nine is for Christians to learn from these developmental theories, assimilating wisdom that is compatible with Christian theology and rejecting claims that explicitly contradict it.

THE IMPORTANCE OF GENESIS 1–3

In both parts I make frequent appeals to the biblical creation narratives in Genesis 1–3 (also called origins narratives). Per Francis Schaeffer (2010, p. 9), "In some ways these chapters are the most important ones in the Bible, for they put man in his cosmic setting and show him his particular uniqueness. They explain man's wonder and yet his flaw." These creation narratives are particularly important to a faith-based *psychological* analysis of personhood. While many sections of Scripture describe human characteristics, the first chapters of Genesis establish characteristics that all humans share. Extracting universal characteristics is necessary for the evaluation of mainstream psychological theories, which make no distinction between theological categories of people (e.g., believers versus unbelievers, righteous versus wicked).

Genesis 1:1–2:3 (henceforth called the *Genesis 1* account or the *first* creation story) establishes that humans were created in the image of God. Many biblical scholars think that Genesis 1 was written in the sixth century BCE during one of Israel's periods of exile by an author who was familiar with many existing Hebrew writings, including Genesis 2–3, psalms that allude to creation (e.g., Ps 74; 90), and texts that wrestle with God's power over evil during Israel's extended periods of foreign captivity (e.g., Jeremiah, Ezekiel, Isaiah 40–55, and likely the book of Job).

With the Genesis 1 creation story, the author "took on" the cosmology of the surrounding cultures, which viewed both the material world and humans as a product of evil chaos in the heavenly realm. The author countered this pessimistic worldview by asserting God's preeminence over evil and chaos, and humans' special status as God's good representatives on earth. The author's purpose was to give hope to an oppressed people.

Genesis 2:4–3:24 (henceforth called the *Genesis 2–3* account) includes the *second* creation story and the events traditionally referred to as "the fall." This origin story establishes that humans sinned. In doing so, we damaged our relationships with God, fellow humans, and the rest of creation. Our good creational structure was not obliterated; we are still able to participate actively in the restoration of our damaged relationships, but we do this in a sin-warped way. Many scholars believe that the transcription of the second creation story predates the first, some dating Genesis 2–3 as early as the tenth century BCE. In contrast to the message of empowerment intended by the author of Genesis 1, the author of Genesis 2–3 sought to explain the pervasive suffering and evil in the world.

So if Genesis 1 was written *after* Genesis 2–3, why does it appear first in the biblical canon? Some scholars believe that the order communicates the importance of Genesis 1. Smith (2010, p. 136) writes, "For although Genesis 1 came at a later point in the order of historical composition (compared with many other creation accounts), it was given pride of first place in the Pentateuch, in what its compilers regarded as more properly reflecting the order of reality. This placement—and all that represented hermeneutically— thus serves as one of the Bible's greatest acts of commentary."

Genesis 1 also receives pride of place in this faith-based exploration of social development. The point of developmental psychology in general (not just a faith-based exploration) is to identify the potential built into the human person and then describe how development is *supposed* to unfold. Without a particular emphasis on the built-in or supposed-to, we have no basis for discerning how and why development goes right or wrong, or the degree to which temporal restoration is possible.

CHAPTER TWO

Essence and Purpose

IN THIS CHAPTER I summarize various Christian beliefs about human essence and purpose. By *essence* I mean the "intrinsic or indispensable"[1] qualities that identify and distinguish humans from other species. By *purpose* I mean the reason that humans were created (i.e., what humans are supposed to do).

ESSENCE

In the image of God. Central to a Christian understanding of human essence is our creation in the image of God (in Latin, the *imago Dei*). The doctrine of the *imago Dei* is derived from Genesis 1:27:

> So God created humankind in his image,
>> in the image of God he created them;
>> male and female he created them.

Evidence for the importance of this doctrine includes its placement at the beginning of the canon and the fact that it is shared by all three Abrahamic religions (Judaism, Christianity, and Islam). Evidence that the doctrine continues to apply, even after humans sinned, can be found in Genesis 9:6.

Despite the importance of this doctrine, biblical authors were not very explicit in telling us what it *means* to be created in the image of God. Colossians 3:10 suggests that the *imago Dei* has something to do with

---

[1]*American Heritage Dictionary of the English Language*, 5th ed., s.v. "essence," www.thefree dictionary.com/essence.

knowledge.[2] First Corinthians 11:7 suggests that it has something to do with relationships.[3]

In contrast to the authors of the Bible, later theologians have had a lot to say about the *imago Dei*. Millard Erickson (2001) concisely summarizes three broad aspects of the *imago Dei*: substantive, relational, and functional (pp. 170-78).[4] Because writings on the *imago Dei* often emphasize one aspect over the others, Erickson refers to the three aspects as "views," but most theologians believe that the *imago Dei* involves all three.

Theologians who write on the *substantive* aspect of the *imago Dei* teach that there are aspects of human nature that are substantively like God's nature in some ways. In other words, humans have God-like qualities in our psychological or spiritual makeup. The most commonly emphasized quality is the capacity for reason. Because humans are endowed with a God-like power of thought, we have the freedom to make moral choices and behave accordingly.

The *relational* aspect builds on the substantive. Theologians who write on this aspect emphasize that God endowed humans with reason so that we can live in relationship with God and with other people. God is relational, as evidenced by the plural pronoun in the proposal "Let *us* make humankind in our image" (Gen 1:26). The relational view characterizes humans as being in the image or displaying the image "when we stand in a particular relationship" (Erickson, 2001, p. 173). Put simply, humans are like a mirror. If there is nothing in front of the mirror, nothing is imaged. The fact that only

---

[2] "[You] have clothed yourselves with the new self, which is being renewed in knowledge according to the image of its creator."

[3] "For a man ought not to have his head veiled, since he is the image and reflection of God; but woman is the reflection of man." Some ancient commentators took Paul's differential treatment of the sexes as a denial of women's creation in the image of God, but this supposition is likely wrong. Augustine challenged this interpretation. See Sullivan (1963, p. 49). Calvin also challenged it. See the two chapters by Børreson in Børreson (1991).

[4] Some theologians in the Reformed tradition distinguish narrow versus broad senses of the image of God. "By the narrower image, we mean active conformity to God's will in a life of obedience, and by the broader image we mean an analogy to God's being, which consists of the possession of reason, will, and other qualities"—in other words, "man's ontological and psychological structure" (Hoekema, 1986, p. 60, summarizing the position of G. C. Berkouwer). Although Berkouwer views scientific scholarship in the broad sense as "a kind of appendix" to theology that places "man's relatedness to God at the center" (Hoekema, 1986, p. 60), it is the broad sense that I will attempt to synthesize with the developmental theories. The narrow sense is central to theology, but the broad sense shares more overlap with mainstream developmental psychology.

humans were created in the image of God has two important implications for a psychological understanding of human essence. First, it means that humans are the only creatures that can participate in spiritual relationships. Second, it means that the relationships that humans have with each other have a value that transcends their instrumental benefits. (By *instrumental* I mean "useful" things a person might get out of the relationship.)

Theologians who promote the *functional* aspect believe that the *imago Dei* is best understood as a function of humans' dominion over the rest of creation. Although some theologians have been reluctant to conceptualize the *imago Dei* in physical terms (preferring to defend the spiritual, non-physical nature of God), the full proposal in Genesis 1:26—"Let us make humankind in our image . . . and let them have dominion"—seems to imply that dominion is a function of the *imago Dei*.

But what does it mean to have dominion? Most theologians teach that dominion involves caring for the world as God does. Contemporary terms for this caring include *stewardship*, *earth-keeping*, and *place-making*.[5] As explained by Cornelius Plantinga Jr. (2002), God intends this care to extend not only to the biophysical sphere (Deut 11:12; Jer 2:7; Mt 6:26) but also to "a vast array of cultural possibilities that God folded into human nature" (p. 32), including the development of language, industry, and institutions.[6]

Compelling evidence for a functional interpretation of the *imago Dei* has been offered by W. Randall Garr (2003, pp. 132-65) and by J. Richard Middleton (2005, chap. 2; 2006). Both conclude that the use of the word *image* in the Hebrew Scriptures typically connotes sovereignty. Archaeological evidence indicates that the surrounding Near Eastern cultures applied the word *image* to humans of significant status who acted as a conduit through which a divine patron was realized. For example, the Babylonian king Marduk[7] was believed to image the sun and was charged to come out of his palace so that the people could reap the benefits of the sun. As a corrective to scholars who shy away from linking the *imago Dei*

---

[5]For discourse on the pros and cons of these terms, see Warners and Heun (2019).
[6]For a discussion of the Hebrew words associated with the Gen 1:28 directive to *subdue* the earth, see Middleton (2005, chap. 2).
[7]*Merodach* in Hebrew; see Is 39:1.

to the physical body, Middleton (2005) argues that "visibility and bodi-liness may well be important for understanding the imago Dei" (p. 25). In the functional view, then, humans were created in the image of God to physically preside over and functionally represent God in the earth. In a later essay, Middleton (2006, p. 81) suggests that the functional view might also be called the *missional* view.

According to God's likeness, embodied, gendered. Humans were also created "according to [God's] likeness" (Gen 1:26). As with *image*, theologians debate the meaning of *likeness*, but contemporary scholarship suggests that likeness connotes a lesser form of an original form (Garr, 2003, pp. 118-32; Middleton, 2005). Likeness elevates humankind by linking our physical form to God's form, even as it keeps us in our place—lest we presume "too close an identification" with the original form (Middleton, 2005, p. 46). It reminds us that we are the created rather than the Creator. Our status as the created is reiterated in Genesis 2 when the author links humans to animals, identifying both as creatures from the ground. In fact, the (apparent) reason animals are created in the second creation account is to serve as a potential partner for the man. Together, these passages suggest that humans share some essential features with God and some with animals, even as we are distinct from both.

Garr's (2003) word study also emphasizes *self-perpetuation* of the form and its associated function. In Garr's analysis, the proposal "according to our likeness" signifies that humankind is supposed to continue God's creative work, perpetually registering the presence of God in the world. We do this generally through place-making and particularly through procreation. Garr's assertion that *image* signals sovereignty and *likeness* signals procreation accords with the prime directives given to humans. In Genesis 1:28 God instructs humans to continue creating more humans (likeness) and to have dominion (image).[8] Middleton (2005) points out that the author of Genesis 1 uses the biological terms for sex (*male* and *female*),

---

[8]These definitions are also accordant with their seeming usage in Gen 5:3, Scripture's only other pairing of the two words. Genesis 5 documents the lineage from God to Noah. Scholars of the Pentateuch have interpreted this not only as a physical genealogy but also as a record of succession identifying the rightful heirs to the divine throne.

instead of the social categories (*man* and *woman*) used in Genesis 2–3. Thus, both Garr and Middleton present biological sex as an important and essential quality of humankind.

Extracting essence from the Genesis 2–3 account elicits controversy. In contrast to the identical description (image, likeness) and identical directives (be fruitful, have dominion) given to males and females in Genesis 1, the author of the second account distinguishes the man and the woman by creating them sequentially and assigning them different punishments after they sin. This very different treatment of sex and gender in the two accounts contributes to two views of creational gender among contemporary Christians.

The first approach is called *complementarianism* and can be found in Christianity, Judaism, and Islam. Adherents of complementarianism hold that men and women were created with different but complementary skills, roles, and responsibilities. In theory, the two groups differ in many important ways, but the primary contrast is men's "responsibility to lead, provide for, and protect" and women's "disposition to affirm, receive, and nurture strength and leadership from worthy men" (Piper & Grudem, 1991, pp. 35, 46). Because this approach focuses on maintaining a hierarchy intended and built in at creation, I have elsewhere referred to it as the "maintenance model" of gender (Gunnoe, 2003). More generally, this position is known as *gender hierarchy*.

A second approach also teaches that differences between men and women were present at creation, but these differences were nonhierarchical and nonrigid. Sin then caused these differences to be warped in gender-specific ways. According to Mary Stewart Van Leeuwen (2002), "Postfall man is continually tempted to turn the legitimate, God-imaging dominion of Gen 1:28 into domination" (p. 74). Conversely, postfall woman is continually tempted to collude with the man's domination. She avoids doing "what is right, if doing so will upset existing relationships, especially those with men." Because advocates of this approach believe that Christians should seek to amend gender differences resulting from the fall and work to restore the equal opportunity and accountability intended at creation, I have elsewhere referred to this perspective as the "restoration model" of gender (Gunnoe, 2003). More generally, this position is referred to as *gender egalitarianism.*

Despite very different explanations for some of the differences between men and women, both perspectives view these differences as rooted in morphology. Regardless of whether one views the account of the woman being created from the man's rib (Gen 2:21-22) as an analogy or an actual physical process, it is hard to ignore the bodily emphasis in this foundational passage of Scripture. Accordingly, many Christians resist psychological definitions of gender as primarily socially influenced.[9] Many Christians view sex and gender as synonymous. Christian *psychologists* tend to take a more nuanced view. For example, Eric Johnson (2017) argues that the plasticity of sex and gender in a fallen world does not negate the "creational norms" whereby humans were created "sexed and gendered" (p. 191). In class I define gender as the complex interrelationship between three dimensions: body, identity, and expression (Gender Spectrum, n.d.). I teach that sex and gender are neither synonymous nor binary, and that gender has a large learned component, *even as* humans were created gendered.[10]

Working model of human essence. A working model of human essence must incorporate our morphology and the emergent qualities that our morphology affords. By *emergent* I mean a higher-order phenomenon that arises out of lower-level structures and is greater than the sum of its parts (e.g., vision and language emerge from brain structures that do not individually see or hear). A concise working model of essence is that humans are *embodied creatures with the capacity for reason, relationships, and dominion.*

This working model does not specifically reference sex or gender because my primary focus in the evaluation of the psychological perspectives

---

[9]For example, in their margin vocabulary terms, Myers and DeWall (2018) define *sex* as the "the biologically influenced characteristics by which people define *male* and *female*" and *gender* as "the socially influenced characteristics by which people define *boy, girl, man,* and *woman*" (p. 152). In the main body of the text, they clarify that "for most people, those biological traits help define their assigned gender" (p. 152).

[10]In this book, I try to use the terms *male/female* when discussing biological sex and *men/women* when discussing gender categories, but there are many sections where this protocol does not work (e.g., when I am quoting authors who make no distinction).

on essence is the theorists' treatment of the *imago Dei* characteristics. I will, however, provide occasional discussion of sex and gender, appropriate to specific theories.

PURPOSE

Two universal purposes: love and dominion work. In his critique of the three broad aspects of the *imago Dei*, Erickson (2001) favors the substantive. One of his arguments is that the substantive aspect *permits* the relational and functional aspects, which are more about what we do than who we are. I find this distinction too simplistic, but I agree that the latter two aspects establish that God has purposed us for certain experiences and activities more explicitly than the substantive does.

Theologians who emphasize the *relational* aspect of the *imago Dei* assert that human beings were purposed for close relationships, or love. First, we were purposed to love God. Asked to identify the greatest commandment, Jesus replied, "You shall love the Lord your God with all your heart, and with all your soul, and with all your mind" (Mt 22:37). Accordingly, the first question and answer of the Westminster Shorter Catechism is as follows:

> Q.1. What is the chief end of man?
> A. Man's chief end is to glorify God, and to enjoy him forever.

Second, we were purposed to love others. In Genesis 2:18 God says, "It is not good that the man should be alone." Readers of Ecclesiastes are told, "Enjoy life with the wife whom you love . . . because that is your portion in life" (Eccles 9:9). Jesus identifies loving our neighbor as the second greatest commandment (Mt 22:39) and instructs us to love our enemies, pointing out that even the tax collectors and Gentiles love those who reciprocate (Mt 5:46-47). The apostle Paul emphasizes Christians' intimate connection as members of the body of Christ (Rom 12; 1 Cor 12).

Theologians who emphasize the *functional* view assert that humans are purposed for sovereign-like dominion. Per Middleton (2005, p. 55), the "*Let there be . . .*" statements in Genesis 1 are both a declaration that something was spoken into being and a designation of the thing's purpose. In the same way that the declaration "Let there be lights . . . to separate the day from the night" (Gen 1:14) establishes separation as the *purpose* of the lights, "Let us make humankind in our image . . . and let them have dominion" (Gen 1:26) establishes dominion as a "necessary and inseparable purpose" of creatures created in the image of God. Sovereign-like dominion as a purpose is also suggested in Psalm 8:4-5, which declares of human beings,

> You have made them a little lower than God,
>   and crowned them with glory and honor.
> You have given them dominion over the works of your hands;
>   you have put all things under their feet.

A less majestic depiction of our intended dominion is offered by the author of Genesis 2, who, according to Smith (2010), "assumes that work is the primary purpose of human life" (p. 135). Genesis 2 opens with a barren earth and the implication that it is barren because there "was no one to till the ground." Then "the LORD God took the man and put him in the garden of Eden to till it and keep it" (Gen 2:15). The second creation story depicts humans as stewards more than sovereigns, but it is not incompatible with the first creation story. Both accounts make it clear that humans were created to work with God and for God, creating and sustaining the world through dominion work.

Confirmation of this purpose appears throughout Scripture. The teacher of Ecclesiastes concludes that "there is nothing better than that all should enjoy their work, for that is their lot" (Eccles 3:22). To the Ephesians Paul writes, "For we are what he has made us, created in Christ Jesus for good works, which God prepared beforehand to be our way of life" (Eph 2:10). The author of Hebrews links work with our other purpose (love), writing, "Let us consider how to provoke one another to love and good deeds" (Heb 10:24). From these passages and others, we can conclude that humankind is dually purposed for love and dominion work.

Motivation for love and dominion work. If humans are purposed for love and dominion work, we should be highly motivated to engage in these activities. Motivation to be in close relationship with God is expressed by

King David, who likens his longing for God to a deer panting for water (Ps 42:1). It is echoed in subsequent psalms (Ps 63, 73, 119, 143) and by the prophet Isaiah (Is 26:9). Motivation to be in close relationship with another human is the theme of the Song of Songs and evidenced in many biblical case studies (e.g., Jacob/Rachel in Gen 29, Ruth/Naomi in Ruth 1:16-17, and Hannah begging God for a child in 1 Sam 1:13).

Humans are also motivated for dominion work. James Peterson (2010) proposes that the Garden of Eden was part of God's *psychological* provision for the man, offering not just sustenance and delight but also a means of satisfying the human motivation "to create within our small sphere, in a way somehow akin to how God creates" (p. 46). Evidence that humans enjoy dominion work can also be derived from scriptural accounts of people rallying when opportunities for meaningful work had been scarce. When Moses offered the recently emancipated Israelite slaves an opportunity to craft articles for the building of God's tabernacle, the response was so great that he had to send out an order to cease work, "for what they had already brought was more than enough to do all the work" (Ex 36:6-7). Similar fervor is seen in the rebuilding of the walls of Jerusalem after the Babylonian exile. Early in his progress report, Nehemiah writes that "all the wall was joined together to half its height; for the people had a mind to work" (Neh 4:6). In the New Testament, we read of believers being "devoted" to good works (e.g., Acts 9:36).

Two ways to conceptualize purpose: telos and particular purpose. Related to purpose and motivation is the concept of telos. Teleology is the attempt to ascribe to natural entities an intrinsic purpose that is irrespective of how they are used and that will be realized (unless they are externally thwarted). A telos is an inwardly directed progression toward a predetermined end goal. For example, an acorn's telos is to grow into an oak tree (Cohen, 2016).

Scripture depicts human development as a process in which we mature cognitively (1 Cor 13:11) and spiritually (1 Cor 3:2; 1 Pet 2:2). The end goal, at least for Christians, is "to be conformed to the image of [God's] Son" (Rom 8:29) and "grow up in every way into him who is the head, into Christ" (Eph 4:15). Scripture establishes that this end was determined before creation (Eph 1), and Scripture guarantees that God "will bring it to completion" (Phil 1:6).

Because Christians have both built-in purposes afforded by the *imago Dei* and a clear end goal, Christians would seem to have a telos. Whether we can ascribe to all humans the same telos is less clear. In Romans 9 Paul likens humans to clay pots, some of which were made for destruction. If God predetermines different end goals for different people, I am hesitant to claim a *universal* human telos, but telos is certainly a relevant construct for Christians.

In addition to presenting humans as universally purposed for love and dominion work, Scripture identifies some individuals (or groups; Gen 22:18) as *particularly* purposed. Some particular purposes are foretold before birth, but often they are revealed at a later point in development.[11] Well-loved stories of particular purpose are the royalty stories of Joseph, Moses, Esther, and Daniel, each of whom was positioned in a palace early in life so that God could later work through them to accomplish some important end.

One reason we love these stories is that they illuminate the psychological processes whereby regular people can grow into a royal purpose. Young Esther required the prodding of a trusted mentor ("Perhaps you have come to royal dignity for just such a time as this" [Esther 4:14]). Young Joseph seems eager for his family to bow down to him (Gen 37:5-11) and required the developmental force of adversity to appropriately reckon his particular purpose. It was an older, wiser Joseph who told his brothers, "Even though you intended to do harm to me, God intended it for good, in order to preserve a numerous people, as he is doing today" (Gen 50:20).

A second reason we love these stories is that the accomplishments of these royals appeal to our own created purpose to work for God. Although most of us appointed sovereign over God's creation do not find ourselves positioned in a literal palace, we aspire to do the prosocial dominion work that good sovereigns do: righting injustices, diminishing suffering, and

---

[11] Isaac was to be the conduit of the covenant (Gen 17:19-21) and Jacob the stronger of two nations (Gen 25:23). Jeremiah is appointed a prophet to the nations (Jer 1:5). Samson's purpose was to deliver Israel from the hand of the Philistines (Judg 13:5).

helping others to flourish. Fortunately, Scripture also provides examples from the hoi polloi. The virgin Mary and the apostles Peter and Paul help illuminate the identity work that may accompany the embrace of particular purpose.

Working model of purpose. The Bible characterizes humankind as universally purposed for love and dominion work. It also identifies some individuals as purposed to love and work in a particular way in a particular context. Although there is a predetermined end goal for Christians, we cannot specify a universal end goal for all of humankind. Thus, the address of purpose in part two will focus primarily on temporal aspects of human purpose rather than a spiritual telos.

CHAPTER THREE

Moral-Ethical Tendencies

IN THIS CHAPTER I introduce various Christian perspectives on moral-ethical tendencies. By *moral-ethical tendencies* I mean propensities toward good or evil in our daily dealings (e.g., helpful or hurtful), not our eschatological status as redeemed or condemned. I establish that humans were created structurally good and are now inclined toward both good and evil. I then consider the difficult question of how evil got "added" to our creational good.

STRUCTURAL GOOD AND INCLINATIONS TOWARD GOOD AND EVIL

The Bible makes universal and particular statements about humans' inclinations toward both good and evil. Universal tendencies toward *good* are established in the first creation account when humans—along with the whole of creation—are declared "very good" (Gen 1:31). Genesis 1 expert Mark Smith (2010) argues that this declaration encompasses not only our creational structure but also our moral tendency. Discoursing on the Hebrew word for good (*tob*), he says,

> Indeed, *tob* in this narrative establishes the norms for holiness and good or moral behavior. Elsewhere the word "good" (*tob*) functions in a moral sense as a term for righteous and upright people. "Good" persons are contrasted with wicked or bad people (Proverbs 2:20-22, 12:2, 13:22, 14:14, and 15:3). Similarly, "good" applies to deeds (Psalm 14:1, 3 = 53:1, 3). In an obvious example, Amos 5:14-15 commands: "seek good and not evil" and

"hate evil and love good." Some creation allusions also show a concern for moral good (see Psalm 33:4-7). So we may conclude that both meanings apply in Genesis 1. (p. 62)

Christian psychologist Eric Johnson (2017) refers to humankind's cognitive and behavioral tendencies toward good as our "good-creation orientation" (p. 196). Johnson grounds this orientation in Saint Augustine's declaration in *The City of God* that every creature's "joy is in the goodness of God" (Augustine, 1958, p. 233).

Universal tendencies toward *evil* are established by the apostle Paul as part of his case for the necessity of Christ in the opening chapters of Romans. Paul begins with an account of the fall. In Romans 1:18-32 he provides a long list of sins establishing the guilt of humankind, using descriptors like *wicked* and *ruthless*. In chapter three he declares that "there is no one who is righteous, not even one" (Rom 3:10) and that "all have sinned and fall short of the glory of God" (Rom 3:23). Paul's assertion that no one is righteous echoes Psalm 14, wherein humankind is described as *perverse*.

Paul's very negative description of humankind illuminates just how evil humans are relative to God. This illustration is foundational to the Christian doctrine of salvation, but as a description of humans' general temporal inclinations, it confounds. Paul claims that there are no righteous people, but Psalms and Proverbs are chock-full of contrasts of the *righteous* and the *wicked*.[1] These and many other passages in the Bible indicate that there *are* people who are righteous, at least in some sense of the word. Additional evidence that moral-ethical tendencies may be *person-particular* comes from Ezekiel 18, which teaches that the son may be different from his father, and the third generation different from the second. In the New Testament, we read of Jews who will not inherit the kingdom of heaven (Mt 21:43) and Gentiles who do what the law requires, even without having the law. The latter are described in Romans 2:14 (sandwiched between

---

[1]According to Cover (1992), biblical authors sometimes used terms like *righteous* and *wicked* to indicate sociological categories based on religious affiliation, but often these terms constituted moral judgments distinguishing sinners who had seemingly brought themselves back into a right relationship with God from "sinners without conscience" (p. 37).

chapters one and three, wherein Paul declares humans universally bad). Good and evil also emerge from the same person. When reporting his obedience to the law in Philippians 3:6, Paul describes himself as *blameless*, but in Romans 7:19 he bemoans his *inability to do the good* that his inmost self wants to do.

Because Paul's objective in Romans is to establish humankind as universally in need of Christ, it may be more appropriate to base our statements about *temporal* inclinations on the Genesis 3 account of the fall.[2] The author of Genesis 3 leaves the moral-ethical tendencies of humankind much more ambiguous than Paul does in Romans 1. Informed by the Romans account, Western Protestants have tended to view Genesis 3 as an account of humanity sharply turning from good to evil, but a global psychological reorientation in moral-ethical tendencies is not explicitly stated in Genesis 3. In fact, God's declaration that there will be enmity between humankind and the serpent (rather than enmity between humankind and God) could signify that humans are still on the good team, albeit as insubordinate members. The most explicit statement about moral tendencies in Genesis 3 is a statement of moral capacity, not orientation: "See, the man has become like one of us, knowing good and evil" (Gen 3:22). This statement confirms that humans are universally equipped with a conscience to discern moral direction, without specifying the direction we lean.

MORAL-ETHICAL TENDENCIES AS INHERENT

Because humans have structurally good bodies that enable the emergence of God-like capacities, we have good *built in*. Most Christians also believe that we have evil built in.

Many Scripture passages support this claim. Whether speaking colloquially or referring to the actual organ (Cooper, 1989), the Bible makes frequent statements about bad things coming out of the heart. Making the shortlist are arrogance, rebellion, envy, evil intention, slander, false witness, adultery, theft, and murder.[3] In one of the few potential biblical allusions

---

[2]As stated in chap. 1, explaining temporal experience was an objective of the Gen 3 account.
[3]Is 9:9; Jer 5:23; Mt 15:19; Mk 7:21; Jas 3:14.

to the unconscious, the prophet Jeremiah explains that we need God to search our hearts because our hearts are perverse and can deceive us into justifying our doings (Jer 17:9-10).[4]

Inherent evil is also suggested in some of the apostle Paul's writings. Unfortunately, Paul's descriptions of the physical body are very difficult to assimilate. Paul not only uses a variety of words for the body, but he also uses them in contradictory ways. In Romans 7:18 he insists that nothing good dwells in his *flesh*, but two chapters later (Rom 9:5) he insists that Jesus came according to the *flesh*, thereby negating the possibility that human flesh is inherently evil (see also Heb 2:14). Likewise, in Romans 6:6 Paul bemoans his "body of sin," but in 1 Corinthians 6 he declares that our bodies are "members of Christ" (1 Cor 6:15) and temples of the Holy Spirit (1 Cor 6:19). Whether Paul ever actually viewed any aspect of the physical body as evil is uncertain. This would have required him to separate the body from its emergent psychological properties. Even commentators who allege that Paul dabbled in dualism in a few passages stress that this was uncharacteristic of Paul. His prior theological training would have caused him to view humans as holistically good, and many other passages reveal his worldview to be "characteristically Hebraic" (Dunn, 1988, p. 320; see also Cooper, 1989; Sanders, 1992). The resolution seems to be that Paul uses the same terms to refer to our structurally good bodies and to lament the fact that even believers are still tempted to *use* their bodies for evil.

Paul also uses the term *nature*, but not in the way that psychologists use it. When psychologists say *nature*, we mean characteristics coded for by genes. When Paul applies the term *nature*, he means either (a) a group's condition (physical or social) bequeathed to them by their ancestors or (b) a set of habitual tendencies honed by prior choices, experience, and cultural norms. In other words, Paul's "nature" may be as much *nurture* as heredity. Because many Christians teach that humans have a sinful nature, it is worth stating that Paul uses the term *nature* to describe both good and evil human tendencies (Rom 2:14-15; 2 Cor 4:16; Eph 2:3) and that most

---

[4]Others include Ps 90 and 139 and Rom 7.

translations of the Bible do not use the phrase *sinful nature*.[5] Theologians' inability to agree on what Paul means when he uses various body words prompted Cooper (1989) to conclude, "The only agreement is that there is no simple way to move directly from Scripture to psychology, biology, or sociology" (p. 6).

HOW DID HUMANS BECOME INHERENTLY EVIL?

Genesis 1 establishes that humans were created good. Genesis 3 depicts evil as something existing outside humankind, in the form of the serpent. So how did something *outside* us get *inside*? In this section I present three possible acquisition processes. The first focuses on spiritual forces. Because spiritual forces fall outside the bounds of scientific inquiry, my presentation of the first acquisition process is brief. The latter two processes are related to the doctrine of original sin. Historically, original sin has been defined as a state or condition of sin caused by a literal Adam that now characterizes all humankind. Because original sin is viewed as hereditary, it is a suitable focus for a synthesis of theology and developmental theory. In contrast to *image of God*, the term *original sin* is not found in Scripture. The doctrine is understood somewhat differently in the branches of Christianity (Protestant, Catholic, Orthodox) and rejected by most Jews (Jacobs & Eisenstein, 1906)[6] and Muslims (Brown, 2007; Cragg, 1984). (The latter two groups teach that individuals are responsible for their own sin.) Because our appraisal of the developmental theories in part two will be facilitated by an overview of *diverse* understandings of original sin, I present the latter two acquisition processes in more detail, providing enough historical/theological context for readers to appreciate the psychological implications of this doctrine in their own and other branches of Christianity.

---

[5]The few that do (NIV, NLT, Phillips) use it as a translation for *sarx* (the Greek word typically translated "flesh"), not *physis* (the Greek word typically translated "nature").

[6]Some sources suggest that Jews have a version of original sin. "The majority, however, do not hold Adam responsible for the sins of mankind" (Jacobs & Eisenstein, 1906). Jewish rabbis hold that all people have an inclination to engage in wrong actions. "This inclination is not, however, equivalent to the Christian concept of original sin. According to rabbinic Judaism, people do not have an inherited corrupt nature; rather, they are subject to temptation, a heinous force that must be constantly fought" (Neusner & Green, 1996, p. 588).

Acquisition process one: evil as a spiritual agent. The first possibility is that evil is a spiritual agent that possesses and enslaves our bodies, even when our "inmost self" delights in good. This acquisition process is suggested by the apostle Paul, who says in Romans 7:18-20, "For I know that nothing good dwells within me, that is, in my flesh. I can will what is right, but I cannot do it. For I do not do the good I want, but the evil I do not want is what I do. Now if I do what I do not want, it is no longer I that do it, but sin that dwells within me." A logical problem with appealing to a spiritual agent to claim that humans are inherently evil is that such evil is not really inherent, at least as science conventionally defines inherent. As Paul himself concludes, it is not even *us* that sin.

Acquisition process two: evil as an emergent property. The second possibility is that evil is not an external force that got added to our creational good; rather, evil as an emergent property has always been supported by our good creational structure. The first systematic treatment of evil as an emergent property is credited to Irenaeus, bishop of Lyons (ca. 125–202 CE). Tradition holds that Irenaeus was taught by Polycarp, who was taught by the apostle John. Thus, Irenaeus's writings provide us "a privileged view of teachings about original sin being circulated in the early church" (Zimmerman, 1998, p. 2 of chap. 12).

To understand Irenaeus's view of how humans acquired sin, we must begin with Christ. Irenaeus taught that it was Christ who created the world (see Heb 1:10), intending from the outset to enter the world as a human to teach humankind how to image God and exercise responsible dominion. Like many of his contemporaries, Irenaeus believed that Adam and Eve were created as children, with limited cognitive capacity to make moral decisions in a God-like way. One reason that Christ created Adam and Eve immature was so that they could model (for the rest of us) the process whereby humans *grow into* the capacity to image God, learning from experience to discern good and evil. To ensure that humans had these experiences, Christ created humans free—and then gave them boundaries. Knowing that it was only a matter of time before free, immature creatures would attempt to exercise more dominion that they were ready for, Christ planned to come and die on the cross, even before we were created (see 1 Pet 1:18-20).[7]

Because Irenaeus reckoned Adam and Eve's disobedience as "an almost necessary step for the education of mankind" (Zimmerman, 1998, p. 1 of chap. 12), he viewed it much less negatively than many later theologians. Humans fell from innocence but rose cognitively. Like a parent, God punished us *and* pronounced our new capacity for enhanced discernment: "See, the man has become like one of us" (Gen 3:22). One component of our punishment was mortality. It is this mortality that constitutes *a form* of what the church has traditionally termed *original sin*.

A theological problem with Irenaeus's explanation for original sin is that both the punishments meted out to the humans and Christ's brutal death on the cross seem disproportionate to the crime. Some Christians also have difficulty with the idea that God would build in evil as an emergent possibility.

Irenaeus's exegesis of Genesis 3 has had the most influence on Orthodox Christianity. Like Irenaeus, Orthodox Christians view Adam and Eve as developmentally immature.[8] According to Hopko who is cited on the official website of the Orthodox Church in America, "the eating of the 'tree of the knowledge of good and evil' is generally interpreted as man's actual taste of evil, his literal experience of evil as such. Sometimes, this eating is also interpreted . . . as man's attempt to go beyond what was possible for him; his attempt to do that which was not yet within his power to realize" (2016, p. 58). Like Irenaeus, the Orthodox Church teaches that humans are still inclined toward good (as does the Catholic Church) and focuses on mortality and estrangement from God as the foremost ramifications of the fall. Unlike Irenaeus, the Orthodox Church reckons the fall a cosmic catastrophe for both humans and the creation we were commissioned to care for—albeit less personally depraving than many Protestants reckon it.[9]

---

[7]Irenaeus's claim that Christ planned to die on the cross *before* humans were even created contrasts with Augustine's view that humans were created as celestial beings and were supposed to stay that way (Zimmerman, 1998).

[8]Developmental limitations have also been suggested by the Reformed scholar Anthony Hoekema (1986, pp. 103-4), who argues that Adam and Eve were not fully developed image bearers because they still had the capacity to sin.

[9]Per Chryssavgis (1992): "Orthodoxy, holding as it does a less exalted idea of man's state before the Fall, is also less severe than the west in its view of the consequences of the Fall. Adam fell,

Acquisition process three: evil as a changed nature. The third possibility is that the nature humans have now is different from the nature we were created with. Historically, most Christians have believed that Adam's act of disobedience changed his nature. Through procreation, Adam then transmitted a changed nature to all of humankind. It is this changed nature that constitutes original sin.

Credit for this explanation generally goes to Augustine of Hippo (354–430 CE). Augustine believed that the first humans were endowed with special gifts, including the capacity to not sin (D. L. Smith, 1994, p. 338). In contrast to Irenaeus who viewed the fall as a misstep by immature beings basically like us (i.e., with no special powers), Augustine viewed the fall as mutiny by mature, celestial-type beings. Accordingly, Augustine viewed postfall humanity as much more sinful than Irenaeus did. At one point Augustine even claimed that the image of God had been lost (Couenhoven, 2005).[10]

One of Augustine's primary objectives was to refute Pelagius, a British cleric, who taught that humans could earn salvation through their own good efforts. To preserve the universal need for Christ, Augustine argued that all people, even infants who had not yet committed an action sin, must have some other kind of sin. Placing particular emphasis on (what most scholars now view as) a poor translation of Romans 5:12,[11] Augustine concluded that sin not only entered the *world* through Adam but also entered *humans* through Adam. As for the process, Augustine asserted

---

not from a great height of knowledge and perfection, but from a state of underdeveloped simplicity; hence he is not to be judged too harshly for his error" (p. 201). Orthodox Christians specifically reject Augustine's doctrine of inherited guilt.

[10]Augustine later retracted this, saying, "I should have said that the Image is so deformed that it needs 'reformation'" (Couenhoven, 2005, p. 367). Per Couenhoven's citations, the qualification was made in *Retractiones* 2.24.2.

[11]The Latin translation of Rom 5:12 favored by Augustine said, "Sin came into the world through one man, and death came through sin, and so death spread to all, in whom (*in quo*) all have sinned." Augustine interpreted the phrase *in whom* to mean that all future humans were physically present in Adam's loins at the time of Adam's disobedience. Collectively we participated in the act of original sin; collectively we took on guilt. This Latin translation of Rom 5:12 has subsequently been rejected in favor of Greek-based translations that state that death spread to all *because* or *in that* all have sinned (i.e., in Greek renderings the most direct cause of an individual's death is their own sin). Augustine drew on other biblical texts as well (e.g., 1 Cor 15:22), but critics often emphasize Rom 5:12 as a focal passage. Per D. L. Smith (1994), "Augustine's whole doctrine of original sin and inherited guilt was founded upon this mistranslation" (p. 291).

that Adam's sin confounded his reasoning and disordered his desires, especially sexual ones.[12] Because each act of postfall procreation involves disordered sexual desire, Adam's changed nature gets re-created in every human. Although Augustine neglected to provide readers with a precise definition of original sin,[13] he often depicted it as an inherited state of disordered desire and ignorance, which Couenhoven (2005) likens to a "constitutional fault" (p. 371).

Different Christian traditions emphasize different aspects of this changed nature. In Catholicism, original sin is understood as the deprivation of endowments and the special grace granted to humans before the fall (Ormerod, 1992, chap. 12; D. L. Smith, 1994, pp. 49-59, 338). First and foremost, humans were *deprived* of the capacity to not sin. Humans also lost the preternatural (beyond nature) gifts of infused knowledge, sexual desire void of lust, and immortality (Hardon, 1999). But humans did *not* lose free will. We lost our (super-good) "bonus powers," but our (good) human nature is still intact.[14]

In many branches of Protestantism, good human nature is not viewed as intact. Rather, our nature was damaged and *depraved*. Credit for this theology goes to the Reformers, whose continued efforts to root out Pelagian themes prompted *some*[15] constitutional-blight-type descriptions of humankind that were even more negative than Augustine's. For example, in his commentary on Romans, Martin Luther (1483–1546) says that original sin is "not merely the loss of man's righteousness and

---

[12]Augustine's pessimistic view of human nature has also been attributed to some personal experiences, including an intense struggle with sexual desire. These experiences have been summarized in a disparaging analysis by Ormerod (1992, chaps. 10–11) and a somewhat more sympathetic one by Couenhoven (2005).

[13]Couenhoven (2005) presents Augustine's concept of original sin as "a handful of doctrines" with varying degrees of compatibility (p. 360).

[14]I acknowledge that the loss of preternatural gifts and the retention of natural ones is not technically a changed *nature* but rather a change in humans' total endowment package.

[15]Because I have students who appeal to John Calvin's doctrine of total depravity to claim that there is *nothing* good in humankind, I am compelled to provide evidence that the Reformers also depicted humans as structurally good. Drawing on a Renaissance idea that humans are a microcosm of the divine, Luther writes, "In the human being . . . He [God] is truly recognized, because in him there is such wisdom, justice, and knowledge of all things that he may rightly be called a world in miniature" (Luther, 1958, p. 68). Likewise, in his commentary on Acts, Calvin asserts, "Man is the offspring of God because, by an excellence of nature, they bear something divine" (CO [*Ioannis Calvini opera*], 48:418; translated by Van Vliet, 2009, p. 96).

ability (*to do good*). . . . In addition to this, it is his inclination to all that is evil, his aversion against that which is good, his antipathy against (*spiritual*) light and wisdom, his love for error and darkness, his flight from and his loathing of good works, and his seeking after that which is sinful" (Mueller, 1976, p. 95). Similarly, in the *Institutes* (2.1.8), John Calvin (1509–1564) characterizes original sin as "a hereditary depravity and corruption of our nature, diffused into all parts of the soul, which first makes us liable to God's wrath, then also brings forth . . . 'works of the flesh'" (McKim, 2001, pp. 35-36). These very negative constitutional-blight depictions of humans were rejected by the Catholic Church at the Council of Trent (1545–1563).[16]

A logical problem with Augustine's view of original sin is the absence of a physical mechanism whereby Adam's nature could have changed. It seems unlikely that a single act of disobedience changed Adam's DNA, although an argument for epigenetic changes could be made as he persisted in disobedience.[17] Augustine's explanation of original sin has also been challenged on the basis of *monogenism* (the belief that the whole human race descended from a single pair; see Ormerod, 1992, pp. 89-90). Mathematical estimates of how many different genomes would be necessary to prevent extinction of the human race by inbreeding suggests that monogenism is not scientifically feasible.[18] Of course, any process that could have occurred in a single Adam could also have occurred in a *group* of human ancestors, so this acquisition process should not be rejected on the basis of monogenism alone. A group of ancestors would also solve the theological problem of incest (Ormerod, 1992, p. 90) inherent in Augustine's articulation of original sin.

---

[16]The council reaffirmed the church's position that infants have original sin *in* them but that original sin is expunged by baptism. After baptism, the regenerated experience the inclination to sin, but this is not sin per se and "cannot harm those who do not consent." Trent Decree on Original Sin, June 17, 1546, Session V (Denzinger, 1957, pp. 246-48).

[17]In the last 20 years or so, there has emerged a "third category" in the nature/nurture debate: epigenetics. The epigenome includes the chemicals surrounding DNA that "tag" a gene on or off. The epigenome is not nature in the strictest sense of the word; the chemicals surrounding the DNA are not DNA. But the epigenome can be passed to offspring, so it can be biologically inherited.

[18]For a relatively easy-to-understand argument that contemporary humans descended from a population of 10,000 rather than two, see the chapter titled "Adam's Last Stand" in Venema and McKnight, 2017.

Some combination of processes? The three acquisition processes need not be mutually exclusive. A contemporary attempt to combine processes two and three has been offered by Christoph Schwöbel (2006), who ponders how nature could have changed in creatures made from "the matter of creation and bound into the regularities which shape all created matter" (p. 49). Schwöbel says,

> Paradoxically, being created in the image of God is for humans the presupposition of the fall. Only images of God can sin. . . . Nevertheless, the fall is not to be interpreted as a necessary stage in the process of human development. It remains a contingent fact that cannot be explained completely from its antecedent conditions. Therefore it is not an essential characteristic of human nature but its distortion. (p. 51)

Schwöbel characterizes evil as both emerging out of our essential *imago Dei* qualities (process two) and distorting these qualities (process three). Although Schwöbel frustrated me by failing to articulate the physical mechanism whereby human nature *became* distorted, I appreciated his explicit preservation of humankind's creational good. Although blighted, our structurally good bodies continue to give rise to emergent God-like properties that indispensably identify our species.

MORAL-ETHICAL TENDENCIES AS LEARNED

Humans' moral-ethical tendencies are also influenced by environmental influences. Sometimes these influences are physical (e.g., the Israelites' lack of water; Ex 15). More often they are social (e.g., Mordecai prodding Esther; Esther 4). Because social influences are so powerful, God instructs his people to provide intentional nurture through both direct instruction and the modeling of good behavior (Titus 2). Particular emphasis is placed on the nurture of children. Proverbs 22:6 says, "Train children in the right way, / and when old, they will not stray." God also reminds his people to keep good company. Sometimes these admonitions are explicit (e.g., 1 Cor 5); other times they come in the form of Proverbs and teachings. One of my favorites is Proverbs 13:20: "Whoever walks with the wise becomes wise; / but the companion of fools suffers harm."

The importance of trust. The relationship between environmental influences and moral-ethical tendencies is often mediated by trust. The role of trust in the development of humankind can be seen in Genesis 3:4-5 when the serpent suggests that God's prohibition on the fruit of knowledge is an attempt to keep Eve down ("You will not die; for God knows that when you eat of it your eyes will be opened, and you will be like God, knowing good and evil"). Once Eve doubts that God is looking out for her best interests, she is motivated to protect these interests herself, and Adam is complicit in this endeavor. As summarized in the *Catechism of the Catholic Church*, "Man, tempted by the devil, let his trust in his Creator die in his heart and, abusing his freedom, disobeyed God's command. This is what man's first sin consisted of. All subsequent sin would be disobedience toward God and lack of trust in his goodness" (Catholic Church, 1997, para. 397).

What is true for the development of the species is also true for the development of the individual. In a time when the psychological processes of children received very little attention, Jesus warned, "If any of you put a stumbling block before one of these little ones who believe in me, it would be better for you if a great millstone were fastened around your neck and you were drowned in the depth of the sea" (Mt 18:6). The apostle Paul also appreciated the importance of early trust, warning parents that the discipline of children must not be harsh and provoking, "or they may lose heart" (Col 3:21).

Trust continues to influence our moral tendencies in adulthood. This can be seen in an analysis of the motivations for Old Testament construction projects. From a vantage of trust,[19] David resolves to build a permanent house for God (1 Chron 17:1). Fearing that they would be "scattered abroad upon the face of the whole earth," corporate humanity begins to build a tower that reaches to the heavens (Gen 11:4). From a vantage of trust, the Israelites commemorate various acts of God's provision by constructing altars to God (e.g., Gen 12:7; Josh 8:30). Fearing that they have been abandoned, they request an idol (Ex 32:1). In the New Testament, the

---

[19]The psalms indicating David's trust in God as his security, rock, stronghold, fortress, refuge, and so on are too numerous to list. A few examples are Ps 18:2; 28:7; 40:4; 56:11; 144:2.

inconsistent behaviors of the apostle Peter (walking on the water, denying Christ three times)[20] cannot be reconciled without appealing to his in-the-moment level of trust.

Scripture also addresses trust directly, specifically linking it to moral tendencies. Many psalms (Ps 9, 31, 32, 52, 78, 125) contrast the wicked with those who trust in God. The most explicit link between trust and moral tendencies occurs in Proverbs 3:5-6: "Trust in the LORD with all your heart, /. . . and he will make straight your paths."

Working model of moral-ethical tendencies. Humans are *structurally good and inherently inclined toward both good and evil.* Good tendencies emerge from our good creational structure. How developmentalists should understand our inherent inclinations toward evil is unclear. The environment also influences moral-ethical tendencies. The relationship between the environment and moral behavior is often mediated by trust.

---

[20]Water-walking: Mt 14:24-28. Denial: Mt 26; Mk 14; Lk 22; Jn 18.

CHAPTER FOUR

Agency and Accountability

IN THIS CHAPTER I summarize various Christian views on agency and accountability. By *agency* I mean the freedom and power to choose what we do and who we become. By *accountability* I mean the degree to which we are liable for what we do and become. Part and parcel with accountability (for self) is *responsibility* (for others). For all three of these constructs, I will emphasize humans' temporal experience rather than what is happening in the spiritual realm.

Perspectives on agency and accountability are typically informed by the consideration of two things.

1. Capacity: Do we have the developmental maturity and requisite life experiences to engage in sophisticated moral discernment?

2. Volition: Are we acting voluntarily, or are we unduly influenced by forces beyond our control?

To the degree that capacity and volition are high, we have high agency. Accountability follows from agency; those with higher agency can be held to higher standards of accountability and responsibility.

TEMPORAL AGENCY

Compared to other species, humans have a lot of agency. We were created with God-like capacities and given dominion over all things (Ps 8:5-6). We are particularly agentic when God empowers us for particular purposes through the spirit of the Lord, or the Holy Spirit.[1]

---

[1] Judg 3:10; 14:6; Is 61:1; Lk 4:18; Acts 1:8.

Compared to God, humans have limited agency. The Bible teaches that human agency is subject to the providence of God, who orchestrates both the life of the individual and the course of human history.[2] Concerning God's orchestration, John Calvin asserted that "the plans and intentions of men . . . are so governed by his providence that they are borne by it straight to their appointed end" (*Institutes* 1.16.8; McKim, 2001, p. 28). Calvin believed that God was always working behind the scenes even when our lived psychological experience was one of agency.[3]

Calvin treats humans as having temporal agency because Scripture treats humans as having temporal agency—*even as* it declares us captive to spiritual forces like sin (Rom 7:19). In Genesis 4 God implies not only that Cain has the capacity to master sin but that he must master sin. In Romans 6:12 the apostle Paul instructs Christians to "not let sin exercise dominion in [their] mortal bodies." These passages indicate that we should view ourselves as having temporal agency. Even if this agency is only perceived (or partial),[4] this perception helps us carry out the *imago Dei* activities for which we are purposed and actively fight sin.

ACCOUNTABILITY FOR SELF AND RESPONSIBILITY FOR OTHERS

Scripture depicts humans as accountable for self. A strong message of accountability accompanies the first recorded sin in Genesis 3. Despite efforts by both Adam and Eve to shift responsibility for their own disobedience to another party, both are punished. One of the most commonly recorded events of the Old Testament is God punishing the Israelites for

---

[2]Life of individual: Gen 45:7-8; Ps 75:7; Prov 16:33. History: Job 12:23; Ps 22:28; Dan 4:35; Acts 17:26.

[3]Calvin attempted to reconcile God's providence with our lived psychological experience in his commentary on Is 10:15, explaining, "If God controls the purposes of men, and turns their thoughts and exertions to whatever purpose he pleases, men do not therefore cease to form plans and to engage in this or the other undertaking. We must not suppose that there is a violent compulsion, as if God dragged them against their will; but in a wonderful and inconceivable manner he regulates all the movements of men, so that they still have the exercise of their will" (Pringle, 1953, Vol 1., p. 352).

[4]An alternative frame is that human agency will not be fully realized in this life. As a qualification to Ps 8, the author of Hebrews explains, "Now in subjecting all things to them, God left nothing outside their control. As it is, we do not yet see everything in subjection to them" (Heb 2:8).

their perpetual disobedience. In the New Testament, the apostle Paul institutes temporal accountability in community living (1 Thess 3:10) and reminds believers of their eschatological accountability (Rom 14:12). The disciple John closes the canon with Jesus' proclamation "Look, I am coming soon! My reward is with me, and I will give to each person according to what they have done" (Rev 22:12 NIV).

Scripture also depicts humans as responsible for others. In the Old Testament, responsibility often focuses on respecting others' rights (e.g., don't murder, steal, or commit adultery; Ex 20). In the New Testament, the concept of responsibility is expanded; God's people must now actively strive to build others up (Rom 14:9; 15:2; 1 Thess 5:11).

DEGREES OF AGENCY

Although humankind is an agentic species, some humans have much less agency than others. In the Old Testament history books, social subordinates were blessed or punished on the basis of their leader's behavior. A king influenced God's treatment of his nation; a father influenced God's treatment of his household.[5] One specific condition of reduced agency is the fourth-generation clause, which appears four times in the Pentateuch.[6] In Exodus 20:5 God declares, "I the LORD your God am a jealous God, punishing children for the iniquity of parents, to the third and the fourth generation of those who reject me." Yet this practice was explicitly challenged by the prophets Jeremiah (Jer 17:4-10; 31:29-30) and Ezekiel (Ezek 18:19-20), the latter declaring that "a child shall not suffer for the iniquity of a parent," not vice versa.

Jesus, too, was troubled by the reduced agency of social subordinates, especially women, and often made a point of increasing their agency. In a culture where women were not permitted to study the Torah, Jesus affirmed Mary of Bethany's boldness to posture herself as a disciple and join the theology lesson (Lk 10:42). With respect to divorce, Jesus denounced the practice of putting away wives for insubstantial reasons (Mt 5:31-32). The apostle Paul also worked to increase the agency of women (1 Cor 7:4) and of slaves (1 Cor 7:21; Phil 1:15-16). In what is often called the Magna

---

[5]King: Gen 20; Ex 7–12; 2 Sam 24. Father: Gen 6:18; 1 Kings 15:4-5.
[6]Ex 20:5; 34:7; Num 14:18; Deut 5:10.

Carta of Christian liberty, Paul declares, "There is no longer Jew or Greek, there is no longer slave or free, there is no longer male and female; for all of you are one in Christ Jesus" (Gal 3:28). Admittedly, conditions on the ground have changed slowly. While the percentage of humanity with high agency has increased from the Old Testament to the contemporary period, there are still many people with very limited temporal freedom and power to choose what they do and who they become.

DEGREES OF ACCOUNTABILITY AND RESPONSIBILITY

Because there are degrees of agency, there are degrees of accountability and responsibility. The most common qualifier of accountability in Scripture is knowledge. Using the example of two slaves who received different punishments based on differential knowledge of their master's desire, Jesus warns, "From everyone to whom much has been given, much will be required; and from the one to whom much has been entrusted, even more will be demanded" (Lk 12:48). The apostles also identify knowledge as a qualifier of accountability. Paul asserts that Jews who have knowledge of the law will be held to higher standards than Gentiles (Rom 2). James cautions that those "who teach will be judged with greater strictness" (Jas 3:1).

One proxy for knowledge is developmental status. Because children are highly impressionable and cognitively immature (Prov 22:15; 1 Cor 13:11), they are less accountable than adults. As stated earlier (in chap. 3), Jesus threatens grave consequences for adults who cause children to stumble (Mt 18:6), and Paul instructs fathers not to provoke and discourage their children (Eph 6:4; Col 3:21). The most explicit evidence that children are less accountable than adults is God's reluctance to prescribe death to children (Num 14:29; Jon 4:11). Children *do*, however, seem to be accountable for obedience. Throughout Scripture, parents are instructed to teach and discipline their children, and children are instructed to obey their parents.[7] These passages suggest that even though children are morally inexperienced, they should be (gently) held accountable for direct obedience when they are made privy to parental knowledge in the form of a direct command.

---

[7]For parents: Deut 11:19; Prov 22:6, 15; 23:13-14; Eph 6:4. For children: Eph 6:1; Col 3:20.

A second proxy for knowledge is social status. When dealing with social subordinates, God sometimes seems to apply a sliding scale—particularly if the subordinates lack the agency to secure justice in upright ways.[8] Genesis 38 tells the story of Tamar, a barren widow deceived by her father-in-law Judah. After waiting years for Judah to honor his promise of providing her another husband, she poses as a prostitute and tricks Judah into impregnating her. For this sin of adultery, she does not appear to be punished by God or by Judah. Rather, Judah acknowledges his role in driving her to sin (Gen 38:26). Jesus also told a woman caught in adultery, "Neither do I condemn you" (Jn 8:11).

But Jesus follows this absolution with a directive for the woman: "Go your way, and from now on do not sin again" (Jn 8:11). In contrast to children who retain some immunity throughout Scripture, New Testament advances in the agency of adult subordinates are accompanied by heightened standards of accountability and responsibility. One of the best examples of this occurs in Acts 5, when a man named Ananias sells some property with the *consent* of his wife and withholds some of the proceeds from the apostles. Individually, each spouse then lies to the apostles and receives the exact same punishment. This account establishes that wives who actively participate in moral decision-making are as accountable as their husbands.

FROM KNOWLEDGE TO LOVE

Although knowledge is the most common biblical qualifier of accountability, a synthesis of theology and developmental science also requires some attention to the developmental process whereby morally mature humans undergird their knowledge with discernment rooted in love. In 1 Corinthians 13:8-13 the apostle Paul writes,

> As for knowledge, it will come to an end. For we know only in part, and we prophesy only in part; but when the complete comes, the partial will come to an end. When I was a child, I spoke like a child, I thought like a

---

[8]God does *not* seem to apply a sliding scale when humans disobey a *direct, personal* command. Beginning in the Garden of Eden, it is clear that disobedience of a direct, personal command from God is grounds for death even when a person has limited moral knowledge (e.g., Adam and Eve in Gen 3) or is a social subordinate (e.g., Lot's wife in Gen 19).

child, I reasoned like a child; when I became an adult, I put an end to childish ways. For now we see in a mirror, dimly, but then we will see face to face. Now I know only in part; then I will know fully, even as I have been fully known. And now faith, hope, and love abide, these three; and the greatest of these is love.

In this passage Paul not only establishes that children think very differently than adults; he also implies that reasoning based on knowledge is good, but not as good as reasoning based on love.

Further evidence that loving discernment is superior to a moral system based exclusively on the knowledge of right and wrong can be derived from God's increasingly sophisticated expectations for an increasingly knowledgeable humanity. Following the exodus, God gave his people many laws that required minimal moral discernment. The tenth commandment says, "You shall not covet your neighbor's house; you shall not covet your neighbor's wife, or male or female slave, or ox, or donkey, or anything that belongs to your neighbor" (Ex 20:17). Precise, detailed laws such as this provided structure for the recently emancipated slaves, whose moral reasoning would likely have been based on expected punishments (cf. Lawrence Kohlberg's [1976] preconventional morality). Seemingly, God wanted his morally immature people to live by the letter of the law—at least until their life circumstances permitted them opportunities to develop moral discernment.

Jesus took a very different approach with those who had been privileged to engage in moral reflection, condensing the whole Mosaic code into two laws: "'You shall love the Lord your God with all your heart, and with all your soul, and with all your mind.' This is the greatest and first commandment. And a second is like it: 'You shall love your neighbor as yourself.' On these two commandments hang all the law and the prophets" (Mt 22:37-40). In this exchange, Jesus alerts the Pharisees and Sadducees to a higher standard than obedience to the law. Having gained knowledge and experience, they must now engage in moral discernment motivated by love.

WORKING MODEL OF AGENCY/ACCOUNTABILITY

The Bible depicts humankind as a species with agency. As *powerful agents*, we are *accountable for ourselves* and *responsible for the well-being of others*.

AGENCY AND ACCOUNTABILITY | 39

However, there are *degrees* of agency, and thus degrees of accountability and responsibility. People with limited cognitive capacity, limited power to exercise agency, and limited opportunity to contemplate moral-ethical issues are less accountable and responsible than educated adults with greater social status. The *developmental model* for agency and accountability established in Scripture for both historical humanity and individuals begins with obedience and progresses to moral discernment motivated by love.

If we combine this working model of accountability with the working models of essence, purpose, and moral tendency delineated in the prior chapters, we have a *working model of personhood* to anchor our critique of the psychological theories examined in part two. This working model of personhood is concisely summarized in the chart.

A Working Model of Personhood to Guide Our Critique of the Developmental Theories

1. Essence: Humans are embodied creatures with the capacity for reason, relationships, and dominion.

2. Purpose: Humans are universally purposed for both love and dominion work. Some humans are purposed to love and work in particular ways in particular contexts.

3. Moral-ethical tendencies: Humans are structurally good and inherently inclined toward both good and evil. Moral-ethical tendencies are also influenced by the environment. The relationship between the environment and moral behavior is often mediated by trust.

4. Agency/accountability: Humans are agentic, accountable for self and responsible for others—in varying degrees. Educated adults with high social status have more agency, accountability, and responsibility than children and social subordinates. The developmental model for agency and accountability begins with obedience but progresses to moral discernment motivated by love.

PART 2

Five Developmental Theories

CHAPTER FIVE

Erik Erikson's Eight Stages of the Lifespan

ERIK ERIKSON (1902–1994) is one of the grand theorists associated with psychoanalytic theory.[1] Psychoanalytic theory was made popular in the early 1900s by Viennese physician Sigmund Freud (1856–1939). Its endurance as a widely accepted developmental paradigm is largely attributable to Erikson. Not only did Erikson return to humans some of the positive qualities that Freud took from us (e.g., conscious rational behavior, responsibility) but also provided a lifespan perspective that organizes the presentation of social development in most developmental textbooks. As one of Erikson's biographers claims, "In the entire twentieth century, he stands alone as the one thinker who changed our minds about what it means to live as a person who has arrived at a chronologically mature position and yet continues to grow, to change, and to develop" (Hoare, 2002, p. 3).

Erikson is best known for his eight stages of development and his work on identity. Psychological terms like *identity crisis* coined by Erikson are now common parlance in the developed world. Erikson is also known for his psychohistorical analyses of Martin Luther, Gandhi, Thomas Jefferson, and Jesus.[2] Haggbloom et al. (2002) ranked Erikson the twelfth most

---

[1] Contemporary psychology distinguishes *psychoanalytic* theory (Freud's version) with *psychodynamic* theory (adaptations of Freud). I will use only one term. I chose the former because Erikson was trained as a psychoanalytic theorist and referred to himself as a psychoanalyst (Erikson, 1996, p. 293).

[2] For *Gandhi's Truth*, Erikson was awarded both the Pulitzer Prize and the National Book Award (Erik Erikson wins Pulitzer Prize [1970, May 5], *The Harvard Crimson*, www.thecrimson .com/article/1970/5/5/erik-erikson-wins-pulitzer-prize-perik). *Young Man Luther* got a less positive reception, but even historians who objected to Erikson going beyond the archival data acknowledged its ingenuity. One critic asked, "*How could so bad a book be so good?*" (Lindbeck, 1973, p. 211).

eminent psychologist of the twentieth century, and Cherry (2019) ranked him ninth.

BIOGRAPHY

Erikson's interest in identity was as much personal as professional.[3] Erikson's mother, Karla Abrahamsen, was a well-educated woman of Jewish-Danish origin. At age 21, Abrahamsen married Valdemar Salomonson, a Danish stockbroker who had some shadowy connections with the underworld. Soon after, the marriage went bad and Salomonson disappeared. Erikson was conceived three years later while Karla was on holiday in Germany and had an affair with another Dane, possibly named Erik. To avoid the appearance of scandal, Karla stayed in Germany under the watchful eye of some spinster aunts and gave birth in Frankfurt to the child initially named Erik Salomonson.

Shortly after Erik was born, Karla received word that her missing husband had died in mysterious circumstances. Free to reenter society as a legal widow, she moved to the Karlsruhe area. On Erik's third birthday, she married Theodor Homberger, a pediatrician who later became the president of a local synagogue. As a condition of marriage, Homberger insisted that Erik be told that Homberger was his biological father. Erik Salomonson became Erik Homberger.

But young Erik was not easily deceived. Karla and Theodor were both short and dark, while Erik was tall, blond, and blue-eyed. Relatives and neighbors gossiped and whispered, and Homberger was seemingly more ambivalent about his stepson than he had anticipated being. At age seven, Erik was under the kitchen table while the oblivious adults above discussed his artist and Gentile father. In some accounts, the ambivalent attachment felt by both stepfather and son was exacerbated by Karla, who went out of her way to keep her son implicitly connected to his birth father. Although she never revealed the man's identity (even when Erik pressed her), she maintained friendships with many artists and encouraged Erik to think beyond what he learned at temple school. Erikson recalled earnest

---

[3]Unless otherwise specified, the events of this biography are recorded by Burston (2007).

conversations with his mother about Kierkegaard (a Lutheran) even before his bar mitzvah and credited her with leading him to understand that Judaism was not antagonistic to the "core values of Christianity."[4]

Erik also felt estranged outside the home. In the years leading up to World War II, his German classmates shunned him because he was Jewish, while members of his stepfather's synagogue called him *goy* (Gentile). This ostracizing contributed to Erik's eventual rejection of the synagogue and some of the Jewish rituals that Erikson (1996) felt had "outlived the ideo-logical conditions of their origins" (p. 312). Erik also rejected his step-father's directive to attend medical school. Perhaps in solidarity with his biological father, he dropped out of university to attend art school and then traveled Europe as an itinerant artist.

Erik was sketching children's portraits when a friend recommended him for a tutoring job at the Heitzing School, a Montessori school run by Sigmund Freud's daughter Anna. He entered into psychoanalysis with Anna (unlimited sessions for $7 a month!) and shortly thereafter became her as-sistant, a role that sometimes permitted him the pleasure of transporting "the professor" (Sigmund) to his medical appointments (On This Day, 1994).

Encouraged by Anna, who noticed his unusual rapport with children, Erik soon began training to be a psychoanalyst himself. But Erik found the psychoanalysts in Vienna to be dogmatically resistant to new ideas, and his relationship with Anna was complicated by his marriage to Joan Serson, a Canadian dancer who had had a bad experience with psychoanalysis at the Heitzing School. Even before the German occupation of Vienna had become apparent, the couple had discussed securing a professional affiliation that would permit Erik to place greater theoretical emphasis on the dynamics of *ongoing* social relationships rather than determinants experienced in infancy. As both political tensions and interpersonal relations at Heitzing heated up— Freud's books were being burned in Germany, and the Freuds refused to vacate[5]—Joan's desire to get the family out of Europe intensified.

---

[4]Erikson to Curfman, 30 December 1976, Item 811, Erikson Harvard papers. Cited by Hoare (2002, p. 8).

[5]The Freuds persisted in denial until Anna was interrogated by the Gestapo some five years later. The Freuds did obtain safe passage out of Europe for most of their extended family, but Burston (2007) has speculated that Anna's lifelong refusal to esteem Erikson's scholarly ideas may be

Despite tension between the Freuds and the Eriksons, in 1933 the Vienna Psychoanalytic Society certified Erik to practice psychoanalysis anywhere in the world. The grateful and relieved family traveled first to Denmark and then to Boston. Although he had never earned a college degree, Erik found positions at Harvard, then Yale, and then Berkeley. Across his various posts, he combined his work as a therapist with his work on identity development. He focused specifically on children, Native Americans, and veterans of war. He also worked on his own identity, psychologically resolving his complicated paternity in 1939 when he assumed American citizenship under the name of *Erik Homberger Erikson*—a name that many have interpreted to mean: my identity includes some Homberger, but I am ultimately *son of myself*.

Erikson also self-crafted his religion. Although he never formally left Judaism, he was drawn to the teachings of Jesus from an early age and married an "ardent Christian" whose father was an Episcopal minister (Burston, 2007, p. 58). As Erikson's writings became increasingly dominated by Christian sentiments and images, people began asking him whether he was Jewish or Christian. In an informal setting Erikson once joked, "Why both, of course" (Burston, 2007, p. 60). In a formal publication Erikson (1996) referred to himself as "a psychoanalyst in the Judaeo-Christian orbit" (p. 293). His most thoughtful response was found in his private correspondence. Asked specifically whether he was a Christian, Erikson labeled himself a "Christian apprentice" who studied the "living implications of Christ's message" without confining himself to any particular denomination (Hoare, 2002, p. 87).

Erikson definitely liked Jesus. Whether he believed in Christ's divinity is unclear.[6] Without discounting the integrity with which he approached Jesus' teachings, at least two of Erikson biographers have speculated that Jesus was a good "fit" for Erikson (Burston, 2007, p. 8; Hoare, 2002, p. 87).

---

defensive; Anna's refusal to close the Heitzing School in a timely manner eventually cost people their lives. Even when Erikson dedicated his book *Insight and Responsibility* to Anna, she insisted that she could not understand it.

[6]Erikson was very explicit about how Jesus' teachings connect to personal relationships. He was less explicit in references to Christ's salvific sacrifice. Some content in *Young Man Luther* (Erikson, 1962, esp. p. 179) makes me suspect that Erikson questioned Christ's divinity. Some content in "The Galilean Sayings and the Sense of 'I'" (Erikson, 1996, esp. pp. 299, 333) makes me suspect that Erikson doubted the historicity of the resurrection.

Jesus' acceptance of both Jews and Gentiles permitted Erikson to integrate his two religious heritages. Burston also speculated that Erikson felt an affinity with Jesus, who knew what it was like to grow up in a family characterized by false pretenses (i.e., Joseph was not Jesus' true father).

Erikson seems not to have fully appreciated the ramifications of false pretenses until he engaged in them. The years 1949–1951 found him wrestling with two particular charades. The first concerned a new policy by the University of California specifying that all faculty must sign an oath stating that they did not belong to the Communist Party. Erikson did not belong to the party, but like most Berkeley faculty (Gendzel, 2010), he objected to the oath for a variety of reasons, including the violation of academic freedom and the nullification of tenure. Despite his public objection to the oath, Erikson found himself clandestinely signing a watered-down version of the oath in order to keep his job, a concession that Burston suspects likely troubled him later. Erikson resolved this ethical dilemma by departing Berkeley for a new job at the Austin Riggs Center in Stockbridge, Massachusetts, in 1951.

This move forced Erikson to reveal a family secret: the Eriksons' fourth child, Neil, had not really died at birth. While Joan was recovering from a difficult labor, Erikson's close friend anthropologist Margaret Mead convinced Erikson that the family would be best served by institutionalizing Neil, who had been born with Down syndrome (a practice that is very objectionable now but was commonplace in the 1940s and 1950s). News that their younger brother was still alive reportedly had a "profoundly unsettling effect" (Burston, 2007, p. 38) on two of Erikson's older children, undermining their *basic trust* in the man who would soon coin the term, even as it eased tension between Erik and Joan. With their new freedom to acknowledge Neil, Erik and Joan engaged in a concerted collaboration to "map" the human life cycle, paying particular attention to how mitigating circumstances influence the normative sequence of human development. This joint project reenergized them both, and Erikson consistently credited Joan as a collaborator in his eight-stage model.[7]

---

[7]"To restate the sequence of psychosocial stages throughout life means to take responsibility for the terms Joan Erikson and I have originally attached to them" (Erikson & Erikson, 1997, p. 155). See also Thomas (1997).

Aside from his disillusioned children, the move to Stockbridge was a good one for the Eriksons, affording them relationships with the likes of Benjamin Spock, Norman Rockwell, and Reinhold Niebuhr. But Erikson became restless once again and rejoined the faculty at Harvard in 1960 as a public lecturer with no departmental affiliation. Although Erikson felt unprepared for the large audiences that greeted him at Harvard, he was wildly popular and finally emboldened to speak critically on a variety of issues ranging from Hietzing-style psychoanalysis (it's too rigid) to American culture (the American moratorium lasts too long and we abandon our commitments too easily).[8] Burston (2007) credits Erikson's extreme popularity with college students in the 1960s to his assurance that it was possible to age "without losing one's moral and spiritual compass" (p. 51). Erikson formally retired from Harvard in 1970 but continued to write for another 10 or so years. He lived to be 91.

ERIKSON VERSUS FREUD

Because I am focusing on theories framing *contemporary* understandings of human development, I have not included a chapter on Sigmund Freud. However, appreciation of Erikson's model is facilitated by a brief comparison with the model of his predecessor. Moreover, it is important to give credit where credit is due. Although contemporary psychologists are inclined to view many of Freud's *specific* claims about human development as erroneous, Freud is credited with at least three principles that are foundational to psychoanalytic theory in general and Erikson's theory in particular. These principles are as follows:

1. Humans are animated by an innate energy or life force. Freud referred to this energy as libido; contemporary psychologists speak generically of inborn drives. These drives, viewed as partially conscious and partially subconscious, motivate emotional attachments and enduring patterns of behavior. These patterns of behavior can

---

[8]Erikson (1968) defined *psychosocial moratorium* as a period "during which the young adult through free role experimentation may find a niche in some section of society" (p. 156). This period of development is characterized by a "delay of adult commitments" (p. 157) and is institutionalized by most cultures, for most youth.

be adaptive and maladaptive. When congealed, they constitute human personality.

2. Human personality develops over time as a series of universal stages. Developmental stages are universal rather than culture-specific because they are part of humans' biological "ground plan."

3. Early childhood experiences are paramount in orientating individuals *toward* or *away from* healthy interpersonal relationships and social competence. Because psychoanalytic theories focus on drives and view psychological experience as scheduled by biological maturation, they are classified as "nature" theories. But they place *almost* as much importance on nurture, at least in the early stages of development. This is because healthy development requires environmental opportunities (nurture) to satisfy inborn drives (nature) in a healthy manner.

Erikson always viewed Freud with a certain amount of awe, but he did not hesitate to reformulate the aspects of Freud's theories with which he disagreed. Three particular areas of disagreement between Freud and Erikson concerned (a) the focus of our primary drives, (b) the duration of psychological development, and (c) the degree to which early experiences determine who we become.

Concerning the focus of our primary drives, Freud proposed that the chief objective of the libido is to obtain pleasure, and that humans derive the most pleasure from zones of the body that are developed enough to work well. Zones change as we mature, moving down the body. Freud articulated five *psychosexual* (i.e., physical-pleasure-based) stages ranging from oral (stage one) to genital (stage five). Erikson viewed Freud's focus on physical pleasure as narrow and misguided. In Erikson's view, humans direct much more of our life energy toward developing the social and cognitive competencies appropriate to our life stage.

The overarching drive in Erikson's model is the drive for mastery over oneself and one's environment. Erikson (1980) said,

> The growing child must, at every step, derive a vitalizing sense of reality from the awareness that his individual way of mastering experience is a successful variant of the way other people around him master experience

and recognize such mastery. In this, children cannot be fooled by empty praise and condescending encouragement. . . . Their accruing ego identity [i.e., portion of the Self that is conscious][9] gains real strength only from wholehearted and consistent recognition of real accomplishment, that is achievement that has meaning in their culture. (p. 95)

This general drive for competence that manifests across various situations has alternatively been called a "mastery motive" or "effectance motive" (Bandura, 1997, p. 13).

Concerning the duration of development, Erikson took a lifespan perspective. Because challenges to our competence as well as opportunities to demonstrate mastery occur throughout life, Erikson asserted that psychological development is not "done" when our genitals are fully mature (as Freud proposed) but is a lifelong process culminating in a psychological "life review" and acceptance of our impending death. As an alternative to Freud's five psycho*sexual* stages, Erikson articulated eight stages of psycho*social* development named to emphasize a contrast of human attributes (e.g., industry vs. inferiority). In each of Erikson's stages, the developing person confronts, and hopefully masters, the opportunities and challenges afforded by his or her current physiological capacity, cognitive capacity, and society. Erikson referred to these developmentally specific challenges and opportunities as *crises* that the person could resolve positively (more in keeping with the first attribute in the stage name) or negatively (more in keeping with the second attribute).

Finally, Erikson's model is less determining than Freud's. With respect to early determinism, Freud proposed that psychological deprivation in infancy could leave a person stuck or "fixated" in the early stages of development. In contrast, Erikson believed that the early stages were foundational but not determining. Erikson's early stages are foundational in that those who resolve early crises in a positive way are better prepared to face the challenges of later stages, whereas those who resolve early crises in a negative way can expect the challenges of that particular stage to reemerge as problems in later stages.

---

[9]I have inserted the bracketed material to provide clarity. The Self as partially conscious and partially unconscious is explained in conjunction with Tenet A (discussed below).

ERIKSON'S EIGHT STAGES OF PSYCHOSOCIAL DEVELOPMENT

Erikson introduced his eight stages in *Identity and the Life Cycle*, first published in 1959.[10] Although many readers will be familiar with a textbook version of Erikson's stages, discussion of this book's four organizing themes will be facilitated by a review of the stages as Erikson developed them across various publications. Textbooks provide the gist of Erikson's theory but tend to describe development through a contemporary and strictly secular lens. They place more emphasis on individual fulfillment than Erikson did, and ignore his writings on faith. Most textbooks also neglect the *eight virtues* linked to the successful resolution of each stage. Although Erikson's (1964) assignment of a specific virtue to each stage came after his introduction of the stages, inclusion of the virtues helps illuminate Erikson's fundamental beliefs about personhood.

Stage one: trust versus mistrust (infancy). Erikson's first crisis is that of trust versus mistrust. Finding themselves out of the womb and in a complex social environment, infants' first attempts at mastery involve an implicit tallying of caregivers' initiatives and responses (*Mom cuddled me, Mom cuddled me again, Mom ignored me, Mom cuddled me a third time*). From this tally, infants preconsciously compute a ratio of supportive experiences to nonsupportive ones.

This ratio is the basis for expectations that influence the *methods* infants use to resolve subsequent crises. Infants who experience the world as primarily supportive develop what Erikson called *basic trust*. This trust makes them open to caregivers' directives in *healthy* forms of mastery (*hold the spoon like this; don't hit; say you're sorry*). They also develop the *virtue of hope*, which is best thought of as trust extended beyond the caregiver to the deep conviction that life has meaning. Erikson viewed hope as sort of an infant version of faith. In contrast, infants who experience the world as primarily unsupportive develop expectations that will make it difficult to develop healthy competence in subsequent stages. Similar to infants with disturbed attachment (cf. chap. 6), mistrustful infants are positioned

---

[10]Page numbers cited in this book are from the 1980 edition.

to "master" themselves and their environments in unhealthy ways (e.g., emotional masking, hyper-attention to threat).

With respect to identity development, the argument could be made that Erikson's first stage is a pre-stage. Infant mastery is prelinguistic, limited in volition, and largely focused on monitoring *others'* behavior to determine what kind of place the world is. It is not until children develop a self-concept at approximately 18 months that mastery consciously informs identity.

Stage two: autonomy versus shame and doubt (18 months to age 3). In late infancy and toddlerhood, gains in motor skills, language, and planning afford children much greater control over their own bodies and some aspects of their environment. Toddlers no longer have to wait for a parent to feed them. Rather, they can formulate a simple plan to stand on a chair, reach a banana, and feed themselves. This newfound control can produce an emboldening. This emboldening prompts Erikson's second crisis, wherein children devote a great deal of psychological energy to positioning themselves along the continuum of autonomy versus shame and doubt.

Stage two focuses on children's sense of control, especially as it pertains to their physical body (stature, motor functions, bowel and bladder, etc.). Children who experience their body as more empowering than embarrassing develop a sense of autonomy and the *virtue of willfulness*, defined as "increased judgement and decision in the application of drive" (Erikson, 1964, p. 118). Healthy children apply willfulness to challenging tasks in subsequent stages. Alternatively, children who are acutely aware of what James Fowler (1981) has termed a "deficiency of being" (p. 60) are likely to experience shame (best viewed as a self-conscious sense of inadequacy) and begin to doubt their abilities.

To be clear, some sense of self-consciousness and limited capacity relative to parents is necessary for children to recognize and benefit from parental instruction. There was no doubt in Erikson's (1980) mind that parent and child are "unequal to each other" (p. 68) and parents must establish themselves as clear authority figures. But children who frequently experience parental authority as shaming often settle for forms of mastery that permit them to psychologically spurn their parents. Some defy shaming with "shameless willfulness" (Erikson et al., 1989, p. 45). Others develop "the character dominated by the wish to 'get away with' things" (Erikson, 1980, p. 73). Still others develop an infantile obsessiveness with having small things a certain way. By becoming "a stickler for certain rituals, the child then learns to gain power over his parents . . . in areas where he could not find large-scale mutual regulation with them" (Erikson, 1980, p. 73).

Children's positioning along the stage two continuum follows directly from their experience of trust versus mistrust in stage one. Those who enter stage two with basic trust in their caregivers are typically able to achieve the appropriate balance between autonomy and shame by establishing themselves as children who act confidently, with intention, within the appropriate limits set by their caregivers. Children lacking basic trust attempt alternative forms of mastery. Clever commentary on this stage has been provided by Fowler (1981), who declared that "the child becomes one who could go far, or indeed go too far" (p. 59).

Stage three: initiative versus guilt (ages 3 to 5). When preschoolers gain the capacity to mentally sequence and evaluate several actions, they face the third crisis of initiative versus guilt. Initiative involves the superimposing of the child's first envisionings of a future self on stage two willfulness. Erikson (1980) put it like this: "Being firmly convinced that he is a person, the child must now find out what kind of person he is going to be. And here he hitches his wagon to nothing less than a star: he wants to be like his parents who to him appear very powerful and very beautiful, although quite unreasonably dangerous. He 'identifies with them,' he plays with the idea of how it would be to be them" (p. 78).

This identification with parents provides the child with the "rudiments of purpose: a temporal perspective giving direction and focus to concerted striving" (Erikson, 1964, p. 120). This *virtue of purpose* often reveals itself in fantasy and play. It also serves as the basis for the development of a conscience, which is formed by the child's internalization of parental standards. When the child violates these standards, or even considers violating them, the child feels a sense of guilt. Again, memorable commentary has been provided by Fowler (1981), who characterized Erikson's stage two as visual and stage three as auditory (p. 60). In stage two, children "see," in their mind's eye, how small or exposed they are relative to others. In stage three, children "hear," in their moral conscience, the constraining and judging voices of authority figures. The importance of well-articulated adult standards to the preschooler's developing conscience is indicated in Erikson's (1980) declaration that the child "now hears, as it were, God's voice without seeing God. Moreover, he begins automatically to feel guilty even for mere thoughts and for deeds which nobody has watched. This is the cornerstone of morality in the individual sense" (p. 84).

Stage four: industry versus inferiority (age 6 to puberty). In middle childhood, children need time for play, but they are also very interested in competent "workmanship" (Erikson, 1964, p. 123). Recognizing that they have some capacity to function as adults, they become "dissatisfied and disgruntled without a sense of being useful, without a sense of being able to make things and make them well and even perfectly" (Erikson, 1980, p. 91). What distinguishes this stage from the previous two is the amount of intentional effort children must exert to show themselves useful. In stages two and three, many of the skills that children acquire are largely maturationally driven. Although toddlers and preschoolers acquire skills at different rates, almost all eventually walk, talk, develop the fine motor skills necessary for tool use, and internalize the values of their community. In contrast, the skills of middle childhood are much more *effort*-driven. Maturation is not the primary contributor to learning to read, multiply fractions, play the piano, or excel on the soccer field. Maturation helps, but the development of desirable (even marketable) talents requires hard work (thus Erikson's term *industry*).

It is these hard-work tasks of middle childhood that offer both the challenge and the opportunity to define oneself as an *industrious* person who can attain mastery if concerted effort is applied or an *inferior* person for whom hard effort will not pay off. The sense of self as a talented, industrious person with the capacity to master the environment facilitates the development of skills necessary for adolescence and adulthood and gives rise to the *virtue of competence*. It also protects us from developing depression. The centrality of work in healthy development is indicated in Erikson's (1964) musings that "ever since his 'expulsion from paradise,' . . . man has been inclined to protest work as drudgery. . . . The fact, however, is that man must learn to work, as soon as his intelligence and his capacities are ready to be 'put to work,' so that his ego's power may not atrophy" (p. 123).

Stage five: identity versus role confusion (adolescence). Erikson's fifth stage, identity versus role confusion, is about developing an identity that is coherent and feels freely chosen. By *coherent* I mean that identity must reconcile what one has been uniquely and "irreversibly given" (body type, temperament, giftedness and vulnerability, infantile models, life experiences) with the choices available (Erikson, 1975, p. 19). Youth do this by gravitating toward social groups, personas, and activities that match their self-assessments. Sometimes youth make healthy, realistic assessments of their potential and position themselves in contexts where they thrive. Other times they do not. For example, a girl who doubts her ability to excel in college might take a factory job, avoiding a situation where it might be revealed that her goals surpass her ability. A boy with low self-esteem might date someone who also holds him in low esteem because this satisfies his need for "sameness" (Erikson, 1980, p. 94) across time and contexts. In other words, the stage-five adolescent feels an intense need to pin down "who I am" and would rather have a coherent identity (*I am not worth much and we all concur*) than be exposed as a fraud.

Youth are not always able to articulate why they choose the contexts they choose. Contemporary textbooks emphasize the conscious and intentional component of adolescent "identity work," but Erikson (1966) asserted that "the core of that inner unification called identity" is mostly unconscious or preconscious (i.e., "accessible only to musings at moments of special awareness"; p. 151). Thus, in a discussion of "'outsiders' who go their lone way," Erikson (1962) said that "therapists can only note that their pride in not having wanted to adjust is a cover up for not having been able to do so from way back. But not always" (p. 100).

The second requisite for successful resolution of stage five is the sense that one has at least assented to, if not freely chosen, one's identity. Toward this end, many youth benefit from an extended period of exploration, termed *moratorium*, during which they "try on" different interpersonal roles, vocations, and beliefs and then discard ones that don't fit. Often the adolescent moratorium includes "falling in love," which involves "projecting one's diffused self-image on another . . . seeing it thus reflected and gradually clarified" (Erikson, 1968, p. 132). It is also typical for adolescents to clarify who they are by being cliquish or actively rejecting those who are different (often for petty reasons such as dress, tastes, and cultural background). Although adults should not condone this meanness, it can protect against identity diffusion.

To appreciate Erikson's perspective on identity, it is important to recognize that contemporary American textbooks place much greater emphasis on moratorium than Erikson did. This is because there are now many more vocational and lifestyle choices than when Erikson was writing *and* because individualistic societies take existing commitments less seriously than Erikson did. (Recall from the biography section that Erikson criticized Americans for this.)

Erikson viewed a moratorium as helpful, but not necessary in all contexts. What is necessary is that youth *feel* as though they have a choice in their commitments, even when their choices are limited. This is because an adolescent's fear "of being forced into activities in which he would feel exposed to ridicule or self-doubt is so strong that he would rather act shamelessly in the eyes of his elders, out of free choice, than be forced into activities which would be shameful in his own eyes or in those of his peers" (Erikson, 1968, p. 129). Adolescents who feel that they have choices generally develop the *virtue of fidelity*, defined as "the ability to sustain loyalties freely pledged in spite of the inevitable contradictions of value systems" (Erikson, 1964, p. 125).

Stage six: intimacy versus isolation (young adulthood). Erikson's sixth crisis, intimacy versus isolation, involves the ability to maintain a healthy level of intimacy and commitment to others: to a lover and to one's friends, and more broadly as a participant in society (e.g., as a member of a religious congregation, tribe, or combat unit). Successful resolution of stage six engenders what Erikson (1964) deemed "the greatest of human virtues, and, in fact, the dominant virtue of the universe": *love* (p. 127).

Erikson believed that the capacity to love well followed directly from the strength of the identity crafted in stage five. Those who know who they are, are better able to initiate relationships with like-minded others and maintain the boundaries necessary to offer themselves on a deep, interpersonal level without completely losing themselves in the offering. Loving well also includes the capacity to distance oneself from intense but unhealthy relationships.[11]

The alternative to intimacy is the lack of healthy adult relationships. Unhealthy relationships can generally be attributed to one of two psychological processes. In the first process, people resist close relationships because they are still absorbed in identity work and fear that an intense relationship might do the definitional work the self has not yet completed. In the second process, the person too-readily relies on close relationships to define the self. With respect to the second process, Erikson (1980) cautioned that some people marry too early and "alas, the early obligation to act in a defined way, as mates and as parents, disturbs them in the completion of" identity work (p. 101).

Stage seven: generativity versus stagnation (middle adulthood). In Erikson's seventh stage, generativity versus stagnation, adults turn their attention to establishing and mentoring the next generation. This shift in attention happens because the human adult "is so constituted as to need to be needed" (Erikson, 1964, p. 130). The virtue associated with this stage is *care.* In Erikson's early writings, this stage centered almost exclusively on childrearing. Later, Erikson (1974) wrote that to be "generative does not necessarily mean that one produces children. . . . But it means to know what one does if one does not. And it means that one participates otherwise in the establishment, the guidance, and the enrichment of the living generation and the world it inherits" (p. 123).

The alternative to generativity is a feeling of stagnation and pervasive disconnect from society. Erikson presented a very unflattering portrayal

---

[11]The importance of this capacity is evidenced in the fact that Erikson (1980) initially named this stage *intimacy and distantiation vs. self-absorption*, defining *distantiation* as "the readiness to repudiate, to isolate, and, if necessary, to destroy those forces and people whose essence seems dangerous to one's own" (pp. 100-101).

of nongenerative individuals, characterizing them as self-indulgent and regressively immature. Erikson (1980) located the cause of stagnation, most commonly, in early childhood problems with parents, proposing that stagnant individuals lack "'belief in the species,' which would make a child appear to be a welcome trust of the community" (pp. 103-4).

Stage eight: integrity versus despair (old age). Erikson's final stage, integrity versus despair, is focused on the psychological "life review" most humans undertake as they approach death. Most directly, this review involves looking back over our life and accepting responsibility for how we lived. When we conclude that our life was well spent, we face death with integrity; when we conclude that we should have lived differently, we experience despair.

Although developmental textbooks often present Erikson's final stage as focused almost exclusively on the evaluation of self, Erikson's own presentation reveals a much more comprehensive task. Acquiring the *virtue of wisdom* means coming to peace not only with ourselves but also with our associates and even historical humanity. Erikson (1980) characterized integrity as

> the acceptance of one's own and only life cycle and of the people who have become significant to it as something that had to be and that, by necessity, permitted of no substitutions. It thus means a new different love of one's parents, free of the wish that they should have been different, and an acceptance of the fact that one's own life is one's own responsibility. It is a sense of comradeship with men and women of distant times and of different pursuits, who have created orders and objects and sayings conveying human dignity and love. Although aware of the relativity of all the various life styles which have given meaning to human striving, the possessor of integrity is ready to defend the dignity of his own life style.... For him all human integrity stands and falls with the one style of integrity of which he partakes. (p. 104)

In his later writings, Erikson also incorporated faith in stage eight. This incorporation will be discussed in connection with Tenet B.

THE FOUR THEMES

Contemporary psychology is grounded in quantitative methods, but early psychologists moved more freely between various ways of knowing. From Erikson's vast array of discursive writings and lectures, I have derived five tenets that summarize his view on the four themes of this book.

A. The central characteristic of personhood is our identity (essence).

B. Humans are inherently purposed for love and care (purpose).

C1. The human ground plan provides psychological equipment to reflect and discern good; how well the equipment works is primarily a function of nurture (moral-ethical tendencies).

C2. Good and evil emerge from the same basic psychological processes (moral-ethical tendencies).

D. Humans need to live as though we have high agency, even as we accept the providence of God (agency/accountability).

ESSENCE

Tenet A: The central characteristic of personhood is our identity. Central to Erikson's view of personhood is the concept of identity. Identity is the *conscious* part of the Self (capital *S*). As we progress through Erikson's stages, we develop many (lowercase) selves (e.g., my preschool self aspired to be queen; my adolescent self failed to make the homecoming court; my adult self is hoping for meager book royalties).

Many selves would make for a fragmented identity. Fortunately, humans are equipped with "a central and partially unconscious organizing agency" (Erikson, 1968, p. 211) that Freud named the ego. According to Erikson, the primary job of the ego is to safeguard our identity by continuously synthesizing our many selves (abandoned, existing, anticipated) into one coherent Self. The ego also works to keep selves that might debilitate us (e.g., an abused self) in our unconscious. Because identity includes only the part of Self to which our ego permits conscious access,[12] Erikson sometimes referred to identity as *ego-identity.*

---

[12]Erikson (1968) defined *identity* as the conscious part of the Self, after admitting that he had previously been very inconsistent in his use of the word (p. 211). On page 208 he says, "I have

Erikson viewed ego-identity as having both a functional and an existential component. In his book on Martin Luther, Erikson (1962) distinguished these as the "horizontal" and "vertical" components of identity (p. 179). Although coverage in textbooks is almost always limited to functional identity, Erikson believed that a healthy functional identity must be anchored in an existential identity derived from religion or a meaning system implicitly based in religion. He drew most often on Christianity but used examples from a variety of meaning systems in his writings, moving seamlessly between psychology and theology.

Both functional identity and existential identity develop in relationship with others. This is because the "ultimate goal of man's wishes is to know even also as I am known" (Erikson, 1964, p. 102). Humans' first significant relationship is with the mother. In healthy development, the child and mother experience *mutuality*, defined as "a relationship in which partners depend on each other for the development of their respective strength" (Erikson, 1963b, p. 421). Erikson believed that the mother-child relationship is so formative that it influences all subsequent relationships, including our relationship with God. Ultimately, a relationship with God replaces our relationship with our mother. Erikson believed that every adult senses God (or gods). He is the only psychologist in this book to present a relationship with God as a universal characteristic of personhood.

Identity is also informed by more corporeal factors such as sex-specific embodiment. In one study, Erikson asked children to imagine that they were making a movie by arranging toys in an exciting scene and then telling the plot. He observed that boys' play space was typically characterized by exterior scenes involving tall structures with protruding cones and cannons, downfall and ruin, and free motion of vehicles, animals, and people. In contrast, girls' play space often involved arranging furniture and a greater quantity of animals and people in "static interiors which were

---

tried out the term identity almost deliberately—I like to think—in many different connotations. At one time it seemed to refer to a conscious sense of individual uniqueness, at another to an unconscious striving for a continuity in experience, and at a third, as a solidarity with a group's ideals."

open or simply enclosed and were peaceful or intruded upon" (Erikson, 1968, p. 271). Erikson explained males' focus on what he called the "outer" space and females' focus on the "inner" space as primarily a function of morphology consciously and unconsciously impacting preferred activities. While many of his contemporaries were downplaying sex differences to promote gender equity, Erikson made people angry with his observation that "sexual differences in the organization of the play space seem to parallel the morphology of genital differentiation itself" (p. 271). Expanding on this idea, he posed and answered this question:

> Am I saying, then, that "anatomy is destiny"? Yes, it is destiny, insofar as it determines not only the range and configuration of physiological functioning and its limitations, but also, to an extent, personality configurations. The basic modalities of woman's commitment and involvement naturally also reflect the ground plan of her body (Erikson, 1968, p. 285)—as do men's modalities reflect that of the male body. (Erikson, 1975, p. 228)[13]

That said, Erikson recognized that morphology interacts with sociohistorical context. Thus, average sex differences should not be used to justify institutional inequities or socially prescribed roles. In fact, they should be parlayed into helping humanity thrive. Arguing that men and women should collaborate in the application of science to ecological and humanitarian tasks, Erikson (1968) said,

> My main point is that where the confinements are broken, women may yet be expected to cultivate the implications of what is biologically and anatomically given. She may, in new areas of activity, balance man's indiscriminate endeavor to perfect this dominion over the outer spaces of national and technological expansion (at the cost of hazarding the annihilation of the species) with the determination to emphasize such varieties of caring and caretaking as would take responsibility for each individual child born within a planned humanity. There will be many

---

[13]The first portion of this quote (prior to the dash) appeared in Erikson (1968, p. 285). Erikson (1975, p. 228) published a letter he had received that included part of the 1968 quote. He defended himself by saying that "'Also' means that the modalities of a woman's existence reflect the ground plan of her body among other things—as do men's modalities reflect that of the male body."

difficulties in a new joint arrangement of the sexes to changing conditions, but they do not justify prejudices which keep half of mankind from participating in planning and decision making, especially at a time when the other half, by its competitive escalation and acceleration of technological progress, has brought us and our children to the gigantic brink on which we live. (pp. 292-93)

A second way that Erikson addressed embodiment was to compare humans with animals. Erikson (1963b) recognized some hardwired psychological similarities between humans and animals, noting that humans—like Harry Harlow's monkeys—can be made "psychotic" in situations of extreme social deprivation (p. 420). But Erikson also viewed humans as psychologically distinct from animals. Objecting to Freud's assertion that humans are brutish because of our "membership in the 'animal kingdom,'" Erikson (1975) quipped, "Far from deserving disdain as our ancestors, then, animals could well take exception to their 'descendants.' No, with his sins, man stands alone among all creatures" (p. 188).

In sum, Erikson's view of human essence focuses on identity. Our identity has a functional component informed by our relationships with significant others, our morphology, and the sociohistorical context in which we live. Our identity also has an existential component rooted in our relationship with God.

Critique A. Our working model of the person (developed in part one) depicts humans as embodied creatures with *imago Dei* qualities. More than any other developmental theory in this book, Erikson's perspective is compatible with the *relational* view of the *imago Dei*, which emphasizes relationships with God and other people.

Which relationships are primary depends on the developmental stage. Erikson designated mother as primary in stage one, with God replacing mother by stage eight. In contrast, Scripture depicts God as primary, paying scant attention to mothers. However, Scripture does depict humans as "standing in" for God, for those who do not yet know God (e.g., the apostle Paul tells the Corinthians that they are Christ's ambassadors, "as though God were making his appeal through us" [2 Cor 5:20 NIV]). Scripture also provides stories which imply that mothers are important to young children's development (e.g., Hannah raising Samuel until he is old enough to serve God at the temple; see 1 Sam 1). Thus, Erikson's explication of a process whereby the young child is defined by the mother until a relationship with God replaces the relationship with the mother would seem to *supplement* rather than compete with Scripture's emphasis on the primacy of humans' relationship with God. (For more on parents "standing in" for God, see Critique A in chap. 6.)

Both Erikson and Christian theology also emphasize the need for humans to define themselves as being in relationship. As a psychoanalytic theorist, Erikson believed that a good deal of identity work happens unconsciously, but he formally defined identity as the conscious part of the Self. Similarly, Scripture implies unconscious processes[14] but is explicit about humans' need for a conscious, relational identity. Isaiah emphasizes that God has called us *by name* and we are his (Is 43:1). In several Old Testament passages, God's people are instructed to craft identity markers such as an emblem on the forehead (Deut 11:18-21) or a pile of stones that will prompt children to ask, "What do these stones mean?" (Josh 4:21). In the New Testament, the apostle Paul seeks to cultivate both a corporate and a unique sense of identity for every member of the body of Christ (see Rom 12; 1 Cor 12).

Erikson's view is also compatible with the other elements of essence presented in chapter two. By shifting attention from (Freud's) unconscious processes to conscious ones, and by drawing a clear distinction between humans and animals with respect to sin, Erikson depicted humanity as a species with the reasoning capacity to make moral choices and behave accordingly. Thus, his perspective is compatible with the *substantive* view of the *imago Dei*. By asserting that identity is rooted in our biological ground plan, Erikson afforded appropriate attention to human embodiment. In proposing that commitments associated with the female ground plan might "balance man's indiscriminate endeavor to perfect this

---

[14]Scripture passages that seem to imply unconscious processes include Ps 90 and 139; Jer 17:9-10; and Rom 7. Theologians who interpret Scripture as establishing unconscious processes include Abraham Kuyper and Cornelius Van Til. For a review of Christian positions on the unconscious, see Payne (2003).

dominion [emphasis added] over the outer spaces," Erikson (1968, p. 292) not only gave a rhetorical nod to Genesis 1; he also validated the *functional* view of the *imago Dei* (with its emphasis on earth-keeping and cultural development) the link between *likeness* and biological sex proposed by Garr (2003) and by Middleton (2005), and a restorative approach to gender. (Recall: the restoration model of gender [Gunnoe, 2003] proposes that nonhierarchical differences were instituted at creation to help males and females jointly fulfill the directives explicitly given to both: to be fruitful and have dominion.) In these many regards, Erikson's view of human essence is very compatible with a Christian one.

PURPOSE

Tenet B: Humans are inherently purposed for love and care. Erikson's eight stages and *nature-intended* virtues constitute a telos-like developmental process with telos-like goals. That is because development is undergirded by the epigenetic principle. Erikson (1968) explained development like this:

> Whenever we try to understand growth, it is well to remember the *epigenetic principle* which is derived from the growth of organisms *in utero*. Somewhat generalized, this principle states that anything that grows has a ground plan, and that out of this ground plan the parts arise, each part having its time of special ascendency, until all parts have arisen to form a functioning whole. This, obviously, is true for fetal development when each part of the organism has its critical time of ascendance or danger of defect. At birth the baby leaves the chemical exchange of the womb for the social exchange system of his society, where his gradually increasing capacities meet the opportunities and limitations of his culture. . . . The maturing organism continues to unfold, not by developing new organs but by means of a prescribed sequence of locomotor, sensory, and social capacities. (pp. 92-93)

In other words, nature provides humans a ground plan (or blueprint) that specifies not only the broad competencies a person should develop across all developmental domains but also a timetable for the mastery of these competencies. The timetable keeps the many domains linked in such a way that the person maintains a "structural unity" (Erikson, 1964, p. 136).

Nature also provides the life force or energy necessary to motivate the individual to develop according to the ground plan, even when new capacities are no longer gifted to us by maturation (stages one to three) but require hard work (stages four to seven).

Nature operates *in tandem* with nurture in Erikson's theory, initially the nurture of the womb and then the nurture of society. The developing individual is pushed from within to reach out to others, who reach back and shape the person. Erikson (1964) said, "Human ego strength . . . depends from stage to stage upon a network of mutual influences within which the person actuates others even as he is actuated, and within which the person is 'inspired with active properties,' even as he so inspires others" (p. 165).

To be clear, nature and nurture are not equally influential at the same level of specificity. Nature motivates us to attain certain social and functional goals, in and through relationships, whereas nurture influences the specific methods and behaviors we use to satisfy our drives toward these goals, channeling us toward mental health or dysfunction. This concept of method was introduced earlier in conjunction with stage two. (I said that maturation provides a toddler the capacity to assert greater control over herself and her environment; the environment influences whether this control manifests as determined striving within parental boundaries or as resistance.) To extend this discussion, the stage-four child satisfies his drive to demonstrate industry by progressing through Boy Scout merit badges *or* through gang-initiation rites; the stage-five adolescent explores her identity by experimenting with volunteer work *or* with drugs.

Nature intends to propel us through the development of eight virtues, but the first five virtues can be viewed as building blocks for the latter three (love, care, wisdom). If humans attain the three adult virtues, they become structural adults. *Structural adult* is a term Erikson coined in his later years, as he himself aimed to exemplify the higher stages of Kierkegaard, whom he referred to as "my great compatriot" (1975, p. 31). Kierkegaard wrote about the adult in the ethical stage and the adult in the religious stage. Erikson synthesized elements of Kierkegaard's stages in many unpublished drafts focused on the structural adult (Hoare, 2002, chap. 5). In brief, Erikson's structural adult manifests love and care (the virtues associated with stages six and seven) *informed* by wisdom (stage-eight virtue) and faith (without which "wholeness"[15] is impossible).

Erikson defined love and care broadly. Love—identified earlier as "the greatest of human virtues, and, in fact, the dominant virtue of the universe" (Erikson, 1964, p. 127)—extends to "works and ideas as well as [our] children" (Erikson, 1964, p. 132). Care extends to "the maintenance of the world" (Erikson, 1974, p. 124), linking the life cycle of the individual with subsequent generations. Assuming a normal process of development, the infant who is loved and cared for emerges as an adult who loves and cares for the next generation, or at least works to leave it a better world. Care also links this world to the next. This is apparent in a 1996 essay Erikson wrote about the teachings of Jesus, titled "The Galilean Sayings and the Sense of 'I.'" One reason Erikson was particularly drawn to Jesus is that Jesus taught that the kingdom of God is in the midst of us (i.e., in our relationships).[16]

Erikson also accorded some individuals a *particular* purpose. For many of us, it is enough to be a structural adult in whatever environment we find ourselves. But Erikson (1966) recognized that "there will be the martyrs of self-chosen or accidently aggravated identity-consciousness, who must sacrifice the innocent unity of living to a revolutionary awareness" (p. 151). By this Erikson meant that some people are compelled to assume a specific, revolutionary way of loving and caring for the world even when this costs them the semblance of normal living. Erikson was very interested in the processes whereby a sense of particular purpose develops. His detailed studies of particularly purposed individuals like Luther and Gandhi are primarily attempts to explain revolutionary behavior in light of earlier life experiences.

Erikson's choice of Luther and Gandhi reveals that he was very interested in faith, but I am refraining (after much deliberation) from claiming that Erikson viewed humans as *purposed* for a relationship with God. I

---

[15]Personal correspondence, Erikson to Curfman, December 30, 1976, Item 811, Erikson Harvard Papers, as cited by Hoare (2002, p. 72).

[16]Erikson (1996) wrote, "If the Kingdom is so vague in its temporal boundaries, where is it? This question Jesus answers in another context. 'Behold the Kingdom of God is in the midst of you'" (p. 319, citing Lk 17:21).

am refraining because inherent purpose should be realizable, and it is not clear that Erikson viewed his relationship with God as such. Although he made frequent references to God (variously called the Ultimate Other and about 30 other names),[17] he also pondered whether the experience of God was a projected human need (Hoare, 2002, p. 88), specifically a need for a supportive father. Erikson (1962) wrote that we need fathers to provide a guiding voice and affirm our identity, but some fathers don't do this very well.

Later in life, Erikson (1996) seemed more confident of God's existence, even if God was "now only vaguely sensed beyond 'a glass, darkly'" (p. 302). He still viewed the human need for God as rooted in childhood, saying, "The way the father can be experienced in childhood can make it almost impossible not to believe deep down in (and indeed to fear as well as to hope for) a fatherly spirit in the universe" (p. 309). He also acknowledged that a projected human need would not necessarily be incompatible with the existence of God, saying, "I do not mean to reduce such faith to its infantile roots. For the literal believer could well respond with the assertion that human childhood, besides being an evolutionary phenomenon, may well have been created so as to plant in the child at the proper time the potentiality for a comprehension of the Creator's existence, and a readiness for his revelations" (p. 309).

Regardless of whether humans are *purposed* for a relationship with God, Erikson believed that all humans reach for God. Anyone who lives long enough to engage in a life review (stage eight) must eventually reckon "man's nothingness"[18] before God (Erikson, 1962, p. 213). As Erikson himself approached stage eight, he often substituted the word *faith* for *integrity* (Hoare, 2002, p. 90; recall that Erikson's last stage is named *integrity versus despair*). As Erikson found himself less needed

---

[17]Hoare (2002, p. 238, note 63) estimated that Erikson applied 30 names to God. In addition to *God* and *Ultimate Other*, Erikson used the terms *Absolute Being, supreme counterplayer, Super-Identity, Maker, Fabricator, True Identity, True Reality, Higher Identity, Prime Planner and Builder, Final Other, Numen, Divine Thou, Grand Ultimate*, and *Great Spirit*.

[18]Zock (1990) attributed this component of Erikson's model to his reading of Kierkegaard, noting the similarity between Erikson's concept of self-realization and Kierkegaard's concept of self-affirmation, both of which arise out of a person's conscious embracing of the finiteness of human existence (p. 92).

in his post-retirement years, he wrote, "One can only hope that the Ultimate does not possess a similar rejectivity."[19] It is Erikson's developmental process centered on human relationships, combined with a reach for a God who may elude us, that prompted Hoare (2002) to conclude that "Erikson held to this as telos, an elusive aim and a developmental growth process" (p. 85).

Critique B. Per our working model, all humans are purposed for love and dominion work, and some are purposed to love and work in particular ways or contexts. Erikson's emphasis on love is not only compatible with Christian theology; it was likely derived from it. His "beyond 'a glass, darkly'" analogy is an explicit reference to 1 Corinthians 13:12. Given his familiarity with verse 12, he was presumably aware of verse 13 when he designated love "the greatest of human virtues, and, in fact, the dominant virtue of the universe" (Erikson, 1964, p. 127). (First Corinthians 13:13 states, "And now faith, hope, and love abide . . . and the greatest of these is love.") Likewise, Erikson's emphasis on care of the world is compatible with Christian theology. It is specifically compatible with the Genesis 1 emphasis on dominion, the Genesis 2 emphasis on caretaking, and Paul's statement that Christians were created for good works as a way of life (Eph 2:10).

Erikson's emphasis on *particular* purpose, and even the verbiage he used to discuss the psychological processes whereby humans assimilate a particular purpose, can be easily applied to various Bible characters mentioned in chapter two. Joseph is a good example of one whose aspirations seem at least partially "self-chosen" (in response to divinely directed dreams); Esther may have viewed herself as a victim of "accidently aggravated identity-consciousness" (both Erikson, 1966, p. 151). More so than any other theorist featured in this book, Erikson recognized the importance of coming to view oneself as uniquely purposed "for just such a time as this" (Esther 4:14).

Erikson stopped short of claiming humans were purposed for a relationship with God, but he did discuss vertical identity as an important part of identity formation (see Tenet A). Although some Christians might wish

---

[19]"Aging" [Typescript], undated, Item 1562, Erikson Harvard Papers, as cited by Hoare (2002, p. 68).

that Erikson had been as explicit as the Westminster Catechism (A1. "Man's chief end is to glorify God, and to enjoy him forever"), others will respect him for his honest existential grappling. In contrast to many other Holocaust-era Jews who gave up on God altogether, Erikson continued to fear, hope in, and reach out to God, and presented this as an *expected* process of human development.

Erikson's perspective on purpose also includes other developmental details not explicitly stated in Scripture but nonetheless compatible with it. A genetic ground plan is compatible with the psalmist's declaration that

> you knit me together in my mother's womb. . . .
> In your book were written
>   all the days that were formed for me,
>   when none of them as yet existed. (Ps 139:13, 16)

The specification of stages and structural unity is compatible with the apostle Paul's observation that when he was a child, he spoke, thought, and reasoned like a child (1 Cor 13:11). Erikson's (1964) assertion that the "person actuates others even as he is actuated" (p. 165) reminds us of Paul's rationale for wanting to see the saints in Rome (so they could be "mutually encouraged by each other's faith" [Rom 1:12]). In these regards, Erikson's perspective on human purpose is very compatible with a Christian one.

MORAL-ETHICAL TENDENCIES

Tenet C1: The human ground plan provides psychological equipment to reflect and discern good; how well the equipment works is primarily a function of nurture. Erikson articulated at least three ways that nature structurally equips us for good. First, nature builds in a "radiant core" to *reflect* the light of influential others. A person's first light source is the mother (a.k.a. "Primal Other"; Erikson, 1996, p. 302).[20] With development, other sources are tapped and the child is illuminated by the father, other intimates, and eventually God. Erikson (1996) used various terms to

---

[20]"All the self-verifications, therefore, begin in that inner light of the mother-child-world, which Madonna images have conveyed as so exclusive and so secure: and, indeed, such light must continue to shine through the chaos of many crises, maturational and accidental" (Erikson, 1964, p. 117).

describe this radiant core, including *luminosity* and *numinosity* (pp. 300-301). The word *numinous* means "divine," and Erikson used this term when he wanted to emphasize that every person has at least a subjective sense that their light is coming from a source that transcends them.[21] In other words, Erikson viewed every human as outfitted (or "in-fitted") with a light that helps us to both know and show God.

Admittedly, not every light is equally bright. Lights shine the brightest when we are manifesting our purpose to love and care for others. Lights are dimmed, and sometimes extinguished, in conditions of mental illness or evil (Hoare, 2002, p. 79). In the worst-case scenario, an infant suffers such evil that the light is never illuminated in the first place. Infants who have known only evil have no basis for the development of trust (which informs hope, which is the "ontogenetic basis of faith" [Erikson, 1964, p. 118]). While many infants experience impaired trust, only a tiny fraction of infants experience so little good that they fail to develop hope.

Second, the human ground plan specifies the development of a moral sense. By *moral* Erikson meant that we assimilate rules and become troubled when we or others violate these rules. We develop a conscience based on the social norms we experience. According to Erikson (1964), a "moral sense . . . has been an intrinsic part of man's evolution" (p. 226) and man is now "by nature, an 'authority acceptor'" (p. 142). Although infants manifest luminosity, humans do not become moral until the preschool years. This is because morality requires enough cognitive capacity to permit our thoughts and behaviors to inform the conscious Self. Awareness of the Self begins in stage two with the child's first linkage of intent to action, which precipitates the development of a conscience in stage three.

Third, nature builds in the capacity to be *ethical*. In contrast to morals, which are "based on a fear of threats," ethics are more freely adopted and are "based on ideals to be striven for" (Erikson, 1964, p. 222). Idealism often appears in adolescence, but Erikson doesn't view people as ethical until they manifest a bit of adult realism and a lot of responsible

---

[21]"This subjective sense [of God as light] dwells on the very border of our conscious existence" (Erikson, 1996, p. 300).

commitment.[22] While most humans become moral, only some become ethical. This is because the development of a system of ethics requires more reflective thought and insight than simply following the rules one has been taught. This requisite has prompted Hoare (2002) to gently criticize Erikson for writing only for those in social classes privileged enough to be able to contemplate ethics (p. 111). While this criticism may be somewhat accurate, it supports Erikson's (1975) own assertion that "the ethical core which is built into all of us phylogenetically must evolve in each of us ontogenetically" (p. 261). In other words, humans are by nature an ethical species (*phylo*), but it is only in healthy conditions that individuals (*onto*) become ethical.

Tenet C2: Good and evil emerge from the same basic psychological processes. Nature equips us for good, but the same equipment can be used for bad. In his analysis of Gandhi, Erikson included a "letter" to the (then deceased) Gandhi. In this letter, Erikson (1969) declared that he could not help but believe in original sin (p. 249) but disparaged the "Calvinist sense of sin" (p. 252). Whereas Calvin depicted the first humans as perfect creatures who soaked up an external evil that reoriented them toward bad, Erikson believed that good and evil emerge from the same basic processes preprogrammed into humans from creation/conception. Throughout the lifespan, antithetical human qualities appear simultaneously. With the capacity to trust comes the capacity to mistrust. With the capacity to will comes the capacity for shameless willfulness. For Erikson, capacity is the currency that funds moral tendencies, and good and evil are two sides of the same coin.

So why does the coin sometimes come up evil? Addressing the development of sin in the individual, Erikson (1963a) said, "Primal sin . . . consists of the first awareness of the violent wish to control the mother with the maturing organs of bite and grasp" (p. 378). In explaining this violent wish, he appealed to the convergence of maturation and environmental

---

[22]Erikson (1964) drew on Kierkegaard, writing, "The true ethical sense of the young adult, finally, encompasses and goes beyond moral restraint and ideal vision, while insisting on concrete commitments to those intimate relationships and work associations by which man can hope to share a lifetime of productivity and competence" (p. 226).

conditions. Concerning maturation, epigenetic processes deliver a toddler many fundamentally good capacities at the same time, among these teeth and will. Concerning environmental conditions, interruptions in a nursing toddler's food supply can prompt anxiety, particularly if the toddler has resolved the crisis of stage one on the side of mistrust. So the toddler bites, or at least becomes aware of the will to bite the breast. In the Godkin Lectures, Erikson explained that "because will is developmentally inescapable in healthy child development, it is likely the ontogenetic source of sin."[23]

Erikson also took issue with Calvin's view of the *mechanism* whereby sin is transmitted across generations. Whereas Calvin viewed original sin as an inherited constitutional blight, Erikson emphasized that the *maturation enabling* various forms of sin (failure, weakness, need, and overt evil; per Hoare, 2002, p. 106) is genetic, but the *clinical presentation* of sin is more the result of family interaction patterns than genes.[24]

Critique C. Our working model depicts humans as structurally good and inclined toward both good and evil. These inclinations are attributable to both nature and nurture.

Erikson's depiction of humans as structurally good is very compatible with our working model. Like other elements of his theory, his proposal that humans are equipped with a radiant core was explicitly derived from Scripture. Discussing the development of a sense of "I" (i.e., the self), Erikson (1996) said, "In the Bible, the most direct reference to the human I is in the form of an inner light" (p. 300). He then referenced Matthew 5:16 ("Let your light shine before others") and Matthew 6:22 ("The eye is the lamp of the body"). Erikson's idea that lights vary in brightness may have been his own, although both Augustine and Thomas Aquinas ascribed varying degrees of brightness to the image of God. Aquinas argued that all humans retain the capacity to image God, "regardless of whether (a) 'this image of God is so thinned out'—clouded over, as it were— . . . as in those who do not have the use of reason, or whether (b) 'it is darkened or

---

[23]"Godkin Lectures: Play, Vision, and Deception" [Author's typescript], April 1972, Item 1521, Erikson Harvard Papers, as cited by Hoare (2002, p. 106).

[24]"Clinically, so to speak, there can be little doubt that ideas of basic sin may be very much aggravated by personal fate and historical circumstance, and are rarely faced existentially" (Erikson, 1969, p. 250).

deformed,' as in sinners, or whether (c) 'it is bright and beautiful,' as in the justified—as Augustine says in De Trinitate 14" (Freddoso, n.d.; translation of *Summa Theologiae* 1.93.8).

To be clear, Erikson did not explicitly equate his *numinous* with the *imago Dei*, and a never-illuminated light seems functionally incompatible with theologians' depiction of the *imago Dei* as a universal characteristic of humankind. But Scripture does suggest that humans could have *installed, nonworking* moral equipment. The author of Proverbs even links this equipment to the parent-child relationship, warning, "If you curse father or mother, / your lamp will go out in utter darkness" (Prov 20:20).[25]

Erikson's claim that a conscience is standard equipment is in keeping with Romans 2:15, wherein the apostle Paul refers to Gentiles who "show that what the law requires is written on their hearts, to which their own conscience also bears witness." Although *nature* is a murky construct in Paul's prescientific worldview (see chap. 3), this verse implies that Paul viewed conscience as at least partially built in. A capacity for ethical reasoning that goes beyond moral obedience is also compatible with the developmental process of moral maturity extrapolated from Scripture in chapter four.

Erikson's depiction of original sin as an *emergent property* is compatible with some theological presentations, even as it challenges others. Erikson proposed that the emergence of sin in the individual coincides with stage-two self-awareness and will. With this, he implies that the stage-one infant is functionally incapable of sin. He also believed that development of the individual paralleled the development of the species.[26] This suggests that Erikson would have viewed the onset of sin in humankind as coinciding with an evolving humanity's development of

---

[25]I am grateful to my former student Maya Rowland for drawing my attention to this verse in a course paper.

[26]Erikson (1996) said, "Here, of course, man's evolutionary capacity for guilt becomes a pointed part of his sense of existence; and, as creation and procreation become one actuality, so the experience of the Father in monotheism recapitulates the experience of the father in ontogeny" (p. 309). This statement is in keeping with Freud's acceptance of Haeckel's recapitulation theory (in brief, ontogeny recapitulates phylogeny). Although this theory has been discredited among biologists studying embryonic development, it is still sometimes applied in the study of cognitive development.

self-awareness and will. Because Erikson (1964) stressed the principle of "structural unity" (p. 136), he would have had difficulty making sense of an Adam and Eve who had the moral culpability of adults before acquiring the knowledge of good and evil.

As stated earlier, Erikson particularly disparaged John Calvin's version of original sin. (Recall from chap. 3 that Calvin's original sin was a particularly pessimistic articulation of Augustine's original sin.) A synthesis of these ideas prompted Mark Mann (2006) to conclude, "The account of the development of the moral image that emerges from our dialogue with Erikson runs counter to the traditional Augustinian version of the Fall" (p. 144). Mann then points his readers to the writings of Irenaeus, who believed that Adam and Eve were less developmentally mature than most Western Christians have believed since Augustine. In Mann's estimation, "not only does Irenaeus's view have clear similarities to Erikson's understanding of the development of moral responsibility, but it also coincides with the biblical picture at least as well, if not better, than that of Augustine" (p. 145).

Regardless of whether the reader favors Irenaeus or Augustine, Erikson's perspective offers an interesting lens through which to view Genesis 3. According to Erikson (and empirical research on the development of an *objective self*), children attain self-awareness in stage two and develop a conscience in stage three.[27] If there was a point in the development of the *species* when humans could not yet discern good and evil (inferred from Gen 3:22), did they also lack self-awareness? This might explain God's

---

[27] An objective self means that you recognize yourself to be an object/body that takes up space. (Close your eyes. Are you able to conjure up an image of what you look like? If so, then you have an objective self.) During the first year of life there is no evidence that children have a mental picture of their whole body as an object. Once they have learned to crawl, they spot a toy through a gap in the fence and crawl right into the fence (smacking their foreheads) because they do not have a mental picture of themselves as a body too large to fit through the gap. Similarly, they do not seem to recognize themselves in photos or in the mirror. An objective self is the prerequisite for the *moral emotions*. In contrast to simple emotions that require the child to react to a situation with joy, sadness, fear, and so on, moral emotions require the child to recognize that other Selves (bigger and more powerful than my Self) holds standards that my Self has met or failed to meet, and are evaluating my Self on the basis of these standards. The child who meets these standards feels the moral emotion of dignity (*I have done a good job coloring within the lines, obeying the rules*). The child who does not meet the caregivers' standards feels the moral emotions of (stage two) shame and doubt (*I am too little to color; I'll tear up my scribbles*) and (stage three) guilt (*I should not have taken the forbidden fruit*).

query: "Who told you that you were naked?" (Gen 3:11). The statement that Adam and Eve heard the "sound of the LORD God" and hid themselves "from the presence of the LORD God" (Gen 3:8) is also intriguing from a developmental perspective. If God was physically close enough to be heard over the breeze, would cognitively mature humans think they could effectively hide in a tree? Or did the first humans hear God in their newly birthed conscience and psychologically hide from God's presence? (Recall Erikson's [1980] statement that, with the development of a conscience, the child "now hears, as it were, God's voice without seeing God" [p. 84].) Erikson's perspective reminds us that Genesis 3 is a story of *both* devolution and evolution. For some Christians (e.g., Polkinghorne, 1998),[28] this dual focus is a way to reconcile the biblical narrative with scientific assertions of a cognitively evolving humanity; although other Christians (e.g., Hoekema, 1986)[29] explicitly resist this potential reconciliation.

Christians who take a pessimistic view of humans' moral-ethical tendencies may also resist Erikson's (1964) belief that "man [is] . . . by nature, an 'authority acceptor'" (p. 142). This assertion is generally accepted within psychology (recall Stanley Milgram's [1974] shocking studies[30]), but some

---

[28]Polkinghorne (1998, p. 89) wrote: "It seems likely that the further power of self-consciousness . . . only dawned with the evolution of the hominid lines leading eventually to Homo sapiens. As that self-awareness developed, I suppose that a corresponding spiritual awareness of the presence of God also became part of the experience of these living beings. One can conceive of a struggle in the hominid psyche between the pole of the self and the pole of the divine, resolved by a turning from God and a concentration on the creature as all-sufficient, a succumbing to the temptation, whispered in Eve's ear by the serpent in that powerful ancient story, to assert autonomy over creaturely dependence, to believe "you will be like God, knowing good and evil" (Gen. 3:5). In Luther's phrase, humanity became "*incurvatus in se.*"

[29]Hoekema (1986) argued that the pair were not fully developed image bearers because they had the capacity to sin, but *did* have *fully developed self-images*. Hoekema depicted the serpent as working directly to pervert the pair's preexisting self-image and interpreted their concern about nakedness to an altered self-image rather than development of self-awareness. He proposed that, before the fall, Adam and Eve "had, we may presume, very positive images of themselves" because they had not yet sinned (p. 103). The serpent then engendered a "perversion of the self-image in an upward direction, [which] was the cause of man's first sin. After the sin had been committed, the second perversion of the self-image occurred, this time in a downward direction. Adam and Eve now felt ashamed of themselves; their self-image became negative. The Genesis narrative continues: 'Then the eyes of both of them were opened, and they realized they were naked'" (p. 104).

[30]In these studies, an "authority figure" (a Yale professor) directed research participants to administer dangerous electric shocks to a person they believed to be another research participant. Although many of the participants were very distressed by the instructions, 65% obeyed until the end of the experiment.

Christian traditions stress that humans are rebellious by nature. Scripture does describe humans as rebellious (Deut 9:24; Is 30:1) and stiff-necked (Ex 32:9; Acts 7:51). But it also likens us to sheep at least 19 times (e.g., Is 53:6; Mt 9:36; Acts 20:28). It even documents a psychological yearning for authority. When Moses lingered on the mountain in Exodus 32, the Israelites begged Aaron to create for them an alternative deity. The fact that structural equipment to help us heed good authority can also prompt us to yearn for bad authority lends credence to Erikson's assertion that good and evil emerge from same basic properties. Whether our good equipment actually works for good is largely a function of environmental conditions in Erikson's model, especially the conditions that promote trust in early childhood.

The Bible also emphasizes environmental conditions and trust, *and* it teaches that Christ can disrupt general patterns of development. In 2 Corinthians 5:17 the apostle Paul declares, "If anyone is in Christ, there is a new creation: everything old has passed away; see, everything has become new!" Knowing how to apply verses like this is difficult. An encounter with Christ can cause dramatic changes in a person (Saul/Paul being an obvious case study), but spiritual transformation is gradual. Just one chapter earlier, Paul bemoans temporal realities that have *not* passed away and admonishes believers to take an eternal/theological view rather than a human/temporal one (2 Cor 4:18). The challenge for Christian developmentalists is to take a theological view with respect to spiritual transformation, even as we articulate principles of development from a human point of view. From a human point of view, the environment has a demonstrably strong influence on our moral-ethical tendencies, making Erikson's model of moral-ethical tendencies compatible with our working model.

AGENCY/ACCOUNTABILITY

Tenet D: Humans need to live as though we have high agency, even as we accept the providence of God. Erikson's perspective on agency and accountability can be derived from two critical clauses in his description of *integrity* (stage eight). The first concerns an acceptance of one's life "as something that had to be and that, by necessity, permitted of no substitutions" (Erikson, 1980, p. 104). Independently, it is difficult to appreciate the significance of this assertion. In the context of Erikson's full corpus, it would appear to be an acknowledgment of the providence of God. The second critical clause is "an acceptance of the fact that one's own life is one's own responsibility" (Erikson, 1980, p. 104).[31] Although these two clauses seem contradictory, Erikson viewed the tension between viewing one's self as highly agentic and accepting the fact that one's agency is limited as something that healthy people learn early. In a statement about toddlers that would seem to apply to the lifespan, Erikson (1964) said that the maturing individual "learns to accept the essential paradox of making decisions which he knows 'deep down' will be pre-determined by events, because making decisions is part of the evaluative quality inherent in being alive. Ego strength depends, above all, on the sense of having done one's active part in the chain of the inevitable" (p. 119).

As for "the elusive question of Free Will" that is begged by this tension, Erikson (1964, p. 118) simply dismissed it. Regardless of whether we have free will, we need to believe we have it, because "no person can live, no ego remain intact without hope and will" (p. 118). Erikson's prescription for a healthy ego is this: "Man must learn to will what can be, to renounce as not worth willing what cannot be, and to believe he willed what is inevitable" (p. 118).[32]

In addition to benefiting the individual, a belief in some degree of agency is good for society. Erikson believed that disenfranchised social groups need to believe that they have the freedom and power to choose what they do and who they become so that they will act responsibly, even when they face difficult circumstances. An example of Erikson applying this perspective can be found in his 1966 address of identity development and race relations. In this essay, he laments the unfortunate circumstances of Black Americans; implicates God and Christians in the shameful exploitation of Black Americans; praises those who actively reckon our

---

[31]Erikson used the word *responsibility* as I use the word *accountability* (to mean liability for self). I use *responsibility* when I am discussing care of others.

[32]Erikson's prescription for a healthy ego calls to mind the oft-quoted Serenity Prayer typically credited to Erikson's Harvard colleague Reinhold Niebuhr: "God, give us grace to accept with serenity the things that cannot be changed, courage to change the things that should be changed, and the wisdom to distinguish the one from the other" (Shapiro, 2008).

painful past as part of the process of moving forward; and questions whether too much emphasis on unconscious determinants, historical events, and communal identities is detrimental for society. Erikson argued that too much emphasis on these determinants undermines the presumption of moral choice and free will. In short, while Erikson clearly empathized with (indeed, was angry on behalf of) Black Americans, he still held that adults must become sons (or daughters) of ourselves rather than our circumstances.

I say *adults* because identity is the crisis associated with adolescence. Beginning in adolescence and continuing into adulthood, most citizens of the developed world have some freedom to seek out environments that permit us to satisfy our drives in healthy ways, even if we still spend significant portions of our day stuck in unhealthy environments. In contrast, children have neither the freedom to choose their environments nor the cognitive capacity to define themselves apart from these environments. The most that Erikson held children accountable for is the acceptance of authority and rule-following within the environments chosen for them.

What is unclear is whether Erikson allowed for some individuals to be so impaired that they are incapable of accountable, responsible behavior. As discussed in conjunction with Tenet C1, our inner "lights" can be dimmed or extinguished by mental illness or evil, and a tiny fraction of infants never have their light illuminated in the first place. Such infants never have the chance to develop hope. Statements like "No person can live, no ego remain intact without hope" (Erikson, 1964, p. 118) suggest that Erikson viewed those with horrible early environments as being impaired beyond accountability. The problem with this interpretation is that Erikson has, just four pages earlier (p. 114), made a point to distinguish his lifespan perspective from the "'originological' approach" of those who "attempt to derive the meaning of development primarily from a reconstruction of the infant's beginnings" (i.e., Freud and attachment theorists). In distinguishing himself from those who view infancy as determining, Erikson seems to be saying that everyone has the potential to become accountable.

Critique D. Our working model depicts humans as temporally agentic, accountable, and responsible in varying degrees. Erikson's recognition that healthy development requires a temporal sense of agency is compatible with various biblical and theological treatments of perceived agency. As stated in chapter one, many theologians believe that a rhetorical goal of the Genesis 1 creation account was to give hope to an oppressed people. The Bible also provides explicit statements about the role of perseverance in development (Lk 21:19; Rom 5:4). It directs us to *choose* for ourselves (Deut 30:19-20; Josh 24:15) and to *do* as we have chosen (2 Cor 9:7). Like the apostle Paul, who preceded his discussion about the power of sin with instructions for the Romans to *not let* sin rule them (Rom 6:12), Erikson understood that perceived agency facilitates accountable, responsible behavior. He sequenced his stages to equip healthy individuals with a sense of agency (stage two) before they wrestle with accountability (stage three) and responsibility (stage seven). He explicitly encourages an emphasis on agency rather than social determinants that undermine agency in his article on race.

One of the primary qualifiers of agency and accountability in our working model is maturation. Erikson addressed maturation more systematically than our other four featured theorists, drawing an explicit distinction between moral and ethical behavior. Erikson's declaration that children have the capacity for moral behavior in stage three accords with the apostle Paul's directive for parents to hold children gently accountable for obedience (Eph 6:4). His declaration that some but not all adults develop the capacity for ethical behavior is compatible with the general maturational process whereby individuals grow into a moral maturity based on love. With respect to the temporal experience of agency, accountability, and responsibility, Erikson's approach is very much in keeping with our working model.

WHAT CHRISTIANS CAN LEARN FROM ERIKSON

Erik Erikson demonstrated that it is possible to be a mainstream psychologist who publicly integrates faith and science. Although this may be obvious to some readers, my graduate school mentors presumed that I would need to compartmentalize (or renounce). The discovery that Erikson had written an article about Jesus' teachings in a nonsectarian academic journal almost knocked me off my desk chair. Admittedly, this is not a common path to success in mainstream psychology, but I am inspired by the fact that one of developmental psychology's grand theorists understood the need for more holistic thinking, writing of "the blame that psychiatry must some day accept as its burden because of the way it had distanced itself from religion" (Hoare, 2002, p. 54).

Erikson's *integration* of psychology and theology likely enhanced his understanding of human development. Scripture provides a broad scaffold for development—children are a vulnerable class who think differently from adults and require instruction—but developmental psychology fills in specific details about *how* children think and *how* they need to be instructed. Psychology specifies developmental trajectories, but theology imparts existential significance. Some particularly important understandings to emerge from the synthesis of Erikson's model and Christian theology include the importance of responsive parental care in enabling our *imago Dei* qualities, and maturational timetables associated with the emergence of moral-ethical tendencies and elements of self-concept like industry and identity.

The maturational timetable associated with industry is an important consideration in Christians' response to the cultural war over racial socialization. As this book goes to press, many Americans are angry that schools are beginning to teach constructs like structural racism. In keeping with his 1966 essay on race relations, I expect that Erikson would insist that Christians have a particular responsibility to grapple with *all* manner of racism as we wisely discern the developmentally appropriate time to emphasize structural determinants of industry in school curricula. Certainly we must address racial bias in young children's interpersonal interactions, and adolescents and adults must wrestle with social/structural factors in the manifestation of industry. But what is the best time for children to be told, in a classroom setting, that personal industry may not be enough in a racialized culture? Tatum (1997) suggests that youth are able to think critically about self and race beginning in sixth or seventh grade. This might mean that schools should hold off emphasizing social/structural determinants of industry until after children have (hopefully positively) resolved Erikson's stage four. Because some Christians scorn concepts like structural racism, it would be helpful for other Christians who recognize structural racism as a manifestation of structural sin in general to lead the way in conducting research on the best stage to teach this concept and the best methods for doing so.[33]

Erikson's most important contribution for Christian developmentalists may be his discourse on original sin. In Erikson's model, sin emerges when good capacities (self-awareness and will) converge with environmental threat. With this, Erikson increases our psychological understanding of moral development in infants and toddlers. He also offers a potential framework for reconciling the first chapters of Genesis with contemporary science's depiction of humankind as a cognitively evolving species. Although some of my students are uncomfortable applying scientific scrutiny to an understanding of the fall, others have reported that a developmental perspective on the species—informed by principles that guide the development of the individual—has given them a way to retain their Christian faith. As a promoter of both faith and science, Erikson is a good theorist for Christians to know.

---

[33] A concise address of racism as structural sin has been provided by Kevin Timpe in "Sin in Christian Thought," *The Stanford Encyclopedia of Philosophy* (Summer 2021 Edition), Edward N. Zalta (ed.), https://plato.stanford.edu/archives/sum2021/entries/sin-christian/.

CHAPTER SIX

John Bowlby's Attachment Theory

JOHN BOWLBY (1907-1990) is the father of attachment theory. In this theory, the most important aspect of development is the quality of our attachments with others, particularly the first few years of life. Concerning early childhood, Bowlby (1951) said, "What is believed to be essential for mental health is that the infant and young child should experience a warm, intimate, and continuous relationship with his mother (or permanent mother-substitute) in which both find satisfaction and enjoyment" (p. 11). Bowlby believed that *without* this foundational relationship, it is very difficult to be mentally healthy in childhood or later in life.

Bowlby is less eminent than the three grand theorists. In Haggbloom et al.'s (2002) rankings, he appears forty-ninth. This may be because the importance of healthy attachment is not readily apparent until we have had a close encounter with disturbed attachment. Additionally, attachment theory does not apply equally well to all individuals. Some people who are emotionally deprived in infancy *are* able to overcome this deprivation and live emotionally healthy lives. But others are not. Attempts to understand the sometimes irrational behavior of the latter group using the other developmental theories reveal explanatory gaps best filled with attachment theory.

Bowlby filled these gaps in two important ways. First, he provided a theory that is rich in humanness, like psychoanalytic theory, but more precise in its articulation of biological drives. Second, he helped illuminate the *mechanisms* whereby maternal deprivation in the first years of life can contribute to lifelong struggles in relationships, self-regulation, and the development of a conscience. Because these aspects of personhood are so central to both Christian theology and developmental psychology, I have included a chapter on Bowlby's attachment theory.

BIOGRAPHY

John Bowlby was born in London.[1] Like many children in the British upper-middle class, he and his five siblings spent their early years in a nursery disconnected from the main activity of the house. To avoid spoiling, Bowlby's mother restricted her contact to about an hour a day, during which she taught about religious and moral values, animals, and nature. As for their father, the children saw him even less—mostly just on Sundays when they walked in a procession to the Anglican church and on various outings.

Bowlby experienced his first major loss at age four with the departure of his dear nurse Minnie, who reportedly loved him best. After Minnie left, he was cared for by Nanny Friend (who reportedly was not a friend and called the young John nicknames such as Admiral Sir Nosey Know-All). When John was 7, World War I broke out and Mr. Bowlby departed for four years at the front. Although he wrote letters, these letters were not read to the children. At age 11, John and a brother were sent to a boarding school. John was not happy there and later told his wife that he would not send a dog to boarding school at that age. At age 12, John saw his godfather fall down dead in the middle of a soccer match.

Although Bowlby viewed his childhood as normal for the time, he later characterized the limited affection he experienced as something that had left him "sufficiently hurt, but not sufficiently damaged."[2] Like the thrice-named Erikson (intrigued with issues of identity), the oft-forsaken Bowlby became absorbed with absence. As a therapist, he worked primarily with mothers and children, but also military personnel separated from their families during World War II. While working with the latter, Bowlby told his wife that he was going to conduct research on separation and "that'll keep me busy for the rest of my life" (Dinnage, 1979, p. 323, as quoted by Van Dijken, 1994, p. 5).

---

[1] Unless otherwise noted, information in the biography section is taken from Van Dijken (1994).
[2] Van Dijken (1994, p. 11) quoting John's wife, Ursula, personal communication.

Bowlby spent his adolescence at a naval academy and then went on to study medicine and psychology at Cambridge. After graduating in 1928, he taught at a school for maladjusted children. Two students in particular had a great influence on Bowlby. The first was a seven-year-old who followed him everywhere, eventually earning the nickname "Bowlby's shadow." The second was a fatherless teen expelled for perpetual pilfering. Because this teen was from an affluent family (i.e., had no financial reason to steal), Bowlby began contemplating socioemotional deprivation as a motivator for the teen's behavior. Bowlby then spent eight years in clinical training for medicine, psychiatry, psychology, and psychoanalysis, becoming a patient himself, as required by the British Psychoanalytical Society.

One of the most prominent figures in the society during Bowlby's training period was Melanie Klein, who held that psychopathology was more a function of unconscious tensions than actual experiences. Although Bowlby initially believed his ideas to be compatible with Klein's, profound differences became apparent in 1936 when Klein, acting in a supervisory role, forbid Bowlby to divert attention from a three-year-old to help the child's mother, who subsequently ended up institutionalized (Grosskurth, 1986, p. 402). Fortunately for Bowlby, he was not the only Kleinian dissident in the society. Immigration of psychoanalysts from the Viennese school had begun in 1933, and the Freuds themselves arrived in 1938 after Anna's interrogation by the Gestapo. Following "King" Sigmund's death in 1939, there emerged what Holmes (1993) has characterized as a battle for the queendom between Melanie Klein and Anna Freud (pp. 5-6). Because Anna also valued experience, treated children *along with* their parents, and showed more modesty and professionalism in her criticism of other viewpoints, Bowlby favored Anna—although he viewed both women as lacking in scientific acumen.[3] To become a full member of the society, those in training were required to present a paper to the society, which Bowlby did in 1939. Against the advice of some of his mentors, he boldly challenged Klein's view that real experiences

---

[3]In a 1981 interview, Bowlby described Klein as "inspirational, the antithesis of what I try to be" and totally unaware of scientific method. He then added, "Anna Freud doesn't know what science is about either" (Grosskurth, 1986, p. 404).

didn't matter. Bowlby was accepted as a full member of the society, but with opposition.

During and after his training, Bowlby worked at various child guidance clinics and began synthesizing his case notes. In 1944 Bowlby presented a report on affectionless children with histories of maternal deprivation titled *Forty-Four Juvenile Thieves, Their Characters and Home Lives* (1947). Many in the society scorned Bowlby for this work, speaking derisively of "Ali Bowlby" and his 40 thieves. In 1946 Bowlby became director of the Children and Parents Department of the Tavistock clinic in London (NHS Foundation Trust, n.d.). Bowlby also testified before Parliament and helped bring about Britain's 1948 Children's Act establishing a comprehensive system of care for children without parents (Reeves, 2005).

In 1949 Bowlby was commissioned to author a monograph for the World Health Organization (WHO) on the mental health of orphans and homeless children in post–World War II Europe. Of particular concern to the general population was that these children seemed incorrigible and lacking in conscience. Although research on maternal deprivation was still in its infancy, Bowlby located enough empirical work to provide a disconcerting portrayal of troubled (mostly institutionalized) children who had experienced significant periods of maternal separation or loss. He argued that their development was almost always delayed—physically, intellectually, and socially.

Central to Bowlby's depiction of these children were two disconcerting characteristics: a lack of genuine relationships and an inability to pursue long-term goals. Concerning the former, Bowlby (1951) said:

> Such children . . . have no friendships worth the name. It is true that they are sometimes sociable in a superficial sense, but if this is scrutinized we find that there are no feelings, no roots in these relationships. This, I think, more than anything else is the cause of their hard-boiledness. Parents and school-teachers complain that nothing you say or do has any effect on the child. If you thrash him he cries for a bit, but there is no emotional response to being out of favor, such as is normal to the ordinary child. . . . Since they are unable to make genuine emotional relations, the condition of a relationship at any given moment lacks all significance for them. (p. 32)

Concerning the latter, Bowlby said,

> Clinically, it is observed that the egos and super-egos of severely de-
> prived children are not developed—their behaviour is impulsive and
> undercontrolled, and they are unable to pursue long-term goals because
> they are victims of the momentary whim. For them, all wishes are born
> equal and equally to be acted upon. Their capacity for inhibition is
> absent or impaired, and without this a limited, precise, and consequently
> efficient mode of response cannot develop. They are ineffective person-
> alities, unable to learn from experience and consequently their own
> worst enemies. (p. 54)

Simultaneous with the WHO monograph,[4] Bowlby was collaborating
with a boiler man named James Robertson[5] in the production of a movie
titled *A Two Year Old Goes to Hospital*.[6] This movie documented one
child's reaction to standard hospital procedures of the time, which were to
permit children no access to family members for the duration of their visit.
Both the movie previews and the monograph hit the scene in 1951, causing
quite a stir. The monograph was translated into 14 languages and sold
400,000 paperback copies in English before Penguin published a trade
edition. Robertson went on a six-week film tour in the United States and
eventually produced a prevention-oriented sequel, *Going to Hospital with
Mother*. Although both efforts were met with continued resistance by the
British Psychoanalytical Society, they greatly improved the care of young
children in institutional settings in many countries.

Bowlby always identified with the psychoanalytic tradition,[7] but during
the writing of the monograph, Bowlby realized that psychoanalytic theory
was insufficient to explain the profound effects of separation in the early

---

[4]Unfortunately, the father of attachment theory was so busy during these years that he had little
time for his own children, putatively prompting Bowlby's oldest daughter to ask whether Daddy
was a burglar because "he comes home after dark and never talks about his work" (Van Dijken,
1994, p. 144, citing personal communication with J. Hopkins).

[5]James Robertson learned methods of naturalistic observation and became interested in psychi-
atric social work while working as a boiler man in Anna Freud's Hampstead residential nursery.
Anna required *all* staff, regardless of their job description or training, to write up observations
of the children on index cards for weekly staff meetings. See Bretherton (1991).

[6]Watch an excerpt of this movie on YouTube (Concord Media, 2014).

[7]Bowlby (1988) described his theory as "a much modified and updated variant of traditional
psychoanalytic thinking in which great emphasis is placed on the particular pattern into which

years. "What was missing in that monograph," said Bowlby, "was how comes it [*sic*] that those experiences can possibly have those effects."[8]

Bowlby's solution came in the writings of Australian ethologist and Nobel Prize–winner Konrad Lorenz (1903–1989), known for his research on imprinting in greylag geese. *Imprinting*, broadly defined, is any learning that occurs rapidly during a critical period and is apparently independent of the consequences of behavior. One of the best examples is filial imprinting, the process whereby young birds, 13–16 hours after hatching, instinctively imprint on a moving object (typically the mother) and then follow this object. Lorenz demonstrated the mechanistic, deterministic inevitability of this phenomenon by imprinting goslings to nonmaternal objects such as a box carried by a mechanical train and to himself (or, technically, his boots).

Bowlby studied ethology extensively for several years and surmised that evolutionary processes also prompt *humans* to form strong attachments with early caregivers, although the human critical period is much longer (months, not hours). Evidence that formation of attachments with early caregivers is instinctive, mechanistic, and independent of consequences—even for humans—can be derived from the grief process seen in children removed from abusive homes. Even when caregivers *should not* be bonded with, children bond and become distressed when separated from such caregivers.[9]

Bowlby formally introduced what is now known as attachment theory in a series of three papers published 1958–1960. Each met with increasing resistance from the British Psychoanalytical Society. The first paper prompted Donald Winnicott, who had worked with Bowlby to ensure the passage of the Children's Act, to declare, "It was certainly a very difficult paper to appreciate without at the same time giving away almost everything

---

each personality comes to be organized during the early years, with its own distinctive working models" (p. 6).

[8]M. J. E. Senn, interview with Dr. John Bowlby in London, England, October 19, 1977 (p. 24), unpublished (National Library of Medicine, USA), quoted by Van Dijken (1996, p. 5).

[9]An analysis of what happens in the brain when early care and abuse are given by the same caregiver has been provided by Regina Sullivan and Elizabeth Norton Lasley (epub, Sept. 2010) and can be found at "Fear in Love: Abuse, Attachment, and the Developing Brain," https://pubmed. ncbi.nlm.nih.gov/23447763/, retrieved September 28, 2021.

that has been fought for by Freud."[10] As the official keeper of her father's legacy, Anna Freud was also distressed by the direction of the paper, but she valued Bowlby and wrote to Winnicott that "Dr. Bowlby is too valuable a person to get lost to psychoanalysis." In the third paper, Bowlby disputed Anna's contention that infants cannot mourn because of insufficient ego development. This paper prompted Winnicott to confess privately to Anna, "I can't quite make out why it is that Bowlby's papers are building up in me a kind of revulsion although in fact he has been scrupulously fair to me in his writings."[11] Another analyst is said to have quipped, "Bowlby? Give us Barabbas!" (Grosskurth, 1986, p. 406).

Bowlby's renown in the academic world was greatly enhanced by his association with Canadian American Mary Ainsworth (1913–1999), who is credited for systematizing many of Bowlby's ideas. Ainsworth joined Bowlby's staff at the Tavistock in 1950 and represented Bowlby at a 1961 WHO meeting where she clarified that the catch-all phrase *maternal deprivation* could actually mean three things: insufficient care, distorted care (abuse or neglect), or discontinuity of care.[12] Ainsworth is best known for developing a laboratory protocol to test Bowlby's ideas called the Strange Situation,[13] the concept of a secure base, and delineating three of the four attachment classifications now used by psychologists all over the world (secure, insecure-ambivalent, and insecure-avoidant).[14] Research on attachment suggests that about 60% of infants in developed countries can be classified as having a secure attachment with their primary caregiver (Van IJzendoorn & Kroonenberg, 1988). Infants and children with secure attachments are oriented toward their caregivers, receptive to their

---

[10]Letter from Winnicott to Bowlby's therapist Joan Riviére, June 21, 1957, quoted by Grosskurth (1986, p. 404).

[11]Interview, January 24, 1982 (unclear with whom), quoted by Grosskurth (1986, pp. 405-6).

[12]Robert Karen (1998, p. 123), as quoted by Mooney (2010, pp. 25-26).

[13]The Strange Situation is a sequence of mild stressors that occurs in a prescribed order in a laboratory playroom (e.g., entrance of a stranger, departure of the mother, return of the mother). Mild stressors are used because they typically activate attachment behavior. Trained researchers code the child's behavior at each step of the sequence paying particular attention to the child's use of the mother as a secure base from which to explore the playroom and the child's response to the mother upon reunion. Watch a Strange Situation at Saul McLeod, "Mary Ainsworth," Simply Psychology, updated 2018, www.simplypsychology.org/mary-ainsworth.html.

[14]A concise table of Ainsworth's three main styles and their subtypes is included in Sroufe and Waters (1977).

caregivers' directives, and use caregivers as a secure base from which to explore the world. This orientation, as well as growing awareness of the caregivers' moral standards, is the basis for emotionally healthy toddlers' emerging sense of moral conscience and eventual competence. In contrast, infants with insecure attachments demonstrate, among other things, resistance to their caregivers and a premature tendency to try to manage their emotions and their relationships.

Bowlby remained at the Tavistock until his retirement in 1972 and was a prolific writer. His magnum opus is a trilogy titled *Attachment and Loss*, in which he examines in great detail attachment (Vol. 1, 1969), separation (Vol. 2, 1973), and loss (Vol. 3, 1980). Bowlby died at age 83 in his summer home on the Isle of Skye (Scotland). In 2005 the Harvard Mountaineering Club named two remote mountains in Kyrgyzstan for Bowlby and Ainsworth.[15]

BASIC PREMISES OF ATTACHMENT THEORY

Our discussion of the four themes will be facilitated by a preliminary delineation of the basic premises of attachment theory. Bowlby provided a 13-point presentation of these premises in the third volume of his trilogy (1980, pp. 39-41) and a 4-point presentation in a 1988 essay, from which I have derived the following nine premises:

1. Attachment behavior is behavior that helps a creature maintain proximity to others of the same species.

2. Because of its survival value, attachment behavior is organized by the central nervous system and characteristic of many species, including humans.

3. In humans, attachment behavior is at least as significant as other instinctive behaviors like feeding or sex.

4. Attachment behaviors are specific to attachment figures with whom we have bonded (i.e., we desire proximity to specific individuals; not just any warm body playing the role of caregiver, lover, or offspring will suffice).

---

[15]"Mount John Bowlby and Peak Mary Ainsworth," www.psychology.sunysb.edu/attachment /mount_john_bowlby/mountains.htm.

5. Attachment behavior is goal corrected. The infant whose caregiver responds quickly to distress bids uses these bids to keep the caregiver in close proximity. The infant who experiences the caregiver as inconsistent may become hypervigilant and clingy. The infant who experiences the caregiver as rejecting learns to mask emotions and not bother the caregiver so that the caregiver will tolerate the infant's proximity. Proximity is paramount because even bad parents typically engage in basic protective behaviors when a child is in grave danger (Bowlby, 1980, p. 73).

6. Over time, both the infant and the caregiver develop sets of expectations (i.e., working models) about others, self, and likely interactions between self and others. Knowing what to expect makes interactions more efficient.

7. Because attachment behavior is so critical for survival, all phases of bonding (formation, maintenance, disruption, renewal) are associated with very strong emotions.

8. Although development permits humans to sustain longer periods of separation from our attachment figures, the attachment system is integral to personhood and active throughout life.

9. Attachment relationships during the "years of immaturity—infancy, childhood, and adolescence" (Bowlby, 1980, p. 41) propel us along various developmental "pathways." Pathways organize personality, which organizes all subsequent relationships, mental health, and morality.

THE FOUR THEMES

When critiquing Bowlby, it is important to remember the context and objective of his writing. Like Augustine and Calvin, whose pessimistic portrayals of moral tendencies were intended to counter the Pelagians, Bowlby's corporeal characterization of humans was intended to counter the Kleinians. Therefore, Bowlby's theory is the most focused in this book. His goal was to explicate the processes of attachment, not to provide a comprehensive model of personhood. This makes it difficult to discern the compatibility of *some* aspects of Bowlby's perspective with a Christian one, even as other aspects lend themselves to critique. From Bowlby's writings I have derived four tenets:

A. The central characteristic of personhood is our working models of self and others (essence).

B. First and foremost, humans are hardwired to survive (purpose).

C. Supportive care fosters moral behavior; rejection fosters deviance (moral-ethical tendencies).

D. We help ourselves along healthy or dysfunctional pathways, but the primary credit for how we turn out goes to caregivers who provide our initial orientation (agency/accountability).

ESSENCE

Tenet A: The central characteristic of personhood is our working models of self and others. Attachment is foundational to human functioning because our earliest interactions inform our expectations about how relationships work. Bowlby called these expectations *internal working models* (IWMs). The first few years of life, relationship patterns are a property of the mother-child dyad, but over time the patterns of interaction, with their associate personality features, "become increasingly a property of the child himself or herself and also increasingly resistant to change. This means that the child tends to impose it, or some derivative of it, upon new relationships" (Bowlby, 1988, p. 5).

The reason IWMs are resistant to change is that they are learned by the body and thus partially unconscious. As an analogy, consider your expectations for how cars work. When you drive an unfamiliar car, you might anticipate that you don't know the location of the wiper switch, but you perform the most fundamental aspects of driving—like braking with the left pedal—outside of conscious awareness. Now imagine what it would be like to drive a car that required you to brake with the *right* pedal instead of the left. You would find it very difficult to stop pressing the left pedal to brake. If you were required to drive this car, you would probably try to have the brake pedal moved to where it is "supposed to be" because it takes so much mental energy to suppress what your body has learned to do automatically. If you were not able to alter the car, you would drive in a constant state of anxiety for a long time.

In the same way that our bodies learn to drive a car, our bodies learn to "drive" relationships. This learning is mechanistic and involuntary, like the greylag geese imprinting to Konrad Lorenz's boots. Already by the second year of life, we are so influenced by IWMs that the most fundamental aspects of relationships happen automatically.

In the driving of relationships, two particular IWMs are critical. First, the child develops a model of their attachment figures, specifically "who his attachment figures are, where they may be found, and how they may be expected to respond" (Bowlby, 1973, p. 203). Second, the child develops a model of self, particularly "how acceptable or unacceptable he himself is in the eyes of his attachment figures" (Bowlby, 1973, p. 203). The two models are *complementary*, meaning that our model of self is the complement of the model we hold of our attachment figures. Again, an analogy is helpful. Bowlby's colleague Winnicott (1971) said that our mothers are our first mirror. In the same way that we look into a glass mirror to evaluate our external attributes (are we attractive or homely?), we look into our "mother-mirror" to evaluate our internal attributes and our worth. If our mother treats us lovingly, we conclude that we are good and behave accordingly; if our mother rejects us, we conclude that we are bad and behave accordingly.

Usually, IWMs help us live efficiently. Knowing what to expect helps us interpret current experiences, forecast new ones, and make plans. But problems arise when we develop IWMs that work to protect us emotionally in a dysfunctional environment, and then carry these models into new environments that *could* be functional for us—*if* we weren't emotionally stuck in the past. We see this in children adopted out of situations of abuse and neglect. New adoptive parents are sometimes baffled when a child behaves in ways that sabotage the parents' bonding attempts and the child's own good fortune. For example, parents report habitual lying even when little is at stake, or the purposeful destruction of a present the child had begged for. Parents try to explain that destructive behavior hurts oneself, and maybe punish, to no avail. While B. F. Skinner (discussed in chap. 7) would have difficulty explaining why these children seem "unable to learn from experience" (Bowlby, 1951, p. 54), attachment theory holds that individuals who are convinced that they will eventually be rejected sometimes act to hurry this rejection along. (Recall: If your body learns to brake with the left pedal, it takes a lot of mental energy to remember to brake with the right. Given the chance, you would alter the car in keeping with what your body already knows to avoid a perpetual state of anxiety.) Because IWMs become part of us and determine critical aspects of our personality, Bowlby would assert that the central characteristic of personhood is our IWMs.

Bowlby identified two other components of human nature: one that competes with attachment behavior and one that complements it. The component that *competes* with attachment behavior is "the urge to explore the environment, to play, and to take part in varied activities with peers" (Bowlby, 1988, p. 3). The relationship between attachment and exploration is that we are better explorers when we are secure in our attachments. This is particularly true in infancy, but

> human beings of all ages are happiest and able to deploy their talents to best advantage when they are confident that, standing behind them, there are one or more trusted persons who will come to their aid should difficulties arise. The trusted person, also known as the attachment figure (Bowlby, 1969), can be considered as providing his (or her) companion with a secure base from which to operate. (Bowlby, 1979, pp. 124-25)

The component of human nature that *complements* attachment behavior is caregiving. Bowlby characterized caregiving as hardwired altruism that facilitates the survival of the species. In his analysis of caregiving, he made a point to counter Freud, who "mistakenly assumed that individuals are by nature essentially selfish and that they consider the interests of others only when constrained to do so by social pressures and sanctions" (Bowlby, 1988, pp. 3-4).

Critique A. Bowlby's "three components of human nature" (the propensity to make strong bonds, the urge to explore, and caregiving[16]) are

---

[16]The three components of human nature are verbatim from Bowlby (1988, p. 3) but do not appear as one continuous string of text.

descriptively compatible with our working model derived in part one. Our working model of essence emphasizes the three manifestations of the *imago Dei*. Attachment theory contributes the most to our understanding of the *relational* aspect. First and foremost, Bowlby emphasized the affective quality of the parent-child relationship. The best theological argument for the primacy of the parent-child relationship is that God is depicted as a parent over 40 times in Scripture. Bowlby also emphasized the importance of our later relationships. Speaking of healthy relationships in adolescence and adulthood, Bowlby (1988) said, "Although food and sex sometimes play important roles in such relationships, the relationship exists in its own right" (i.e., has a transcendent value that exceeds it instrumental benefits; p. 3).

Bowlby did not address humans' relationship with God, but subsequent theorists have. Bowlby articulated the sequence whereby early care generates an IWM of close relationships, which in turn generates a self-concept. Catholic psychoanalyst Ana-Maria Rizutto (1980) took this process one step further, claiming that self-concept serves as the basis for a person's God-concept. Individuals who view self as worthy of love typically view God as loving. Alternatively, individuals who view self as unworthy of love often view God as distant, disappointed, angry, or non-anthropomorphic (i.e., as an impersonal energy force).

Other scholars who have examined the link between attachment and God-concept include Lee Kirkpatrick, Pehr Granqvist, and Jane Dickie. Granqvist and Dickie (2006) delineated ways that God serves as an attachment figure. First, God can serve as a secure base; in Scripture, God is repeatedly depicted as a rock, stronghold, fortress, tower, cornerstone, foundation, refuge, and sanctuary. Second, humans desperately desire proximity to and acceptance by God (Ps 27:9). Third, God's evaluation informs our self-concept (Ps 139:23).

Granqvist and Dickie (2006) also proposed two hypotheses for the development and maintenance of humans' relationships with God. According to the *correspondence hypothesis*, a secure attachment with parents serves as the basis for a secure relationship with God. Other relationships are better described by the *compensation hypothesis*. According to this hypothesis, individuals who lack a secure relationship with their parents often look for compensatory relationships (with other humans and with God) to regulate distress.

Bowlby's perspective is less compatible with the *substantive* aspect of the *imago Dei*. Theologians who emphasize the substantive aspect depict humans as rational and contemplative, able to recognize and choose right. Bowlby did prescribe a hardwired conscience (see Tenets B and C) but focused his clinical writings on how the conscience can be overridden by IWMs that are subconscious and irrational and may even prompt us to choose wrong. Thus, Bowlby's perspective is more compatible with the psalmist's awareness of our "secret sins" (Ps 90:8)[17] than our capacity for reason. Bowlby's perspective also comes up short on the *functional* aspect of the *imago Dei*. Bowlby's brief address of humans' urge to explore overlaps with some Christians' understanding of dominion, but even Christians who believe that humans must explore God's creation to manage it view exploration as only one component of dominion.[18]

Bowlby's perspective on human essence is much more compatible with Scripture's emphasis on embodiment. The notion of IWMs is in keeping with the apostle Paul's understanding of *nature* as cognitive and relational patterns so known by the body that they seem instinctual. The idea that parents represent God to their children in embodied form/function is compatible with word studies of *likeness*. (Recall Garr's [2003] proposal that our creation according to God's likeness permits us to perpetually register God's presence in the world; see chap. 2.)

Bowlby also recognized that humans share characteristics with animals. Indeed, his theory is typically presented as an extrapolation of the ethological work of Konrad Lorenz. Although a psychological theory inspired by birds might seem reductionist, biblical authors also use animals to help

---

[17]See chap. 5, note 14.

[18]In his description of the functional view of the *imago Dei*, Erickson (2001) says that some Christians believe that humans are commissioned "to make full use of our ability to learn about the whole creation. For by coming to understand the creation, we will be able to predict and control its actions" (p. 174). In Reformed circles, the Gen 1:28 directive to have dominion is often referred to as the *cultural mandate*. This mandate is one of the reasons that Reformed Christians emphasize rigorous scientific inquiry.

God's people understand human behavior. In Scripture, a soul can long for God like a deer pants for water (Ps 42:1); evildoers have under their tongues the venom of vipers (Ps 140:3); if we wait for the Lord, we will mount up with wings as eagles (Is 40:31); and when we are lazy, we should consider the ant and learn its wisdom (Prov 6:6). In Matthew 23:37 Jesus himself bemoans, "Jerusalem, Jerusalem, the city that kills the prophets and stones those who are sent to it! How often have I desired to gather your children together as a hen gathers her brood under her wings, and you were not willing!" Although it is unclear whether we should interpret Jesus' words as an allusion to attachment processes or simply a metaphor, it is interesting that both Jesus and Bowlby appealed to chicks in their address of dysfunctional relationships.

Most Christians also view embodiment as the primary vehicle for procreation and gender. Bowlby's emphasis on caregiving as one of the three components of human nature is compatible with *likeness* defined as procreation. Bowlby (1951) addressed gender, but only implicitly, in his emphasis on a good mother-child relationship as "essential for mental health" (p. 11).

PURPOSE

Tenet B: First and foremost, humans are hardwired to survive. Erikson (see chap. 5) depicted development as a telos-like succession of potentialities scheduled by nature and channeled by nurture. Bowlby's view of development overlaps with Erikson's in that both emphasize nature's scheduling function and nurture's channeling function, but Bowlby avoids the concept of telos. Erikson viewed nature as propelling us toward noble ends (love and care), and maybe even a relationship with God; Bowlby (1969) warned that we must not get ourselves "trapped in theories of a teleological kind" (p. 124).

For Bowlby, hardwired motivation is first and foremost for the survival of the species. Therefore, Bowlby's theory is more firmly grounded in (or hostage to) empirical science than Erikson's theory.[19] Whereas Erikson

---

[19]In describing his approach, Bowlby (1980) said, "I have been developing a new paradigm that, whilst incorporating much psychoanalytic thinking, differs from the traditional one in adopting a number of principles that derive from the relatively new disciplines of ethology and control

proposed several concepts that were scientifically imprecise (e.g., the concept of numinosity), Bowlby used precise language to describe sets of behaviors (feeding, proximity seeking) that were organized into adaptive behavioral systems. In volume one of his trilogy, Bowlby (1969) considered various reasons for the behavioral systems that activated attachment behavior, and concluded that "protection from predators seems by far the most likely" (p. 228).

Regardless of what tendency Bowlby was contemplating, he sought to "understand behavioural equipment by reference to the contribution it makes to the survival of members of the species and their kin in the natural habitat of that species" (1969/1982).[20] For example, in explaining the conscience, Bowlby (1951) stated that one of our primary psychological needs is "to remain on friendly and co-operative terms with others"; thus "we differentiate, within our ego, machinery specially designed for the purpose—our conscience or super-ego" (pp. 52-53).[21] Bowlby (1969) characterized this approach as "a direct descendent of the theory outlined by Darwin in *The Origin of Species*" (p. 172).

Emphasis on the species (over the individual) helps us understand one of Bowlby's most important contributions to the discipline of developmental psychology: the documentation of a *critical period* for psychosocial development. Whereas Erikson depicted development as a lifelong exchange between nature and nurture, Bowlby stressed that nature permits a high sensitivity to the environment but only for a small window of time (in humans, our first few years). Likening psychological development to prenatal embryonic development—wherein undifferentiated tissue *must* be exposed to certain chemical organizers during certain critical periods—Bowlby (1951)

---

theory. By so doing, the new paradigm is enabled to dispense with many abstract concepts, including those of psychic energy and drive, and to forge links with cognitive psychology. Merits claimed for it are that, whilst its concepts are psychological and well suited to the clinical data of interest to psychoanalysts, they are compatible with those of neurophysiology and developmental psychology, and also that they are capable of meeting the ordinary requirements of a scientific discipline" (p. 38).

[20]This quote is from the second edition of *Attachment and Loss*, Vol. 1 (1982, p. 55) and differs slightly from the 1969 edition.

[21]Bowlby did not explain how humans gained such sophisticated equipment. He simply acknowledged that explaining the structure of the ego "still leaves the problem of understanding how in living organisms such ingenious structure comes into existence" (1969, p. 126).

said, "In the same way, if mental development is to proceed smoothly, it would appear to be necessary for the undifferentiated psyche to be exposed during certain critical periods to the influence of the psychic organizer—the mother" (p. 53). The way the mother organizes the child's psychic machinery is by organizing the child's world and life. "She orients him in space and time, provides his environment, permits the satisfaction of some impulses, restricts others. She is his ego and superego. Gradually he learns these arts himself and, as he does so, the skilled parent transfers these roles to him. . . . Ego and superego development are thus inextricably bound up with the child's primary human relationships" (Bowlby, 1951, p. 53).

Like embryonic critical periods, psychological critical periods are adaptive for a species as a whole, *within* the environment experienced by most members of the species. Bowlby (1969) called this the "environment of evolutionary adaptedness" (EEA; p. 58). Unfortunately, there are some individuals who pay for the critical periods that preserve the population. When early organization by the mother works as it is supposed to, it is helpful that maturation *locks in* good organization of the psyche for the rest of a person's life (rather than leaving the person susceptible to every environmental change that comes along). But when an early environment deviates too much from the species' typical environment (e.g., a mother who organizes the child to reject intimacy) the locking in of a dysfunctional organization can be debilitating. This is especially true for individuals who begin life in a maladaptive environment and then transition to a species-typical environment (e.g., children who begin life in an impersonal, under-staffed orphanage and then transition to a family). For such individuals, it would be better if the window of time in which the developing organism was sensitive to the attachment environment had not closed so early.

In brief, humans are hardwired to survive. Nature aids us by scheduling critical periods that lock in psychological-behavioral tendencies that work in each person's early environment. Although these locked-in tendencies typically engender higher-order characteristics that transcend their instrumental functions, Bowlby's foremost focus is survival of the species.

Critique B. Our working model depicts humans as universally purposed for love and dominion work. Bowlby's emphasis on survival of the species is not incompatible with love and dominion work. In John 15:13, Jesus teaches that the greatest manifestation of love is to lay down one's life for one's friends. Likewise, a good deal of dominion work is geared toward helping our species thrive.

Our working model also designates some individuals as particularly purposed. Bowlby's emphasis on early psychosocial critical periods offers a possible mechanism whereby individuals grow into particular purposes. I have already listed many individuals predetermined by God for noble purposes (see chap. 2, note 11). The Bible also identifies a few individuals predetermined for ignoble purposes that contribute to the corporate good. Concerning Esau, the apostle Paul wrote,

> Even before they had been born or had done anything good or bad (so that God's purpose of election might continue, not by works but by his call) [Rebecca] was told, "The elder shall serve the younger." As it is written,
>
> "I have loved Jacob,
>   but I have hated Esau." (Rom 9:11-13)

While early critical periods are just one temporal determinant, Esau's relationship with a mother renowned for favoritism and deceit was likely a major influence on his social-psychological development. The case of Esau is in accord with Bowlby's claims that certain aspects of psychic organization and their sequelae can be determined early, and that deterministic social processes sometimes benefit the species at the expense of individuals.

The theological deficiency in Bowlby's presentation is his seeming disavowal of any teleological tendencies that locate survival of the species in an eschatological master plan.[22] Whether we appeal to the Genesis creation accounts, the greatest commandment (Mt 22:36-40), or the Westminster Catechism, Christians believe that humans are purposed to do more than temporally survive. Scripture teaches that we must "not fear those who kill the body" (Lk 12:4) and that "living is Christ and dying is gain" (Phil 1:21). Christians believe that temporal survival is secondary to our relationship with God (at least for those called by God to be conformed into the image

---

[22]I say "seeming" because Bowlby does not explicitly disavow a human telos. Rather, he eschews the use of teleology as an organizing framework for scientific explanations of attachment behavior.

)m 8:29-30). So Bowlby is not wrong in his claim that the
s purposed to survive, but he is reductive. As long as we
 ...of the fact that Bowlby's scientific goal was to ground psychoanalytic ideas in natural processes, Bowlby's explication of these natural
processes can be incorporated in a more comprehensive, theological view
of purpose.

MORAL-ETHICAL TENDENCIES

Tenet C: Supportive care fosters moral behavior; rejection fosters deviance.
Bowlby believed that nature builds in a predisposition for a conscience/
superego. The job of parents is to nurture this "natural behavioral disposition to comply with the wishes of the principle attachment figure"
(Ainsworth & Bowlby, 1991, p. 338), keeping the child oriented toward the
parent and their standards. This orientation is best maintained by sensitive
responsiveness, especially during infancy and early childhood. When a
child's sense of security is bound up in a sensitive caregiver, the child has
an audience worth pleasing and will presumably try to please. When the
child does not, conscience is muted and the child tends toward deviance.

Bowlby articulated two processes whereby a child may lack sufficient
motivation to please a caregiver. The first is when care has been inconsistent (e.g., a series of foster homes; high staff turnover at an institutional
facility) and the child fails to develop a functional attachment figure. A
child is predisposed to be "good" but will not be good unless the child has
a tangible person to be good for.

The second process is when a child has experienced so much rejection
that the need to self-protect usurps the natural predisposition to please the
attachment figure. In the WHO monograph, Bowlby (1951) characterized
children who had experienced maternal deprivation as being "unable to
learn from experience" (p. 54). If Bowlby had written this monograph later
in his career, he might have said that it *seems* that these children are unable
to learn from experience. In fact, children whose primary objective is self-
protection may have already learned that certain immoral activities permit
them to "meet" attachment needs in a self-protective way. Stealing—
especially from a pseudo-intimate—can be a way of keeping close

something that *represents* the person, when keeping the person close would be emotionally risky. Promiscuity is a way to experience intimacy (of a sort) and then walk away before a partner has a chance to reject them. Both stealing and promiscuity have been documented in children who have experienced maternal deprivation (Bowlby, 1951, p. 57).

Moral behavior is *always* a function of the mother-child relationship in Bowlby's writings. To the best of my reading, he never appealed to an external moral standard, nor even natural law. Beyond the functional desire to please a caregiver, he acknowledged no inherent moral tendencies that a child might bring to the socialization process. To the contrary, Bowlby (1951) sought to distinguish attachment theory from theories that explained dysfunction as inherited, saying, "Theories which place the origins of mental disturbances in these intimate domestic events are, of course, in strong contrast to theories . . . which stress constitutional and inherited factors, at times to a point of Calvinistic predestination" (p. 13).

Critique C. Our working model specifies both inherent and environmental contributions to moral-ethical tendencies. It asserts that the relationship between environmental factors and moral behavior are often mediated by trust. Bowlby's emphasis on the emotional tenor of early relationships contributes to our understanding of the importance of trust.

Early emotions are not an explicit emphasis in Scripture. With a few exceptions (e.g., Mal 4:6; Eph 6:4), the Bible says little to link positive emotions in the parent-child relationship to the development of morality. It does, however, provide case studies of humans' relationships with God that lend credence to the specific links between support/rejection and moral tendencies that Bowlby proposed.

A particularly good human in the Bible is Job. Per God's commendation: "There is no one like him on the earth, a blameless and upright man who fears God and turns away from evil" (Job 1:8). The explanation offered by Satan for Job's blamelessness is that God had been particularly supportive of Job. Satan asks God, "Does Job fear God for nothing? Have you not put a fence around him and his house and all that he has, on every side? You have blessed the work of his hands, and his possessions have increased in the land" (Job 1:9-10). An attachment-informed analyses of Job's moral development would conclude that God's early support helped Job sustain trust in and loyalty to God in his later adversity.

A particularly bad human in the Bible is Cain, who had his offering rejected by God and was physically banished from God's presence after killing his brother (Gen 4). An attachment-informed analysis of Cain is frustrated by the fact that Scripture does not tell us *why* God rejected Cain's offering. Perhaps God rejected Cain because Cain had done something wrong. Perhaps God rejected Cain—like God rejected Esau, before he had done anything—to advance a greater purpose, salvific or pedagogical or both.[23] Regardless, Cain's subsequent development is compatible with attachment theory. Following his rejection, Cain gives us self-sabotaging efforts to control the attachment environment, a muted conscience ("Am I my brother's keeper?" [Gen 4:9]), and an emotional breakdown at the prospect of abandonment. Cain even provides a mechanism for contemplating the intergenerational transmission of IWMs. If the reader will indulge a little speculation, we might imagine a conversation around the campfire of Cain's clan. The children inquire, "Why is it that we are marked as the rejected people?" And Cain defensively reports that he was rejected for doing exactly what God told his father to do (work hard and till the earth). If Cain's clan had IWMs of God as rejecting, and self as publicly rejected, we have a framework for understanding how Cain's descendant Lamech might murder a man for striking him and then brag about avenging seventy-sevenfold (Gen 4:24).

Other biblical accounts that lend themselves to attachment-based analysis include Eve doubting that God had her best interests at heart; the Israelites feeling abandoned when Moses lingered on the mountain; Peter feeling abandoned after Jesus' arrest; and Peter's re-emboldening following

---

[23] Most commentators believe that Cain's rejection was due to the condition of his heart or a failure to obey instructions for worship given to the first humans but not mentioned in the text (e.g., M. Henry, *Concise Commentary on the Bible*, on Gen 4:1-7, www.studylight.org/commentaries /mhn/view.cgi?bk=0). Support for the claim that Cain knew he needed a lamb for a sin offering is derived from Gen 4:7, wherein God tells Cain that he must master sin. Another possibility is that Cain's rejection had little or nothing to do with the merits of his heart or his offering. According to Brueggemann (1982), unfounded speculation on the condition of Cain's heart distracts from the primary point that the author of Gen 4, like the author of Job, wanted to make: that a free God does not have to operate within a human understanding of fairness, and humans still have to choose and act for good.

Jesus' resurrection. In these and other accounts, Scripture validates Bowlby's assertion that moral behavior is rooted in our *perception* that we have a supportive, consistent relationship with a secure base. It illuminates the importance of trust.

Bowlby also specified *inherent* influences on moral-ethical tendencies (a conscience and the tendency toward altruistic caregiving), but his presentations of these built-ins were so reductive that it is difficult to ascribe them any transcendent moral value. Concerning sin, Bowlby focused almost exclusively on clinical dysfunction, qualifying humans as sinful but only in a particular realm. This limited treatment of sin has been faulted by Hall and Maltby (2014), who write that Bowlby's

> emphasis on the relational environment in development and psychopathology leaves little room for the role of original sin. While it is impossible to isolate the "variance" in development due to original sin, our Christian worldview would suggest all humans are inclined toward sin from the very beginning of life. As such, it stands to reason that infants and young children bring their proclivity to sin to the processes involved in experiencing, internalizing experience, and responding to attachment figures, even if unknowingly. Therefore, even in a perfect relational environment, infants would still develop less-than-perfect internal working models. . . . In short, an overall shortcoming of attachment theory is its lack of accounting for original sin and sinful acts in the development of insecure attachment and psychopathology. (p. 205)

Although Hall and Maltby's conception of original sin may be more reified than Scripture requires,[24] Bowlby's failure to reckon sin as inherent in any way would make his perspective incompatible with a Christian one *if* he claimed to proffer a comprehensive view of personhood (which he did not).[25]

---

[24]Hall and Maltby seem to view original sin as "something added" to a literal Adam. If so, the only humans to experience a "perfect relational environment" would have been Adam and Eve. If we presume that the pair had perfect IWMs—*until* the serpent created insecurity—then an appeal to a "perfect relational environment" would seem to support Bowlby's model as much as undermine it.

[25]In the previously quoted disavowal of "constitutional and inherited factors," Bowlby (1951) was speaking specifically of the "origins of mental disturbances"—presumably the type one would see in a clinical setting, not immorality in general (p. 13).

Some readers may also fault Bowlby for failing to appeal to any moral standard beyond the attachment relationship. As Jerome Kagan (1984) observed, "Bowlby, like most commentators on human nature, argues that each person has a private judge who approves or disapproves of each day's actions. Whereas Saint Augustine argued that God is the judge, and Emerson maintained that it rests with one's private conscience, Bowlby places love objects in the position of evaluator" (pp. 55-56). Whether Kagan intended this as a criticism of Bowlby, or simply a description of the developmental process wherein parents function as the primary evaluators for young children is unclear. Most developmentalists believe that children do not develop a concept of an unseen God until the preschool years, and may not ascribe feelings to God (e.g., *God will be sad if I hurt my brother*) until approximately age seven (Fowler, 1981; stage two). Likewise, children do not develop a conscience until the preschool years, and they do this by internalizing parental standards (see chap. 5, stage three, and chap. 8, Tenet B). Per Johnson (2017), parents are "the first images of God to which children are exposed" (p. 191). Thus, it is not only appropriate but even desirable for young children to have "love objects" in the position of evaluator. (Yes, it would have been nice if Bowlby had extended his discussion of conscience beyond the early years, but we should not fault him for focusing on parents as evaluators in scientific discourse on the development of conscience in the very young. Most psychologists agree that this is exactly what needs to happen.)

In sum, attachment theory helps elucidate the natural processes whereby our built-in psychological equipment inclines us toward relationships, and the quality of these relationships influences moral-ethical tendencies. Although Bowlby's perspective is theologically incomplete, his specific claims are largely compatible with Scripture and can be incorporated in a Christian perspective on moral-ethical tendencies.

AGENCY/ACCOUNTABILITY

Tenet D: We help ourselves along healthy or dysfunctional pathways, but the primary credit for how we turn out goes to caregivers who provide our initial orientation. In keeping with the psychoanalytic tradition, Bowlby viewed the early years as very determining. To distinguish his theory from Freud's (wherein psychological development actually gets halted or *fixated* at an early stage), Bowlby (1988) depicted development as a pathway. Bowlby acknowledged that life conditions could cause one's path to veer to one direction or the other, but he made little provision for a person to get off the initial path their caregivers start them down. Bowlby (1973) said,

> In order to limit epigenetic sensitivity and so ensure consistent development despite fluctuations of environment, physiological and behavioural processes are evolved that buffer the developing individual against the impact of the environment. Acting in concert, these processes tend to maintain an individual on whatever developmental pathway he is already on, irrespective of most of the fluctuations that might occur in the environment in which further development will be taking place. (p. 367)

Unfortunately,

> such early sensitivity provides no guarantee of an adaptive outcome; for, when the environment of development lies outside certain limits, an organism's sensitivity to environment may result in a developing personality's not only taking a maladaptive pathway but . . . becoming confined more or less permanently to that pathway. (Bowlby, 1973, pp. 367-68)

One reason people have trouble getting off their initial pathway is that the IWMs we develop in childhood are self-perpetuating. IWMs influence what we notice versus ignore, how we interpret what we notice, and the responses we make. IWMs also "determine what sorts of person and situation are sought after and what sorts are shunned. In this way an individual comes to influence the selection of his own environment; and so the wheel comes full circle" (Bowlby, 1973, p. 369).

Bowlby's notion of a full circle can be illustrated with a somewhat extreme but pedagogically helpful example.[26] Imagine a young girl whose

---

[26] Although it is easier to exemplify maladaptive adjustment, Bowlby (1973) said that early sensitivity "commonly results in an adaptive outcome" (p. 367). Children who trust their parents and transfer this trust to their teachers are likely to interpret ambiguous situations in favor of support rather than rejection. If they continue to be friendly to their teachers, peers, and romantic partners, they are likely to have their IWMs of *others as supportive* and *self as worth supporting* repeatedly verified.

birth parents abandon her near the city dump. Her foster parents intend to keep her, but she mistrusts them and resists their authority. After years of acrimony, she finds herself living on the streets. She chances to begin a potentially healthy romantic relationship but is so attuned to behaviors that *might* signal another rejection that she misinterprets an ambiguity and accuses her boyfriend of unfaithfulness. He breaks it off. In keeping with her IWM of *others as rejecting* and her IWM of *self as likely to be rejected* (thrice verified), she then settles for an abusive partner who treats her like the "trash" she believes herself to be. In this example, Bowlby would say that the birth parents started the girl down a maladaptive pathway and at each possible juncture her own behavior further entrenched her.

A second reason we have trouble getting off our initial pathways is that IWMs are partially unconscious. People with mental illnesses are particularly likely to have difficulty articulating dysfunctional IWMs lingering from childhood. Bowlby (1973) noticed that "in a person suffering from emotional disturbance it is common to find that the model that has greatest influence on his perception and forecasts, and therefore on his feeling and behaviour, is one that developed during his early years and is constructed on fairly primitive lines, but that the person himself may be relatively, or completely unaware of" (p. 205).

Even when disturbed persons are able to notice patterns in their own behavior, they may view this behavior as inevitable. Bowlby (1951) wrote,

> In other cases the child has suffered so much pain through making relationships and having them interrupted that he is reluctant ever again to give his heart to anyone for fear of its being broken. And not only his own heart: he is afraid too, to break the heart of new persons whom he might love because he might also vent his anger on them. Older children are sometimes aware of this and will remark to a therapist: "We had better not become too familiar, for I am afraid I shall get hostile with you then."[27] (pp. 56-57)

How long Bowlby gives the developing person to get off a bad pathway is unclear and likely depends on the severity of maternal deprivation. In

---

[27]For this remark, Bowlby credited N. H. C. Tibout (1948), in *International Congress of Mental Health, London, 1948*, 2, 46.

the WHO report (focused primarily on institutionalized children), Bowlby (1951) was optimistic about babies adopted between six and nine months, but declared "good mothering in time" to be "almost useless if delayed until after the age of 2½" (p. 49). Speaking about development more generally, Bowlby (1973) said, "The psychological processes that result in personality structure are endowed with a fair degree of sensitivity to environment, especially to family environment, during the early years of life, but a sensitivity that diminishes throughout childhood and is already very limited by the end of adolescence" (p. 367). This later statement suggests that reorientation can still occur in early adolescence.

What is not clear from Bowlby's writings is whether he viewed the determinism of early attachment relationships as an excuse for bad behavior. Bowlby (1951) acknowledged that with development "we become less and less at the mercy of our immediate environment and of its impact upon us, and more and more able to pursue our own goals, often over long periods of time, and to select and create our own environment" (p. 52). But if IWMs are *so* self-perpetuating that a person with dysfunctional models cannot help but create new environments in keeping with these models, their capacity for accountability would seem to be reduced. Certainly Bowlby the therapist would have tried to help his patients become accountable, and Bowlby the activist (see Reeves, 2005) pressed society to assume greater responsibility in preventing dysfunction. But what of Bowlby the theorist? Unfortunately, I could find no explicit theoretical statement concerning the accountability of those who begin life as victims but then persist in being "their own worst enemies" (Bowlby, 1951, p. 54).

Critique D. Our working model depicts humans as agentic, accountable, and responsible in varying degrees. Bowlby helps us understand how attachment influences the degree to which we manifest these capacities.

Like Bowlby, the Bible often depicts human development as a path and teaches that children's orientation down a good or bad path is influenced by early caregiving.[28] In the NIrV, Proverbs 22:6 is translated, "Start children off on the right path. / And even when they are old, they will not

---

[28]See Deut 5:33; Ps 1:1; 16:11; 139:3; 119:105; Prov 4:26; 10:17.

turn away from it." Scripture also depicts children as easily misoriented (Mt 18:6; Mk 9:42; Lk 17:2) and declares how difficult it is for those who are accustomed to evil to change and do good, likening such a dramatic reorientation to leopards changing their spots (Jer 13:23).[29] Concerning children, Bowlby's perspective is compatible with biblical principles.

Bowlby's perspective is somewhat less compatible when dealing with adults. Although Bowlby characterized adolescents and adults as *less* at the mercy of their environment than children, attachment theory rests on the premise that adult mental health is all but determined by the quality of our early caregiving. Many Christians find Bowlby's approach to adults to be overly deterministic.

One reason Christians do not hold humans hostage to natural, temporal processes initiated by early caregiving is that we believe in spiritual transformation. But transformation takes time. As discussed in the critique of Erikson (chap. 5, Critique C), the apostle Paul proclaims everyone in Christ a "new creation" spiritually (2 Cor 5:17), even as he bemoans the determinism of his natural tendencies (Rom 7). Unfortunately, I could find nothing indicating whether Bowlby retained (from his Anglican upbringing) any hope for spiritual transformation. A second reason Christians do not hold humans hostage to early caregiving is that Scripture identifies God as one of the agents "helping us along" particular pathways. Scripture says that God leads his people in the right paths (Ps 23:3). He makes our paths straight (Prov 3:6) and easier to navigate (2 Sam 22:33).

Of course, God's helping us along is not necessarily discordant with Bowlby's claim that humans are determined by early caregiving. God's supernatural-distal determination may come *through* the temporal-proximal determination of early caregiving sending us down particular paths, *both* good and bad. Concerning the latter, the apostle John implicates God as the agent who blinded Israel's eyes so that they might not turn (Jn 12:40). Although most Christians believe that God is not the author of evil, some passages suggest that God entrenches people on paths they are already on.[30]

---

[29]I am grateful to my former student Simone Frame for directing me to this verse.

[30]See Ex 9:12; Mk 4:12; Rom 1; 11:8. Knowing how to interpret these passages is difficult. Some commentaries teach that God sets some people on "bad" paths as part of a master plan; others teach that God only consigns people to paths they have already chosen for themselves.

The practical task for Christians is to discern how to start all children down the best possible path in the first place. Both the Bible and attachment theory espouse the value of emotional support and moral-ethical instruction. But what should we do when we disagree with the moral-ethical-spiritual instruction a child is (or is not) receiving? Some Christians think it is better for children to linger in foster care than be adopted into the "wrong kind" of family. Some Christians think that parents who give birth to children out of wedlock do not deserve the financial assistance necessary for them to function as a secure base for these children. When we deprive children of basic stability because their parents' values or behavior do not completely align with our own, we may actually aim these children down the bad pathways we are trying to keep them off—both temporally and spiritually. (Recall from Critique A that humans have difficulty viewing God as loving if they do not first develop IWMs of others as loving and of self as lovable.)

In 1 Corinthians 3 the apostle Paul establishes that God is the one responsible for spiritual growth, but God builds on a foundation laid by humans. The language Paul uses to describe this foundation-work appeals to natural processes (we plant, we water, we give milk to those who are still "people of the flesh," still "infants in Christ" [1 Cor 3:1-3]). Jesus also demonstrated that natural processes (e.g., hunger in Mt 14:13-21 and 15:32-39) must be attended if we want our spiritual instruction to be effective. In attending to the temporal attachment needs of all children, we show ourselves to be not just moral people but ethical people who ground our methods of responsibility-taking in love.

WHAT CHRISTIANS CAN LEARN FROM BOWLBY

Bowlby's perspective on human development is eschatologically reductive but empirically rich, offering a much-needed sensitization for Christians who discount the role of embodiment in both temporal and spiritual development. There are at least three very practical things that Christians can learn from Bowlby's attachment theory.

First, high-quality care during the earliest years must become a public health priority. Infants without parents need to be promptly placed with parents who will love them. Parents who lack the resources to function as a secure base for their children need communal assistance. Compared to many other industrialized countries, the United States is miserly in its support of parents with young children. Bowlby helps Christians understand that putting a stumbling block in front of a child may be as much a sin of omission as one of commission.

Second, natural processes associated with early deprivation seem to "lock in" dysfunction and deviancy for some children. Awareness of these processes is critical for adoptive/foster parents seeking to practice the "pure religion" of caring for orphans (Jas 1:27) and for those in a position to support these parents when the children they are attempting to love seem unable to love back. To be clear, not every child who has experienced severe deprivation exhibits attachment difficulties.[31] But greater awareness of the attachment difficulties shown by many children who are emotionally deprived during their early years can help Christians care better. Families considering fostering or adopting emotionally deprived children may want to wait until other children in the home are old enough to understand and protect themselves, physically and emotionally. Friends and relatives in supporting roles must realize that children's enduring attachment problems are often *not* the fault of the child or subsequent caregivers, and that discipline techniques that work well with securely attached children may be useless—or even counterproductive—with emotionally deprived children. Reinhold Niebuhr prayed, "God, give us grace to accept with serenity the things that cannot be changed" (Shapiro, 2008). John Bowlby provided some of the scientific wisdom necessary to understand

---

[31]Psychological functioning is almost always the result of an interaction between genes and environment. Concerning attachment specifically, several contemporary studies (e.g., Drury et al., 2012) have found that previously institutionalized children with a short version of a serotonin transporter gene (5-HTT) are more likely to have difficulties than those with a longer version of this gene. This means that early environmental deprivation is *more* determining for some children than for others. Further evidence of heterogeneity in response to early emotional deprivation—and some children's amazing resilience—comes from studies seeking to estimate the prevalence of attachment-based disorders. Attachment problems are somewhat difficult to quantify, but two longitudinal studies of international adoptees (Gorter et al., 2017; Rutter et al., 2007) revealed that about a third of these children did not show attachment-related difficulties during a five-year period of evaluation, and about half were symptom-free by the last wave of data collection. These studies indicate that even when deprivation is severe, entrenchment is not inevitable.

why some emotionally deprived individuals seem unable to change despite dramatic changes in their attachment environments.

Third, spiritual development is an outgrowth of natural, temporal processes. Although Bowlby himself did not discuss God, theorists who have extended his ideas to the formation of a God-concept believe that our capacity to feel loved by God (and love God back) arises out of our concept of self as lovable or not, which arises out of our relationships with early attachment figures. This means that emotionally supportive *non-Christians* can lay a basic foundation for children's eventual love of God, and *Christians* who neglect attachment needs within the family or society can undermine children's capacity to eventually love God. For his detailed explication of the natural processes impacting psychological development, Bowlby is a good theorist for Christians to know.

CHAPTER SEVEN

B. F. Skinner's Radical Behaviorism

B. F. SKINNER (1904-1990) has been deemed the most important psychologist of all time (Cherry, 2019; Haggbloom et al., 2002; Korn et al., 1991). His methods helped make psychology a science, and his claims about the causes of behavior have shaped contemporary society's collective understanding of personhood.

Skinner is renowned for his conditioning of rats and pigeons and for attempting to explain human behavior *without* ascribing causal status to cognitive processes like choice or free will. Skinner believed that a person is born with a genetic inheritance that predisposes them to find some experiences reinforcing and some not, and to behave accordingly. Although the person is the *vehicle* for the behavior,[1] the cause is located in the environment acting on the person, rather than within the person.

By locating cause in the environment, Skinner was able to create a technology of behavioral control. This sparked controversy in the scientific community as well as the American public. Critics accused Skinner of dehumanizing. They said that Skinner's deconstruction of concepts like choice and responsibility reduced humans to animals or machines. Proponents lauded Skinner because he "took his science out of the laboratory and into the world, where it could help people" (Bjork, 1997, p. xii). Some of the most common applications of Skinner's principles are mental health professionals treating phobias and addictions, teachers improving pupil performance, and business people raising employee morale and productivity.

---

[1]The vehicle analogy was made by Ahearn (2010).

BIOGRAPHY

Burrhus Frederic Skinner (B. F. in scientific discourse; Fred to his friends) was born in 1904 in Susquehanna, Pennsylvania. His childhood home was generally "warm and stable" (Cherry, 2016), but family members judged their own and others' shortcomings harshly, and personal improvement was perpetually emphasized. Although physical punishment was never employed, the Skinner children were controlled through appeals to social evaluation, shame, and fear. Sometimes these appeals leveraged religion, a practice Skinner later deemed spiritual torture. Skinner (1976b) wrote,

> The first religious teaching I can remember was at my grandmother Skinner's. . . . I remember being shown the coal in the fire in the heating stove and told that little children who told lies were thrown in a place like that after they died. . . . Not long afterward I did tell a real lie to avoid punishment and that bothered me for years. I remember lying awake at night sobbing, refusing to tell my mother the trouble, refusing to kiss her goodnight. I can still feel the remorse, the terror, the despair of my young heart at the time. (p. 60)

Susquehanna was a typical railroad town on the Erie line. Faced with a dearth of intellectual challenge and a surplus of mechanical debris, Skinner spent his childhood inventing contraptions. Most of these contraptions were common amusements, but some represented empirical attempts to test scientific or religious tenets—for example, a beam with suspended scales to test whether "faith will move mountains."[2] Other contraptions foreshadowed Skinner's eventual desire to get away from his parents.[3] Ubiquitous in Skinner biographies is his age 10 creation of a hook-pulley system to escape his mother's nagging him to pick up his pajamas. When the hook was empty, a sign that said HANG UP YOUR PAJAMAS hung down in the middle of the doorframe, obstructing his exit from the room. When

---

[2]B. F. Skinner, *Levitation*, June 18, 1971, basement archives at the B. F. Skinner home, quoted by Bjork (1993, p. 19).

[3]In reflecting on his departure for college, Skinner describes a state of "uneasy joy." "I did not know what lay ahead, *but I was getting away from my parents.*" B. F. Skinner, *My Attitude Toward My Parents*, February 19, 1969, basement archives at the B. F. Skinner home, quoted by Bjork (1997, p. 28).

the pajamas were hung, their weight lifted the sign out of his way. Young Skinner also explored the hills and forest surrounding Susquehanna, trapping various creatures for observation.

In 1922 Skinner matriculated at Hamilton College, where he studied English literature and creative writing. His freshman year, he began publishing volumes of poetry. The Skinner unknown to most psychologists once claimed "the wind is sad" (Skinner, 1976b, p. 204), and the great American author Robert Frost wrote in a letter to Skinner, "You are worth twice anyone else I have seen in prose this year" (Skinner, 1976b, p. 249). Upon graduation, Skinner convinced his parents to support him while he wrote a novel, intending to deliver to the world some new philosophy of life or truth (Bjork, 1997, pp. 54-57). Unfortunately, young man Skinner had nothing revolutionary to say.

Thus began "The Dark Year" during which he produced very little that satisfied him. The socially awkward Skinner was also lonely. Several key people in his life were deceased, and he had already begun rejecting organized religion. According to Bjork (1997), this process started in his midteens when a speaker at a revival meeting deemed the accidental electrocution of a Susquehanna resident to be divine punishment (p. 16). Later Skinner wrote, "I strongly resented it when the evangelist referred to his death as punishment for not attending the meetings. . . . I saw suddenly the frail humanness in religion and I must have revolted, not quickly, but over a period of years."[4] However, Skinner's revolt was not total. If Susquehanna tried to instill in him a Protestant work ethic and social gospel, Skinner abandoned only the Protestant and gospel parts, always retaining a strong work ethic and the desire to create a tangibly better life for himself and others.

This desire to make a difference set the stage for Skinner's embrace of the burgeoning science of behaviorism, which Skinner viewed as an objective, concrete means to human progress. Abandoning fiction, Skinner began writing reviews of books on the philosophy of science. It was in the midst of writing a critical review of Lewis Berman's 1927 book, *The Religion*

---

[4]Untitled note, n.d. (probably early 1970s), basement archives at the B. F. Skinner home, quoted by Bjork (1997, p. 16).

Called Behaviorism, that Skinner first defined himself as a behaviorist, admittedly without knowing very much about behaviorism.[5]

In 1928 Skinner enrolled in a graduate psychology program at Harvard, having never taken a course in psychology. He spent his first year dividing time between the departments of psychology and physiology. Physiology seemed more scientific, but the psychology department afforded him a venue to construct more contraptions (Skinner, 1979, pp. 31-32). Indeed, it seems that Skinner's early experiments were as much driven by the fun of making contraptions as a priori hypotheses. Skinner would make gadgets for rats (because rats were cheap) and then follow what struck him. This free approach did *not* always yield theoretically meaningful results. Summarizing his first gadgets experiment, Skinner (1956) wrote, "The major result of this experiment was that some of my rats had babies" (p. 223).

Skinner's research took on focus when he realized that he could use a string wound on a spindle to quantify the rate of lever pressing in food-deprived rats. Replications yielded remarkably smooth data curves that could be used to *predict* rats' rate of lever pressing. Skinner had just turned 26 and explained in a letter to his parents that the greatest birthday present he got was a scientific finding: "What heretofore was supposed to be 'free behavior' on the part of the rat is now shown to be just as much subject to natural laws as, for example, the rate of his pulse. My results seem to be very conclusive, and barring some slip-up in technique, are really important."[6] After receiving his PhD in 1931, Skinner stayed on at Harvard as a researcher for five years before teaching at the Universities of Minnesota and Indiana. He then returned to Harvard, where he taught from 1948 until his retirement in 1974.

Following retirement, Skinner continued to write, and according to John Chirban (a friend who tape-recorded hundreds of informal interviews with Skinner over 25 years), to wrestle with the concept of God. Although Skinner (1983) declared that he had escaped from hellfire to agnosticism (p. 404), he was always interested in matters of theology. In

---

[5]Interview with B. F. Skinner, December 14, 1989, quoted by Bjork (1993, p. 61).
[6]B. F. Skinner to his parents [late March 1930], basement archives at the B. F. Skinner home, quoted by Bjork (1993, p. 91).

Chirban's (2014) analysis, Skinner viewed religious beliefs as a positive thing for others but felt that spiritual grace had been denied to him. This deprivation prevented him from enjoying God, although he did acknowledge spiritual "feeling states" that were "very important" to him. He also recognized the need for a causal force outside of science, which he referred to as "the Other" or "It."[7] He was open to this force being somewhat anthropomorphic. As Skinner told Chirban, "I'm not averse to the idea of some intelligence or some organizing force that set up the initial conditions of the universe in such a way that ultimately generated stars, planets and life. It's easier to imagine the creation of intellectual force than a creation force that was able to create the Big Bang."

In contrast to the two theorists already critiqued (Erikson and Bowlby), Skinner was a learning theorist, meaning that he placed more emphasis on nurture than nature. Within learning theory, Skinner is distinctive for his research on contingency-based behavior (i.e., behavior that depends on what happens *after* a response; as opposed to his predecessors Ivan Pavlov and John B. Watson, who focused on stimuli that preceded behavior). Skinner's principles of contingency-based behavior (first demonstrated with rats and pigeons and standard to most psychology textbooks), include positive and negative reinforcement, punishment, shaping, extinction, discrimination, and fixed versus variable schedules of reinforcement. Many of these Skinner discovered somewhat serendipitously. Skinner's first conditioning of rats happened accidently, and studies of extinction ensued when the lever of the food magazine jammed. Reinforcement schedules were conceived when he did not want to spend a beautiful Sunday afternoon hand-shaping food pellets to provide continuous reinforcement on Monday (Demorest, 2005, p. 85). Skinner recognized the fortuitousness of these events, insisting that "most of the major turning points of his life and the discovery of his science had been sheer accident" (Bjork, 1997, p. 2). Skinner died of leukemia at age 86, 10 days after accepting an APA Lifetime Achievement Award.

---

[7]As discussed in chap. 7, Tenet A, some attachment theorists have proposed that children who experience God as rejecting may eventually abandon the notion of a personlike God in favor of an impersonal energy force. Skinner seems to be an example of this process.

BEHAVIORISM AND RADICAL BEHAVIORISM

Behaviorism is "the theory that human and animal behavior can be explained in terms of conditioning, without appeal to thoughts or feelings, and that psychological disorders are best treated by altering behavior patterns" (Oxford University Press, n.d.). Behaviorism is predicated on Thorndike's law of effect[8] and Morgan's canon of parsimony.[9] Thorndike's law states that rewarded behavior is likely to increase and punished behavior is likely to decrease. Morgan's canon states that when two explanations suffice, scientists should use the simpler one. (In other words, if we can explain behavior solely on the basis of observable causes external to an organism, we should not appeal to mental processes that we cannot observe.)

The birth of behaviorism proper is commonly set as 1913, when Watson (1913) asserted, "Psychology as the behaviorist views it is a purely objective experimental branch of natural science. Its theoretical goal is the prediction and control of behavior. Introspection forms no essential part of its methods" (p. 158). By insisting on objective investigations of observable behavior, behaviorism was an important historical antidote to psychoanalytic theory's imprecisely defined "drives." Behaviorism made the discipline of psychology much more scientific.

Most contemporary behavioral psychologists are (what I am going to call) methodological behaviorists,[10] meaning that their methods exclude the assessment of mental contributors to behavior, but they do not deny the causal role of mental processes in behavior. Methodological behaviorism is different from Skinner's radical behaviorism in that the latter expressly denies that mental processes play *any* causal role in the production of behavior. The term *radical behaviorism* was used a few times to describe Watson's approach in the 1920s (because Watson argued against

---

[8]Edward Thorndike (1874–1949) was an American psychologist.

[9]C. Lloyd Morgan (1852–1936) was a British ethologist-psychologist. He said, "In no case may we interpret an action as the outcome of the exercise of a higher psychical faculty, if it can be interpreted as the outcome of the exercise of one which stands lower in the psychological scale" (Morgan, 1894, p. 53).

[10]Not to be confused with *methodological behaviorism*, an umbrella term encompassing several intellectual positions inside and outside psychology (Moore, 2001).

consciousness; Schneider & Morris, 1987), but Skinner (1964) co-opted the name for his own paradigm, saying, "I am a radical behaviorist simply in the sense that I find no place in the formulation for anything which is mental" (p. 106). Skinner also referred to his approach as *operant conditioning* and a *science of behavior*.

To be clear, Skinner did not deny the existence of mental processes; he just did not ascribe them *causal status*, and he thought that psychologists' attention to them muddied our predictive models (Skinner, 1976, p. 4). Skinner believed that a predictive model of behavior should be composed solely of *observable contingencies* (from a Latin word meaning "to touch on all sides"). Contingencies include antecedents (i.e., what comes before a behavior), observable responses to antecedents, and observable consequences of the responses (important because they provide information about likely consequences, should a specific behavior be repeated). Contingencies are best illuminated by isolating the discrete behaviors that make up a complex behavior pattern within an experimental procedure so that the complex pattern can be better understood.

Skinner particularly challenged the "homunculizing"[11] of mental processes, wherein behavior is attributed to a nonphysical inner agent residing within our physical body. Among other names, this nonphysical agent has alternatively been labeled the self, mind, will, personality, and autonomous man. Skinner (1976a) called this practice

> a vestige of animism, a doctrine which in its crudest form held that the body was moved by one or more indwelling spirits. When the resulting behavior was disruptive, the spirit was probably a devil; when it was creative, it was a guiding genius or muse. Traces of the doctrine survive when we speak of a personality, or an ego in ego psychology, of an I who says he knows what he is going to do and uses his body to do it. (p. 184)

Skinner (1972) insisted that contemporary science permits us to move beyond discourse about inner agents, writing that "science does not dehumanize man, it de-homunculizes him" (p. 200).

---

[11] A *homunculus* is a very small human or humanoid creature. In sixteenth-century alchemy, it was believed that a fetus developed from a microscopic but fully formed human creature present in the sperm.

It was this caricaturizing of the human decision-making process that Skinner's contemporaries found so provocative. If Skinner had stuck to elucidating the conditions under which organisms learn, and the application of these conditions in therapy and educational settings, he would have still been a great psychologist whose behavioral techniques help many people. But Skinner went beyond the explication of learning, deconstructing a myriad of concepts most contemporary humans view as foundational to personhood. In addition to the self, the will, and personality, Skinner had little use for creativity, purpose, freedom, dignity, or an eternal soul. To Skinner, all these concepts were "explanatory fictions" (i.e., terms nonbehaviorists employ to explain behavior when they do not fully understand the behavior itself or the comprehensive pattern of contingencies associated with the behavior; Skinner, 1953, p. 157; 1957, pp. 6-7; 1972, p. 24).

Skinner is also considered radical for his position that those who are knowledgeable of the science of behavior should reengineer society to improve the lives of those less knowledgeable. Finally realizing his postcollege dream in 1976, he published a utopian novel wherein a character named Frazier speaks for Skinner,[12] acting as a tour guide and salesman for an engineered community named Walden Two. Although sales were initially slow, the book eventually made the *New York Times* Best Sellers list.

Whether Skinner genuinely believed all the claims he made through Frazier and in his academic writings or was engaging in calculated exaggerations to drive home a point is not entirely clear to me. The latter is certainly plausible given Skinner's unabashed readiness to self-promote. Even before he had declared himself a psychologist, Skinner wrote to a mentor at Hamilton, "I have almost gone over to Physiology, which I find fascinating. But my fundamental interests lie in the field of psychology and I shall probably continue therein, even, if necessary, by making over the entire field to suit myself."[13]

---

[12]"I received a telegram reading: KINDLY REPLY COLLECT WHETHER OR NOT WALDEN TWO WAS WRITTEN SATIRICALLY. MATTER IN CONTROVERSY ON CONTROVERSIAL WASHINGTON CAMPUS. PREFER AUTHOR'S OPINION, I replied: WALDEN TWO BY NO MEANS SATIRICAL. FRAZIER'S VIEWS ESSENTIALLY MY OWN—MORE SO NOW THAN WHEN I WROTE" (Skinner, 1983, p. 9).

[13]B. F. Skinner to Arthur Percy Saunders, December 5, 1928, Harvard Archives, as quoted by Bjork (1993, p. 81). Inconsistent capitalization in the original.

Skinner did not succeed in making over the entire field, but in his attempt he pushed Western culture to think hard about some fundamental assumptions of personhood. Some aspects of Skinner's perspective are discordant with basic Christian doctrine, meaning that all Christians should reject them. But other aspects are accordant with *some* Christians' beliefs even as they offend others. This makes Skinner an interesting and provocative figure to examine in this book.

THE FOUR THEMES

Like Erikson, Skinner was a prolific writer. From a broad survey of his writings, I have derived six tenets relevant to this book's organizing themes.

A. The central characteristic of personhood is our learned behavior (essence).

B. Purpose is an "explanatory fiction," but effectiveness and good relationships are reinforcing (purpose).

C. Humans are not inherently good or bad; moral tendencies are learned (moral-ethical tendencies).

D1. Behavior is predictable and determined, not freely chosen (agency/accountability).

D2. Even though behavior is determined, humans have a great deal of control over our environment and ourselves (agency/accountability).

D3. Responsibility is a meaningless concept, but people should be taught "self-control" (agency/accountability).

ESSENCE

Tenet A: The central characteristic of personhood is our learned behavior.
Skinner believed that all creatures are best characterized as the sum of their learned behaviors built up over time. In other words, creatures are almost entirely the product of nurture. Nature gives creatures basic morphology; beyond that, it does little to distinguish one creature from another.

To appreciate Skinner's marked disregard for nature, we can consider how his view differed from that of his contemporaries. When Skinner was writing, most scientists viewed genetic endowment as very species-specific. Directives in an organism prompted specific behaviors labeled *instincts*;

sets of instincts were used to define a species. In contrast, Skinner asserted that the psychological part of genetic endowment was best thought of as just one generic directive that all creatures share: *do what is reinforcing.*

By way of example, consider the process of imprinting described in chapter six. Ethologists like Konrad Lorenz viewed imprinting as a chick's "instinctual approach" behavior. Skinner (1976a) viewed imprinting as "the capacity to be reinforced by maintaining or reducing the distance between itself and a moving object" (p. 46). In the natural environment, it is a chick's approach that elicits these consequences, but if a mechanical system is constructed whereby distance is reduced by the chick's movement *away* from an object, the chick learns to move away to keep the target in close proximity.

While this reconceptualization shows that the chick has the capacity to adjust its behavior to achieve proximity, it doesn't tell us why this behavior is reinforcing to chicks in the first place. Most scientists would say that the chick seeks proximity because of a genetically endowed drive for proximity, and that this drive is one of the defining characteristics of chicks. In contrast, Skinner (1976a) dismissed the drive for proximity and then defined the chick by the behavior it used to satisfy the drive he had dismissed, claiming that "genetic endowment is nothing until it has been exposed to the environment, and the exposure immediately changes it" (p. 165).

Skinner (1976a) appealed to the same processes to explain the development of humans, providing this definition:

> A person is first of all an organism . . . possessing a genetic endowment of anatomical and physiological characteristics, which are the product of the contingencies of survival to which the species has been exposed in the process of evolution. The organism becomes a person as it acquires a repertoire of behavior under the contingencies of reinforcement to which it is exposed during a lifetime. . . . It is able to acquire such a repertoire under such control because of processes of conditioning which are also part of its genetic endowment. (p. 228)

Within the discipline of psychology, Skinner's reduction of persons to their repertoire of learned behaviors constituted a direct challenge to psychoanalytic theory, which defined humans with internal psychological constructs. In response to Erikson, who equipped humans with a central organizing agent that synthesizes many selves into one coherent Self, Skinner disavowed both the agent and the synthesis. He refuted the agent by declaring that humans have no sense of self until a verbal community arranges the contingencies that permit such self-perception (Skinner, 1976a, pp. 186, 242). He refuted the synthesis by reducing both self and personality to context-specific repertoires. Personality, argued Skinner (1972), is based on variations in levels of "traits" (e.g., aggression, industry, attention), which are inferred from behavior, which is fully attributable to contingencies in a specific environment (pp. 185-87). Thus, "a self or personality is at best a repertoire of behavior imparted by an organized set of contingencies. The behavior a young person acquires in the bosom of his family composes one self; the behavior he acquires in, say, the armed services composes another. The two selves may exist in the same skin without conflict until the contingencies conflict" (Skinner, 1976a, pp. 164-65).

Beyond the discipline of psychology, Skinner's reduction of personhood to learned behaviors constituted a direct challenge to anyone who maintained motivational differences between species, individuals, or the sexes. In the same decades that Erikson was offending women by emphasizing hardwired sex differences (see chap. 5), Skinner was offending women by failing to appreciate sex differences. Skinner designed Walden Two as a functionally genderless society wherein children were separated from their parents and raised communally by a balanced number of males and females. Skinner reported that one of the reasons he wrote the novel was to help women. He was thus baffled when even his own wife, Eve, resented and hated the book.[14] In personal correspondence, he mused, "The curious thing is that I wrote it in an effort to solve some of their [women's] problems—to give them a genuine equality and to free them from the traditional slavery implied by the role of women in Western Culture. Little thanks did I get!"

---

[14]Eve's response was reported by Skinner in an interview with Bjork, December 19, 1988. The quote is from Skinner correspondence to Wade Van Dore, April 21, 1969, Harvard Archives, as quoted by Bjork (1997, p. 151).

Finally, Skinner's reduction of persons to learned repertoires of behaviors constituted a challenge to those who believed that humans are endowed with transcendent characteristics like an eternal soul. As stated, Skinner declared the soul an explanatory fiction. For Skinner, environmental contingencies develop us, and learned behavior defines us. Ironically, for the one theorist thoughtful enough to provide us an explicit definition of a person, the construct of essence barely applies.

Critique A. Central to our working model of essence is humans' creation in the image of God. Most Christians interpret this to mean that humans are hardwired with capacities that make us *qualitatively* distinct from animals—although MacKay (1986) has argued that differences could be only quantitative (p. 41). Regardless, Skinner's insistence that nature makes only two contributions to personhood (morphology and the generic directive to do what is reinforcing) is incompatible with the doctrine of the *imago Dei*. Skinner recognized this and in one of his autobiographies (1983) explicitly contrasted the self-denial of "assigning one's achievements to one's genetic and environmental histories" with "the self-aggrandizement of those who claim to have been born in the image of God the Creator" (p. 408).

Likewise, Skinner's definition is incompatible with humanity's other essential characteristics articulated in part one (save procreation, which all species seem to find reinforcing). His definition is incompatible with the non-procreative aspects of likeness for the same reason it is incompatible with the doctrine of the *imago Dei*: it makes no distinction between humans and animals who were not made according to God's likeness. It is incompatible with most Christians' beliefs that gender has an essential element.

Skinner's definition is also incompatible with Christians' belief in an eternal soul. Admittedly, Christians do not agree on how to define the soul. Many Christians view the soul as a distinct entity that persons "have," but Christian neuroscientists are increasingly depicting the soul as an emergent property arising out of humans' advanced cognitive and emotional capacities. Scholars like Warren Brown, Nancy Murphy, and H. Newton Malony (1998) have referred to this latter approach as *nonreductive* physicalism to distinguish it from the reductive physicalism advanced by Skinner and later by evolutionary psychology.

Finally, Skinner's reductionism is incompatible with innate individual differences that likely contribute to different spiritual gifts (1 Cor 12; Eph 4). I say *likely* because spiritual gifts could be entirely a product of nurture, but Scripture seems to imply that spiritual gifts are at least partially rooted in morphology. In 1 Corinthians 12:11-12, Paul speaks of these gifts being "activated" by the Spirit and likens Christians with different gifts to a physical body with many parts. Although scientific research on the association between spiritual gifts and nature is very limited (one example is a dissertation by Joachim [1985] linking gifts to temperament), Scripture would seem to call for a greater appreciation of heritable individual differences than Skinner provides.

Incompatibilities notwithstanding, we *can* esteem Skinner for his emphasis on behavior as an important measure of personhood. We don't read very far into the Bible (try Leviticus) to see that observable behavior was *central* to the Hebrew identity. Proverbs 20:11 tells us that "even children make themselves known by their acts." Even in the New Testament, where Christians are defined by Christ's behavior, not our own, the apostle James reminds us that faith without works is dead (Jas 2:17). While behavior is not the primary factor in a Christian view of personhood, Skinner reminds us that it is a very important factor.

PURPOSE

Tenet B: Purpose is an "explanatory fiction," but effectiveness and good relationships are reinforcing. Skinner relegated purpose to his list of explanatory fictions. (Again, *explanatory fiction* is a term Skinner used to dismiss concepts created by nonbehaviorists to explain behavior when they do not fully understand the behavior itself or the comprehensive pattern of contingencies associated with the behavior; Skinner, 1953, p. 157; 1957, pp. 6-7; 1972, p. 24.) Skinner did not deny that people can *feel* purposed; he denied an inwardly directed progression toward an a priori end goal. Skinner (1976a) argued,

> The point is made that motives and purpose are in people while contingencies of reinforcement are in the environment, but motives and purpose are at best the effects of reinforcements. The change wrought by

reinforcement is often spoken of as "the acquisition of purpose or intention," and we are said to "give a person a purpose" by reinforcing him in a given way. These are convenient expressions, but the basic fact is that when a person is "aware of his purpose," he is feeling or observing introspectively a condition produced by reinforcement. (p. 63)

In this denial of purpose Skinner also denies inherent motivation, but the latter denial was more difficult to sustain. We see this in a conversation about pedagogical methods Skinner had with Richard Evans (1968, p. 62), who interviewed Skinner for a National Science Foundation series on great thinkers. The interview goes like this:

Skinner: "Any little indication of progress, such as being right so that you can move on to the next step, is enough. . . . The human organism is reinforced simply by being effective. . . ."

Evans: "Your mention of 'being right' as a reinforcer is very interesting. You are not suggesting that this is something 'internal' or 'self-satisfying' in the individual, are you? . . ."

Skinner: "No. All reinforcers are defined by their effects. . . . We classify events according to their demonstrable effects on a given organism."

Having been caught alluding to what others conceptualize as motivation, Skinner dismissed Evans's question on the grounds that self-satisfaction does not meet *behaviorists'* operational definition of a reinforcer. Instead of explaining why or how effectiveness is reinforcing (if it is not satisfying an inherent desire to be effective), Skinner engages in circular logic: How do we know that something is reinforcing? It is reinforcing because it changes behavior. And why does it change behavior? Because it is reinforcing.

Skinner also alluded to inherent motivation in *Walden Two* (1976c). Speaking through the character of Frazier, he says, "Even hard work is fun if it's not beyond our strength and we don't have too much of it. A strong man rejoices to run a race or split wood or build a wall. When we're not being imposed on, when we choose our work freely, then we want to work. We may even search for work when a scarcity threatens" (p. 147). Continuing his sales pitch, Frazier explains how the whole community has been structured to permit the Good Life, which includes "a chance to exercise talents and abilities," have "intimate and satisfying personal contacts," and enjoy "relaxation and rest" (p. 148). Although Skinner the behaviorist explicitly denies both inherent purpose and motivation, Skinner the novelist implicitly defines human purpose as living the Good Life and depicts humans as desiring effectiveness, good relationships, and rest.

Critique B. In Christian theology, humans have God-given purposes. In Skinner's theory, we have no purpose at all. This makes it short work to declare Skinner's perspective on purpose incompatible with our working model.

For motivation, a more nuanced critique is required. Skinner explicitly denied inherent motivation but sometimes let down his rhetorical guard, especially when speaking through Frazier. Frazier's account of the Good Life reveals that Skinner ascribed to humans several basic human motives suggested in the Genesis creation accounts. In Frazier's discourse, it is difficult not to hear echoes of Eden wherein humans were introduced to work that afforded a sense of dominion, inherently valuable relationships, and rest. The creational motive Frazier neglects is humans' yearning for God. Asked about religion, Frazier says, "The simple fact is, the religious practices which our members brought to Walden Two have fallen away little by little, like drinking and smoking. It would take me a long time to describe, and I'm not sure I could explain, how religious faith becomes irrelevant when the fears which nourish it are allayed and the hopes fulfilled—here on earth" (Skinner, 1976c, p. 185).

Skinner gets some temporal characteristics of humanity right. He recognizes humans' motivation for love and dominion work, in spite of his attempts to deny such motivation. Alternatively, he consistently neglects humans' motivation to love God.

MORAL-ETHICAL TENDENCIES

Tenet C: Humans are not inherently good or bad; moral tendencies are learned. Because Skinner attributed such a minimal role to nature, it should not surprise us that he accorded humans no inherent moral bent. Per Frazier: "We have no truck with philosophies of innate goodness—or evil, either, for that matter" (Skinner, 1976c, p. 182). For both Frazier and Skinner, moral-ethical tendencies are fully attributable to environmental contingencies. Yes, hardwiring might cause me to involuntarily perform simple behaviors that contribute to something good or bad happening (e.g., I sneeze and strike a pedestrian with my car), but behavior that is complex and operant enough to qualify me as *bent* toward good or evil requires the environment to shape my simple reflexive behaviors into more complex ones.

Skinner's dismissal of natural moral proclivity can be seen in his treatment of sin. Skinner (1972) mused,

> Does man sin because he is sinful, or is he sinful because he sins? Neither question points to anything very useful. To say that a man is sinful because he sins is to give an operational definition of sin. To say that he sins because he is sinful is to trace his behavior to a supposed inner trait. But whether or not a person engages in the kind of behavior called sinful depends upon circumstances which are not mentioned in either question. The sin assigned as an inner possession (the sin a person "knows") is to be found in the history of reinforcement. (The expression "God-fearing" suggests such a history, but piety, virtue, immanence of God, a moral sense, or morality does not. As we have seen, man is not a moral animal in the sense of possessing a special trait or virtue; he has built a kind of social environment which induces him to behave in moral ways.) (p. 198)

As stated in the biography section, Skinner was quite knowledgeable of theology. With the phrase *the sin a person "knows,"* I suspect that Skinner was alluding to God's declaration that "the man has become like one of us, knowing good and evil" in Genesis 3:22. As discussed in part one, Western Christianity has often depicted this knowledge as something humans possess (original sin) or something that possesses humans (sometimes referred to as the Old Adam). Skinner (1972) particularly disparaged the reification or personification of evil tendencies, arguing that Christians' Old Adam (and Freud's id) were simply behavior patterns that developed out of humans' genetic susceptibility to reinforcement, a capacity that is in itself morally neutral (p. 199).

Skinner did acknowledge that humans have strong moral feelings, but believed that these, too, were the products of reinforcement. We feel "right" after behaving in ways we know to be reinforcing, and "guilty" after behaving in ways we know to be punishable (Skinner, 1976a, pp. 69-70). Moral feelings can be particularly strong when conditions of reinforcement and punishment have been codified into legal, political, and theological systems. For example: "A person who has been exposed to the promise of heaven and the threat of hell may feel stronger bodily states than one whose behavior is merely approved or censured by his fellow man. But neither one acts *because* he knows or feels that his behavior is right; he acts because of the contingencies which have shaped his behavior and created the conditions he feels" (Skinner, p. 213).

Because Skinner linked morality to environmental contingencies, he was sometimes accused of being a *moral relativist* (someone who bases moral decisions on situational outcomes rather than absolute principles that transcend the situation). Skinner (1976a) responded, "To attribute moral and ethical behavior to environmental contingencies seems to leave no room for absolutes. It suggests a kind of relativism in which what is good is whatever is called good. . . . But an environmental account is not relativism in that sense. . . . Ethical and moral contingencies of reinforcement have their own consequences" (p. 216). This quote suggests that Skinner believed in a transcendent natural law that did not require a deity to reveal it. Rather, it was revealed in the consequences of human actions. Thus, people can be moral without organized religion, although religious systems bolster moral behavior.

Critique C. Our working model depicts humans as structurally good and inherently inclined toward both good and evil. It also specifies contributions from the environment.

Skinner clearly appreciated the contributions of the environment to moral-ethical tendencies. He not only documented the specific processes by which our moral thoughts and behaviors are shaped; he also drew our attention to how a moral environment helps illuminate transcendent moral law. Skinner believed that humans do not need codified religious beliefs to behave in accordance with moral absolutes, but codified systems and explicit training help humans articulate moral precepts, and produce strong moral feelings when precepts are violated. In Romans 5:13, the apostle Paul explains that "sin was indeed in the world before the law, but sin is not reckoned when there is no law." Good environments help us discern moral precepts. That is why Scripture repeatedly directs parents to train their children, and the author of Hebrews reminds us that "solid food is for the mature, for those whose faculties have been trained by practice to distinguish good from evil" (Heb 5:14).

Skinner was not wrong to focus on the environment. The problem is that he focused *only* on the environment. In part one, I summarized various Christian perspectives on humans' inherent moral-ethical tendencies. The most scientifically plausible of these is that both good and evil are emergent properties. Of all the theorists in this book, Skinner is the least willing to ascribe humans *any* emergent capacities. This reductive approach is particularly evident in his book *Verbal Behavior*. Contemporary psychologists are virtually unanimous in the belief that the human brain is preprogrammed to develop language. But Skinner (1957) characterized language as the result of "undifferentiated, previously unorganized, and undirected movements" coming into contact with a verbal community (p. 464). "No special kind of mind stuff is assumed" (Skinner, 1972, p. 242). In the same way that he disavowed human language as a preprogrammed emergent capacity, Skinner disavowed moral tendencies as emergent.

Skinner's stance is discordant with the first chapters of Genesis, which emphasize both moral tendencies and language (in Adam's naming of the animals). The knowledge of good and evil *does* have a learned component (it is *after* humans have sinned and been punished that God says, "See, the man has become like one of us, knowing good and evil" (Gen 3:22), but Christians believe that this knowledge is supported by inherent tendencies—as do most psychologists, even if they are not people of faith.

Skinner also refused to treat sin as an animate agent. This stance is likely to please some Christians even as it troubles others. The apostle Paul depicts sin as a personified agent living inside humans, but most commentators attribute this personification to creative rhetoric rather than a dualistic worldview wherein spiritual forces dwell in a material body (see chap. 3). Thus, Skinner's refusal to personify sin is compatible with the majority opinion of academic theologians, but not all Christians.

In sum, Skinner rightly drew our attention to the very important role of the environment in the development of moral-ethical tendencies. If he had focused on the environment and just neglected the contribution of inherent tendencies, we could declare his ideas generally compatible with our working model. It is Skinner's explicit disavowal of emergent moral tendencies that requires us to declare his model inconsistent with a Christian one.

AGENCY/ACCOUNTABILITY

Tenet D1: Behavior is predictable and determined, not freely chosen. Psychology is based on the premise that human behavior is predictable. By this I mean that something about my past (genetic endowment, experience, behavior) explains something about my present, which predicts something about my future. Take away these patterns and we not only dismantle psychology as an academic discipline; we divest humanity of the primary mechanism by which we have faith in ourselves and our associates (e.g., a job applicant's past job performance has no bearing on future performance; the marriage my spouse and I build today has no bearing on our subsequent fidelity).

While most people are grateful that behavior is predictable, they resist hearing that behavior is determined, and particularly the school of thought known as determinism. As defined by Baumeister (2009), "Determinism is a belief in the inevitability of causation. Everything that happens is the only possible thing that could happen." In other words, *if* we knew all the causes involved—*and* could accurately measure them—we could predict human behavior with 100% accuracy. Asked about his own behavior in an interview with Elizabeth Hall (1972), Skinner said,

> I certainly believe that my own behavior is entirely a function of three things—my genetic endowment, my past history as an individual (my family, my religious experience, my government, my schooling, the physical environment in which I have lived, and so on), and the present

situation. I am absolutely sure that that is all there is in the determination of what I'm going to do at this very moment. (p. 69; see also Skinner, 1983, p. 400)

A concrete example may be helpful. As I write this paragraph, I am drinking milk. I am drinking milk because of a complex set of factors that just converged, *causing* me to drink this milk. These converging factors include genetic endowment, past experience with milk, availability of milk, temporary writer's block that caused me to wander over to the fridge, and so on. So the question is, Could I have chosen to *not* drink milk? And the answer is yes, but only if I had been experiencing a slightly different set of conditions just before beginning to imbibe—in which case my *not drinking milk* would have been determined by a different set of conditions than the ones that determined my drinking. (Specifically, I might *not* be drinking milk if my kids had left me some juice. Or I might *not* be drinking milk if I was trying to prove Skinner wrong by abstaining. But then my abstaining, rather than my drinking, would be the determined behavior in question.) For Skinner, whether I drink, don't drink, or drink something else, it is the only possible outcome of the *exact* set of complex conditions converging immediately prior to whatever I do.

While determinism in general can be difficult to accept, Skinner's version of determinism is particularly offensive to many people. There are at least three reasons for this.

First, Skinner's divesture of personhood cut deeper than scientifically necessary. He could have just said, *If you can't measure something, leave it out of your predictive model.* Instead, he attempted to deconstruct a long list of reified constructs (purpose, will, creativity, self, agency, etc.) that people rely on to fill in the gaps between observable behaviors. Skinner (1976a) tried to leave these gaps unfilled, insisting, "A scientific analysis of behavior must, I believe, assume that a person's behavior is controlled by his genetic and environmental histories rather than by the person himself as an initiating, creative agent" (p. 208).

Second, Skinner defined terms in odd ways. For example, he defined *freedom* as "lack of *any* [emphasis added] prior determination" (Skinner,

1976a, p. 59). Defined that broadly, freedom is an easy-enough construct to let go. (Who among us would like it to be said that our behavior is completely random, free of *any* prior determination?)

Third, Skinner made provocative declarations before his theory was fully developed. A decline in provocativeness over time (on some topics) can be seen in his application of the word *machine*. In his 1968 interview with Evans, Skinner said, "If by 'machine' you simply mean any system which behaves in an orderly way, then man and all the other animals are machines" (p. 24). In 1972 Skinner said, "Man is a machine in the sense that he is a complex system behaving in lawful ways, but the complexity is extraordinary" (p. 202). And then in 1976a Skinner explained that humans did *not* have "the character of a puppet, robot, or machine" (p. 245). This change over time seems to reflect not only a more careful use of terms but also a refined perspective.

Tenet D2: Even though behavior is determined, humans have a great deal of control over our environment and ourselves. Behavior is determined in Skinner's model, but humans have a lot of control over a lot of things. Already in his first book, *The Behavior of Organisms* (1938), Skinner had replaced the term *instrumental conditioning* (preferred by Thorndike and Watson) with the term *operant conditioning*. He did this to emphasize the organism's active role in operating on the environment.[15]

Skinner allotted humans more and more control in the course of his career. His early focus was on observable actions, but eventually "behaving" came to include cognitive processes that he termed *covert behavior*. Arguing that behavior is *not* just a reflexive response to a stimulus, Skinner (1976a) said,

> Human beings attend to or disregard the world in which they live. They search for things in that world. They generalize from one thing to another. They discriminate. . . . They solve problems by assembling, classifying, arranging and rearranging things. They describe things and respond to their descriptions, as well as to descriptions made by others. They analyze the contingencies of reinforcement in their world and extract plans and rules which enable them to respond appropriately without direct exposure

---

[15]Skinner said in an interview, "I prefer to use the word 'operant' in the sense of behavior which operates on the environment and produces reinforcing effects" (Evans, 1968, p. 19).

to the contingencies. They discover and use rules for deriving new rules from old. In all this, and much more, they are simply behaving, and that is true even when they are behaving covertly. (pp. 245-46)

In "behaving" to control the environment, humans also control ourselves and our futures. In his interview with Evans (1968), Skinner explained,

Man can control his future even though his behavior is wholly determined. It is controlled by the environment, but man is always changing his environment. . . . He avoids extremes of temperature; he preserves food to avoid hunger. He builds a world in which he is more likely to get on with his fellowman, in which he is more likely to educate himself so that he will be more effective in the future, and so on. . . . Man controls himself, but he does so by controlling his environment. (p. 107)

Indeed, Skinner was so confident that his technology of behavior could be used to usher in a better future for humankind that he was sometimes grandiose. In the closing line of *About Behaviorism*, Skinner (1976a) boasted, "Man can now control his own destiny because he knows what must be done and how to do it" (p. 277).

Tenet D3: Responsibility is a meaningless concept, but people should be taught "self-control." Skinner used the term *responsibility* in the way that I use the term *accountability* (i.e., in connection to self rather than care of others). In this section, I will use the term *responsibility* as Skinner did, and then return to a distinction between accountability and responsibility in the critique.

Skinner began challenging the concept of responsibility in his first scientific book on humans. In a very unpersuasive passage, Skinner (1953) likened the determinism of whispering in church to the involuntariness of coughing, arguing that "there are variables which are responsible for whispering as well as for coughing, and these may be just as inexorable. When we recognize this, we are likely to drop the notion of responsibility altogether and with it the doctrine of free will as an inner causal agent" (p. 116).

Fifteen years later, Skinner took a less combative approach. Rather than disavowing personal responsibility outright, he attempted to deconstruct it by exploring what responsibility means in different cultures. In his interview with Evans (1968), Skinner explained that in ancient societies (and post–World War II Communist countries), control was exercised primarily through aversive, external means. In these contexts, responsibility is nothing more than obedience to avoid punishment. In contrast, societies shaped by the Protestant Reformation tend to focus on "inner" sources of control, with people doing what they want to do rather than what they have to do. But this emphasis on "inner" control works only with people who have emerged from a tradition like the Judeo-Christian one, which gives them reasons for behaving well. The reason they behave well is that they find this behavior reinforcing. For people who don't find it reinforcing (e.g., lawbreakers), society still requires external controllers. Therefore, "the notion of personal responsibility just isn't relevant. The control is still there" (Evans, 1968, p. 31).

Having deconstructed personal responsibility, Skinner was understandably reluctant to blame people for either misfortune or misbehavior. Concerning misfortune, he expressed frustration over the grievous role that "autonomous man" played in all spheres of academic and public opinion. Skinner (1972) cited a study revealing that more than 50% of White Americans blamed the socioeconomic status of Black Americans on lack of "motivation/will," viewing will as distinct from *both* genetic and environmental factors (p. 198). Concerning misbehavior, Skinner called for a rethinking of punishment, explaining, "In the traditional view, a person is free. He is autonomous in the sense that his behavior is uncaused. He can therefore be held responsible for what he does and justly punished if he offends. That view, together with its associated practices, must be re-examined when a scientific analysis reveals unsuspected controlling relations between behavior and environment" (pp. 19-20).

Instead of punishment, Skinner preferred systematic and intentional modification of behavior using positive reinforcement. An example of this systematic positive reinforcement can be found in the nursery at Walden Two, where preschoolers are given lollipops that are sugarcoated to detect licks. The children are told that they can eat the whole lollipop at systematically increased intervals if they can resist licking it now. (Although a guest at Walden Two labels this "sadistical tyranny" [Skinner, 1976c, p. 99], contemporary psychologists have demonstrated that such restraint can, in fact, be taught.)[16]

If we juxtapose Skinner's *deconstruction* of responsibility with his *construction* of the nursery at Walden Two, we see that Skinner was *not* attempting to relieve humans of responsibility as the concept is commonly understood. To the contrary, his intent was to teach "responsible" behavioral tendencies that would help humans thrive. One reason Skinner is often misunderstood is that this intent is often overshadowed by his insistence on logically consistent rhetoric (whereby *determined* people cannot be *responsible* people). Both his intentions and this overshadowing are evident in the conversation that precipitates Frazier's presentation of the Walden Two nursery. Frazier says,

> You can't foresee all future circumstances, and you can't specify adequate future conduct. You don't know what will be required. Instead, you have to set up certain behavioral processes which will lead the individual to design his own "good" conduct when the time comes. We call that sort of thing "self-control." But don't be misled. The control always rests in the last analysis in the hands of society. (Skinner, 1976c, p. 96)

Critique D. Scripture presents humans as agentic, accountable for self, and responsible for others. Skinner *explicitly* characterized humans as none of these, but the two perspectives are not as incompatible as they initially seem. Rather, there are *some* aspects of Skinner's perspective that are compatible with *some* theological positions. Areas of overlap can be articulated for Skinner's views of determinism, freedom, agency, accountability, and responsibility.

Determinism. Skinner himself touted the overlap between radical behaviorism with a theological stance on determinism. In one of his autobiographies, Skinner (1983) wrote, "My early religious experience was important" (p. 402). Particularly important was his encounter with the

---

[16]Studies initiated in the 1960s and 1970s using the Stanford Marshmallow test (described on *Wikipedia* and demonstrated in many YouTube videos) showed that preschoolers who could resist one marshmallow for 15 minutes to earn a second one are characterized by a variety of better life outcomes; see Mischel et al. (2010). Variance in this capacity was initially attributed to nature, but more recent studies have provided robust evidence that the ability to delay gratification is at least as much nurture as innate ability; see Kidd et al. (2013).

theology of Jonathan Edwards (1703–1758), an influential philosopher-theologian of the colonial era. Working within the larger Reformed-Puritan tradition, Edwards attempted to explicate the metaphysics of theological determinism. In brief, Edwards asserted that humans have freedom to act according to our desires, but our desires are determined by forces outside us, such as the sovereignty of God and the corrosive influence of sin (Everhard, 2016; Wainwright, 2016). Many elements of Edwards's description of the human psychological experience resonated with Skinner. For example, Skinner (1983) liked Edwards's view that "consciousness was a delusion implanted in man to give him a sense of moral responsibility" (p. 403). After perceiving several connections between Edwards's position and his own, Skinner declared, "These seem like a remarkable set of similarities. If a. God is all powerful; b. nature is an orderly determined system, then man's freedom, responsibility, awareness, achievements, and worth must be interpreted in new ways. Much of my scientific position seems to have begun as Presbyterian theology, not too far removed from the Congregational of Jonathan Edwards" (p. 403).

Although his determinism is not theological, Skinner had no qualms appealing to the theological when he thought it would enhance his credibility. Appeals can be seen in filmed talks (Gl0balElite, 2009; see the last half minute of the video) and in books. *Walden Two* contains a passage in which Frazier characterizes a guest's declaration of personal freedom as erroneous. He then attributes this error to the guest "not being a good behaviorist—or a good Christian, for that matter" (Skinner, 1976c, p. 243). But this accusation works for only some Christian traditions. It *works* for Christians in the Reformed tradition who espouse the total sovereignty of God. Per John Calvin, God arranges events to direct our mental life, permitting humans to psychologically experience planning, willing, and choosing, even as God retains total sovereignty.[17] It does *not work* for Christians whose theological roots run through Jacobus Arminius and John Wesley. Many contemporary evangelical Christians teach that salvation depends on each individual personally deciding for Christ.

---

[17]For Calvin's explanation on how sovereignty plays out psychologically, see chap. 4, note 3. For a psychologist's linking of Skinner's determinism to God's, see Bufford (1981, p. 54).

A theology of salvation that requires humans to have free will cannot be reconciled with Skinner. Thus, Skinner's perspective on determinism is more compatible with some Christian traditions than others.

Freedom. Skinner defined freedom so narrowly (as lack of *any* prior determination) that the construct is not worth fighting for. But even if he had employed a broader definition, his assertion that humans are not free is compatible with some biblical and theological postures. The apostle Paul often spoke of the freedom that we have in Christ (1 Cor 9:1; 2 Cor 3:17; Gal 5:1; 5:13), even as he made it clear that we are not really free. Paul said that if we are not slaves of sin, then we are "slaves of righteousness" (Rom 6:18; cf. 1 Cor 9:21). Other theologians who have depicted us as not really free include Jonathon Edwards and contemporary Catholic theologian Neil Ormerod. Edwards said that we freely choose what we most desire, but our desires are determined by God or by sin. Ormerod (1992) says that "each time sinners sin, they sin freely, even if they are not free not to sin!" (p. 51). All of these authors depict humans as inescapably tethered to determinants. While the theological authors tether us to spiritual forces (presumably working through temporal means), Skinner limits his explanation to the temporal. Thus, Skinner's perspective on freedom is incomplete but generally compatible with some aspects of basic Christian theology.

Agency. Skinner gave humans a great deal of agency. Likewise, the Bible teaches that humans were created to have dominion (Gen 1) and locates us "a little lower than God" (Ps 8:5). If we want to criticize Skinner for his perspective on agency, the most valid criticisms are that some of his comments go too far (e.g., we can control our own destiny) and that Skinner maybe thought too highly of himself.[18] While it is good to celebrate our

---

[18]Interesting discourse on Skinner's wrestling with conceit is provided by Bjork (1993). Bjork (pp. 152-53) cites Skinner's personal correspondence to Stephan Feinstein (October 7, 1969, Harvard Archives), wherein Skinner says, "The scene on the hill when Frazier lies in the position of a crucified Jesus has disturbed many people, but I wanted to deal with the God-complex which a man in his position would almost certainly suffer from." In Bjork's analysis, Skinner "mockingly but half seriously, saw himself as a sort of savior to humanity," (p. 152) but his tendencies toward conceit were kept in check by his mother's warning about "what people will think" (p. 153). Skinner also credited his early religious training for keeping him humble, saying, "It seems to me that Frazier represents the confluence of a Judaeo-Christian or Protestant Ethic culture and Western science reaching at last human behavior" (Bjork citing B. F. Skinner, February 9, 1968, *Who Will Control? Who Controls the Controller?*, basement archives at Skinner's house).

status as a little lower than God, it is clear from Genesis 3 that we must not attempt to be as God.

Accountability. The Bible promotes accountability as the goal for all adults. Skinner was grudging in his endorsement of *self*-control, but this does not mean that he had no regard for the biblical goal. Rather, it means that his regard for accountability was trumped by his even greater regard for consistent rhetoric. From the nursery at Walden Two, we can discern that Skinner *did* want people to exercise self-control as it is commonly conceptualized. Moreover, Skinner thought hard and pragmatically about how best to cultivate this quality. In this regard, his position complements a biblical one. The Bible identifies self-control as a fruit of the Spirit; Skinner offers growing instructions.

Skinner was also reluctant to punish, believing that those who behaved poorly did so because they had not been trained to do otherwise. His presumption that bad behavior is solely attributable to training is incompatible with a Christian perspective but compatible with the observation made in part one of this book that the most common qualifier of accountability indicated in Scripture is knowledge. In this way, Skinner implicitly endorsed degrees of accountability.

Responsibility. Skinner did not assign responsibility for others to humankind en masse, but he was keen on taking responsibility himself. In his programs of behavior therapy, his efforts to reform education, and his utopian vision for a society where all people thrive, Skinner presumed that those who have valuable knowledge should take it to those who don't (cf. Rom 10:14-15). Skinner (1972) hoped that his technology of behavior would be used to address threats to environmental sustainability such as overpopulation, nuclear stockpiles, pollution, and the depletion of natural resources (p. 152). Although Skinner had no use for the doctrine of the *imago Dei*, he had high regard for the cultural responsibilities associated with the functional view of it and viewed earth-keeping as a pragmatic necessity.

A frustrating deficit in Skinner's perspective on responsibility (even if we limit our critique to the temporal) is his scant attention to the cognitive processes that accompany responsibility-taking. Eventually, Skinner did subsume cognitive processes as *covert behavior* but persisted in presenting them as determined rather than determining. In part one, I asserted that God desires Christians to grow into a moral maturity based on love. Skinner's refusal to ascribe causal status to any feeling or internal motivation makes his perspective incompatible with the love component of a Christian perspective on responsibility.

WHAT CHRISTIANS CAN LEARN FROM SKINNER

Skinner's (1976a, p. 228) definition of personhood is incompatible with a Christian view of human *essence*. His primary theological offense is that he explicitly denied humans' creation in the image of God, but his extreme reductionism rankled the psychological community and the general populace as well. Concerning *purpose*, Skinner explicitly dismissed it as explanatory fiction. These two aspects of Skinner's worldview should be troublesome for all Christians.

Skinner's perspective on *moral-ethical tendencies* merits greater consideration. His refusal to acknowledge any structural or emergent moral tendencies is problematic, but his refusal to reify moral tendencies is shared by many Christians in the field of neuroscience working to articulate a more scientifically feasible understanding of sin as integral to personhood. I have not so much learned *from* Skinner's discourse on moral-ethical tendencies as learned *because* Skinner made provocative statements that compelled me to think hard about what it means to say that sin got inside of us. Skinner's treatment of sin made me realize that a Christian psychologist needs a more empirically grounded conception of sin than just something humans possess, or something that possesses humans.

I am especially grateful to Skinner for prodding me to think hard about *agency/accountability*. Although I grew up with one foot in the Reformed camp, it was not until I read Skinner as a primary source that I began to appreciate the extent to which humans are determined. Skinner's discourse on environmental determinism was the concrete grounding that helped me wrap my mind around theological determinism and eventually pitch my tent with Christians who emphasize God's sovereignty. Obviously, many Christians will not respond to Skinner in this way, but even

Christians who champion free will can benefit from a greater appreciation of the many, many influences on human behavior. Familiarity with radical behaviorism can help Christians temper our contempt for those who perpetually "choose" poorly. It can also help us systematize our attempts to grow self-control. For these reasons, it is beneficial for Christians to know B. F. Skinner.

CHAPTER EIGHT

Albert Bandura's Social Cognitive Theory

ALBERT BANDURA is considered the fourth most eminent psychologist of the twentieth century after Skinner, Piaget, and Freud (Cherry, 2019; Haggbloom et al., 2002). Bandura is *best known* for his studies of observational learning wherein children behaved aggressively with punching toys (called Bobo dolls) after observing adults do so. Bandura was *most interested* in helping people take better control of their lives (Goode, 2021).

Toward this end, Bandura worked to articulate the conscious cognitive mechanisms that humans use to evaluate and regulate behavior. He then created programs to help them accomplish this. Therapies based on Bandura's social cognitive theory (SCT) have helped people improve themselves in a wide variety of domains, including physical and mental health, literacy, and parenting. In the estimation of his APA biographer, Bandura "led the profession in explicating the . . . self-regulatory determinants of meaningful learning and behavior change" (Evans, 1989, p. ix).

Like Skinner, Bandura's programmatic attempts to modify bad behavior made him the target of public controversy,[1] but Bandura's view of the person is much less controversial than Skinner's. This is because Bandura returned to humans *some* of the self-determination that Skinner rhetorically abdicated to the environment and that Erikson and Bowlby relegated to the unconscious. Concerned that people often "do not exercise the personal control that is fully within their capabilities" (Bandura, 1997, p. 17), Bandura (1999, 2001) specifically promoted SCT as "an agentic perspective."

---

[1]When describing a particularly turbulent time with the executives of the major TV networks, Bandura said: "I began to feel a kinship with the battered Bobo doll" (Goode, 2021).

BIOGRAPHY

Bandura was born in 1925 in a small farming community near Edmonton, Alberta. His parents emigrated from Eastern Europe as teenagers and modeled for him the agency that underpins social cognitive theory. They scrimped and saved, became entrepreneurs, and then scrimped and saved again after dismantling their thatched roof to feed the cows. Although Bandura's father had no formal education, he taught himself to read in three languages, served on the school board, and supervised the construction of the road system in their homestead district. Bandura, too, worked as a teenager: on the family farm, in construction, and re-graveling highways to keep them from sinking into the Yukon bog (Pajares, 2004).

Although Bandura's parents did not agree on everything (his mother was "deeply religious," whereas his father "drank holy wine with the priest"), both encouraged their son to look beyond the confines of their tiny hamlet (Foster, 2006). Bandura's mother told him, "You can work in the field and get drunk in the beer parlor, or you might get an education" (Foster, 2006). Initially this education had to be self-driven. Of the two teachers at his 20-student high school, Bandura said, "They really didn't know the subjects they were teaching very well. It was in an environment of limited resources. The benefit in this kind of situation is that you had to develop a capacity for self-learning" (Görlach, 2013).

At age 21, Bandura matriculated at the University of British Columbia. He enrolled in a psychology course to fill an open hour generated by an inconvenient carpool. Bandura fell in love with psychology and completed his bachelor's degree in three years. When it was time to apply for graduate school, Bandura asked his adviser, "Where are the stone tablets of psychology?" His adviser replied, "University of Iowa of course" (Bandura, 2006, p. 46). Warned that Iowa would be a "taxing experience," Bandura was surprised to find it supportive and hospitable, and later characterized it as a place where a Canadian student (ineligible for fellowships) could get hired to apply *needless* coats of paint (Pajares, 2004). As with his baccalaureate, Bandura completed his doctorate in just three years.

Although Iowa was a stronghold of behaviorism, Bandura spent his short time there experimenting with reciprocal determinism and mental representation. *Reciprocal determinism* means that a person is not only determined by the environment but also determines the environment. *Mental representation* involves the use of language and symbols to mentally manipulate the world. One particularly important category of language is self-labels, first assigned by others, and then by the self. By redrawing a distinction between humans and other species, and by treating cognition and self as *causal* agents, Bandura worked to reclaim important human qualities like freedom and responsibility that others in his program were attempting to deconstruct. After graduate school, Bandura completed a brief internship at the Wichita Kansas Guidance Center.

In 1953 Bandura joined the faculty at Stanford and became well known inside and outside psychology. His research was the impetus for the 1972 surgeon general's report on televised violence and a response in *TV Guide* that mocked Bandura and the surgeon general (Bandura, 2006). In 1973 his career took an unexpected turn when he was elected president of the American Psychological Association (APA). He writes in his autobiography,

> This was a difficult time for our profession both internally and publicly. A media frenzy was whipping up public fear of the looming peril of behavior modification. In his disaffection with the social sciences, President Nixon issued an executive order terminating psychology training grants. Psychologists had no effective vehicle for speaking in a collective voice on legislative issues and sociopolitical influences that affected our discipline. (Bandura, 2006, p. 53)

To remedy this situation, Bandura created a separate advocacy arm of the APA. He then spent much of his presidency working to bring "psychological knowledge to bear on public policies and informing the general public about the relevance of our discipline for matters of social concern" (Bandura, 2006, p. 54).

In 1981—in what we might term a turning of the TV tables—Bandura was contacted by a producer from Mexico City who wanted to create a soap opera–like series that modeled the benefits of literacy and family planning. This series was very effective; enrollment in the national literacy program increased almost tenfold during the broadcast year, and contraceptive sales increased by 23%. Other dramas for radio and television followed. In India the enrollment of girls in school rose from 10% to 38% in one year of broadcast (Bandura, 2015, pp. 422-25). Another program ran for two years in Ethiopia, during which requests for contraception rose 157% and the birth rate fell from 5.4 to 4.3 births per mother (Foster, 2006). Subsequent programs have targeted sanitation practices, dowries, HIV/ AIDS prevention, and environmental conservation (Bandura, 2015). All told, international development projects based on Bandura's theoretical principles have been launched in over 60 countries (Foster, 2006).

Bandura was obviously motivated by humanitarian concerns and planet preservation. Whether his motivation was also faith-based has been difficult for me to discern. For each of the featured theorists, I read closely for any hint of a religious worldview, but Bandura was very guarded in this respect. Bandura (2015) made reference to both "ancient theology" (seemingly Genesis) and nonteleological pre-sentient "Evolutionism" from the same dispassionate distance (p. 16). In an interview with *The European*, Bandura told Görlach (2013), "I'm not interested in what happened in caves ages ago. I look at what evolution has given us: It has given us capacities and mechanisms to influence the future."

When I emailed Dr. Bandura requesting assistance with this section, he pointed me to his website, which includes links to both *Fortuity* and *Spirituality*. Concerning fortuity, Bandura (1982) cited his early college carpool and meeting his wife on a golf course as evidence that "chance encounters play a prominent role in shaping the course of human lives" (p. 747). Concerning spirituality, he stated,

> Most people acknowledge a spiritual aspect to their lives. They seek meaning and social connectedness to something greater than oneself, without being tied to a formal religion or deity. They embrace secular forms of spirituality rather than intrinsic religiosity. The secular forms link spiritual beliefs to spiritual practices that embrace a common sense of humanity. This is expressed in daily living that makes a difference in people's lives. (Bandura, n.d.)

Bandura (2003) identified positive functions of spirituality, such as enhanced coping. From these writings we can discern that Bandura viewed faith as beneficial for many people, but nothing about his own theology or lack thereof.

Bandura continued writing well into old age. In his longer biography, written at age 80, he said, "As I reflect on my journey to this octogenarian milepost, I am reminded of the saying that it is not the miles traveled but the amount of tread remaining that is important. When I last checked, I still have too much tread left to gear down or to conclude this engaging odyssey" (Bandura, 2006, p. 73). Bandura went on to publish my favorite of his books, *Moral Disengagement* (2015), at age 90. Bandura died in 2021, at age 95.

SOCIAL COGNITIVE THEORY AND RECLAIMING THE SELF

Bandura (1977) initially referred to his perspective as social learning theory. Social learning is based on expectations gleaned from one's social context and does not require direct reinforcement/punishment of the learner. Because expectations can be subjective, social learning does not require sophisticated cognition and occurs across many species. To emphasize the sophisticated cognition that occurs when *humans* engage in social learning, Bandura (1986) renamed his perspective social cognitive theory. I will use the term *social cognitive theory* (SCT) to refer to Bandura's perspective, regardless of whether I am referencing his earlier or later publications.

Like all learning theories, SCT emphasizes environmental determinants. But unlike behaviorism, SCT does not limit its explanatory models to outwardly observable events (i.e., Skinner's contingencies). Rather, it fills the gaps between contingencies with a unified cognitive *self* that *causes* some of these contingencies.

As stated in chapter seven (Tenet A), Skinner attempted to do away with the concept of self. Skinner defined *self* as a repertoire of context-specific behaviors, meaning that a person could have as many different selves as contexts in which they behave. Erikson (chap. 5, Tenet A) proposed many (lowercase) selves, synthesized by the (uppercase) Self. Taking on both Skinner and Erikson, Bandura (1997) argued, "There is only one self that can visualize different desired and undesired futures and select courses of action designed to attain cherished futures and escape feared ones. Actions are regulated by a person, not a cluster of selves doing the choosing and guiding" (p. 26). This declaration of one unified self as a causal agent underlies the three aspects of SCT most often included in psychology textbooks: observational learning, triadic reciprocal determinism, and self-efficacy.

Bandura's attention to *observational learning* emerged from his conviction that reinforcement and punishment are insufficient to account for all types of learning, particularly the learning of new behaviors. Rather, a great deal of learning occurs when a self/agent observes a model, evaluates the appropriateness of the model's behavior, and then chooses whether to imitate the model. A summary of observational learning and three types of models has been provided by Cherry (2017), who explains that models can be

- live/physically present (e.g., an adult hitting a Bobo doll);
- symbolic/fictional (e.g., a character on TV or in a book); or
- verbal (e.g., a set of instructions about how to engage in a specific behavior, permitting us to imagine ourselves engaging in the behavior, thereby serving as our own models).

Because some models are observed and then *not* imitated, learning does not always manifest itself in behavioral change. This understanding of learning is in direct contradiction to behaviorism, which operationally *defines* learning as observable behavioral change. (Put another way, if Skinner did not see a change in behavior, he said that no learning had occurred. In contrast, Bandura said that a lot of learning occurs just by watching others, even if we do not change our outwardly observable behavior in any way.)

More central to SCT and themes of this book are the concepts of reciprocal determinism and self-efficacy. *Triadic reciprocal determinism* (TRD) is a developmental model in which three sets of determinants—personal, behavioral, and environmental—each influence the other two. Bandura (1997, 2015) presented TRD by locating the three sets of determinants at the three angles of a triangle and using double-headed arrows to form the three sides of the triangle. (This helps convey that each set of determinants influences the other two and is reciprocally influenced by the other two.) Which determinants are most influential varies by situation. Bandura (1997) clarified that "reciprocity does not mean that the three sets of interacting determinants are of equal strength. Their relative influence will vary for different activities and under different circumstances" (p. 6).

One of the primary contributions of the personal set of determinants to behavior is the pattern of thoughts that Bandura (1994) termed *self-efficacy*. Perceived self-efficacy is the belief in your own capacity to exercise control over your own functioning and situations that affect your life. People who have high self-efficacy and believe they can control aspects of a situation act in a confident, agentic manner.[2] People who doubt their capacity do not attempt to make things happen. In Bandura's (1997) perspective, "beliefs of personal efficacy constitute the key factor of human agency" (p. 3).

THE FOUR THEMES

Bandura was not as prolific as Skinner, nor as rhetorically creative and full of self-regard. He did not speak as the tour guide of a utopian society, but he did produce in his later years several books and articles explicitly addressing some of the very themes scaffolding this book. From these writings, I have derived five tenets about personhood.

A. The central characteristic of personhood is agency (essence).

B. Humans benefit from a learned purpose rooted in moral standards that transcend the individual and promote the common good (purpose).

C. Moral agency is learned, but nature tries to orient us toward good (moral-ethical tendencies).

---

[2]Self-efficacy is generally presented as domain-specific; a woman may feel highly efficacious at work even as she feels helpless to save her marriage. Self-efficacy is not the same as global self-esteem; a man who is a klutz on the athletic field may still have high self-esteem, provided that athletic competence is not that important to him (Bandura, 1997, pp. 11-12).

D1. Behavior is determined, but a partially free self is one of the determinants (agency/accountability).

D2. Humans are partially accountable and should be trained to take greater responsibility for self and others (agency/accountability).

ESSENCE

Tenet A: The central characteristic of personhood is agency. Bandura formally introduced SCT in Asian (1999) and American (2001) journals. He gave both articles the same title: "Social Cognitive Theory: An Agentic Perspective." In these articles, Bandura identified psychological processes that permit human agency. These processes include universal capacities (e.g., intentionality, forethought, self-reactiveness, and self-reflectiveness) as well as core beliefs about the self that are specific to an individual—most notably self-efficacy (see also Bandura, 2015, pp. 4-6). Bandura opened the abstract of the 2001 article with this claim: "The capacity to exercise control over the nature and quality of one's life is the essence of humanness" (p. 1).

Bandura regularly distinguished SCT from psychology's other major schools of thought by appealing to the cognitive processes that enable agency. Some examples of this are as follows:

1. Bandura rejected the psychoanalytic personification of unconscious mental processes. He believed that ascribing power to unconscious determinants would undermine volitional agency. Instead, Bandura (1978) emphasized a "self-system" composed of "cognitive structures and subfunctions for perceiving, evaluating, and regulating behavior, not a psychic agent that controls action" (p. 344).

2. Bandura rejected Skinner's assertion that nature provides all species the same generic processes for learning. Instead, he drew a wide divide between humans and animals. He argued that animals' ability to make associations is prepared or constrained by "specialized associative apparatus that determine how an organism is influenced by experience" (Bandura, 1977, p. 73).[3] In contrast, human development is characterized by plasticity. This plasticity affords humans an amazing control of the

---

[3]For example, animals will more readily associate illness with a specific taste than with a sight or sound (Garcia & Koelling, 1966).

environment not enjoyed by animals. Plasticity, said Bandura, "is the distinctively universal feature of human nature" (interview with Evans, 1989, p. 33).

3. In response to epiphenomenalists[4] who regard cognitive activities as illusory "by-products of low-level physical states," Bandura (2015) asserted that SCT views the mind as "the embodiment of higher-level cerebral processes" that enable "humans to function as mindful agents" (p. 41).

4. To counter "one-sided evolutionism" wherein humans are viewed as the passive product of environmental conditions, Bandura (2001, pp. 18-20) asserted co-evolution. He claimed that the environment fosters changes in cognitive processes, which in turn foster changes in the environment. Bandura (2015) listed many ways that "people use their ingenuity to circumvent and insulate themselves from environmental selection pressures" (p. 22)—even to the point of genetic engineering. Humans are so agentic that we can "alter evolutionary heritages and shape the future" (p. 23).

Further evidence that Bandura viewed agency as the defining aspect of personhood can be derived from a few publications wherein Bandura reduced the value of *relationships* to their agency-promoting functions. While writing about the role of social support in times of distress and difficulty, Bandura (1999) claimed that "social support has beneficial effects only to the extent that it raises perceived coping efficacy" (p. 31; see also Bandura, 2003, p. 171; 1977). Bandura (2003) even addressed humans' relationship with God from the vantage of agency, asserting that "displacement of control to divine agency to solve one's problems . . . can foster dependent passivity that detracts from development and exercise of personal efficacy" (pp. 172). Alternatively, divine agency "viewed as a guiding supportive partnership requiring one to exercise influence over events in one's life . . . can serve as an enabling belief that strengthens a sense of personal efficacy" (Bandura, 2003, pp. 172-73). For Bandura, the essence of personhood is agency.

Critique A. Our working model depicts humans as embodied creatures with emergent capacities for reason, relationships, and dominion. Christians

---

[4]Epiphenomenalists often appeal to work by Libet demonstrating that the unconscious initiates a finger movement before we consciously decide to do so. See BBC Radio 4 (2014) or Libet (1985). Libet (1999) later clarified that "the volition process is . . . initiated unconsciously. But the conscious function could still control the outcome; it can veto the act. Free will is therefore not excluded" (p. 47).

locate these capacities in the doctrine of the *imago Dei*. Bandura's depiction of humans is very compatible with at least two views of the *imago Dei*. His focus on agency accords with the *functional* view wherein humans were created to have dominion. His attention to the sophisticated cognitive processes that *permit* agency accords with the *substantive* view. Bandura's focus on agency is also compatible with *likeness*, understood as humans registering God's presence in the world in form and function. Bandura (2015) even linked human agency to the Genesis 1 declaration of *likeness* in a discourse on human origins (p. 16). (See full quote in Tenet D1 below.)

Bandura placed less emphasis on the value of human relationships. Proponents of the *relational* view of the *imago Dei* depict humans as endowed with sophisticated cognitive capacities *so that* we can participate in relationships with God and other people. Some of Bandura's writings do suggest that agency "serves" relationships. For example, Bandura (2001) cited three collaborative studies that linked agency in the form of high self-efficacy to "a pro social orientation characterized by cooperativeness, helpfulness, and sharing, with a vested interest in each other's welfare" (p. 15). But other writings (cited earlier) depict relationships "serving" agency. Scripture also depicts relationships serving agency. The Israelite judge Deborah facilitated Barak's agency going into battle (Judg 4:8). The apostle Paul claimed, "I can do all things through him [Christ] who strengthens me" (Phil 4:13). Paul's claim is a great example of Bandura's (2003) recommended view of divine agency "as a guiding supportive partnership requiring one to exercise influence over events in one's life" (p. 172). However, a Christian theology of relationships involves a lot more than the promotion of personal agency. In Matthew 5:43-44, Jesus commands us to love our enemies—who likely undermine our sense of agency when they persecute us. A broad view of Bandura's theoretical and humanitarian work suggests that his view of relationships is generally compatible with a biblical view of relationships, even though he directs only implicit attention to the inherent value of relationships.[5]

---

[5]Ideally, Bandura would have treated relationships as did Schneewind (author of a chapter in Bandura's 1995 edited book). Schneewind declared humans' need for both "communion" and "agency." He alerted readers that his subsequent discourse would focus on agency, but "it should be emphasized that both themes are intrinsically interwoven aspects of human life" (p. 115).

Conspicuously absent from Bandura's description of the person is a systematic address of sex and gender. Perhaps he did not want to distract from his emphasis on universal agency, but he seemingly viewed nature as making only a minimal contribution to sex and gender, noting that that nature holds humans on a "loose" rather than "tight leash" (Bandura, 2015, p. 17). Bandura's limited discourse on sex and gender makes it difficult to assess the compatibility of this aspect of Bandura's perspective with our working model.[6]

PURPOSE

Tenet B: Humans benefit from a learned purpose rooted in standards that transcend the individual and promote the common good. Bandura's approach to purpose is grounded in two characteristic elements of learning theory: a reluctance to accord humans any intrinsic motivation[7] and an extrinsic "kick-start" to development. Explicitly challenging those who promote "an intrinsic need to deal effectively with the environment . . . satisfying in its own right," Bandura (1977, p. 13) explained that even when people engage in activities that appear to be intrinsically motivated (e.g., reading, athletics, musical performance), these activities are composed of discrete skills that people often have to be encouraged or compelled to develop. Eventual proficiency in these skills activates "self-evaluative reactions that serve as reinforcers of performance" (Bandura, 1977, p. 106). Accomplished performance then increases "self-regard," which is a primary determinant in how a person behaves (Bandura, 1977, p. 115).

While Bandura expanded Skinner's model on the back end (effectiveness informs our view of self), he too skirts the question of why

---

[6] I found only two explicit mentions of sex or gender in Bandura's writings. In a (very dated) comparison of humans and animals, Bandura (1973) claimed that "human sexual responsiveness is, in large part, socially rather than hormonally determined" (p. 21). In a discussion of proxy control, Bandura (1997) noted that "female type A's are willing to yield provisional control to someone who is more skilled if they can reclaim it at will. But many male type A's will not surrender control even provisionally" (p. 17). But he gave no hint as to whether this difference is innate or learned.

[7] Bandura (1986) does acknowledge "sensory incentives." As infants we "repeatedly perform acts that produce new sounds and sights." This may be related to "a need to sustain an optimal level of sensory stimulation" (pp. 233-34).

effectiveness would be reinforcing at the front end, *if* it is not satisfying an innate drive to be effective. (By analogy, food is reinforcing to pigeons because pigeons are hardwired with a hunger drive. Wouldn't other reinforcers also need to satisfy *some* intrinsic drive?) The closest Bandura came to acknowledging an intrinsic contributor to purpose was to explain how "nonteleological" evolutionism, "devoid of deliberate plans or purpose," has been *superseded* by the evolution of "neuronal structures for supplanting aimless environmental selection" (Bandura, 2015, pp. 16-17). In Bandura's model, it is these advanced brain structures that permit humans to internalize ideologies that originate outside us and, once learned, help us craft *particular* purposes.

In sharp contrast to Skinner (who dismissed purpose as an explanatory fiction), Bandura viewed purpose as necessary for healthy individuals and a healthy society. Bandura (1991) wrote that without purpose and the internalized standards on which purpose is based, "people would behave like weathervanes, constantly shifting a direction to conform with whatever is expedient at a given moment" (p. 64). Concern for future generations prompted Bandura (1995) to assert that people must "commit to shared purposes that transcend narrow self-interest" (p. 2). Bandura (2015) lauded Gandhi, Nelson Mandela, Martin Luther King Jr., and the religious martyr Thomas More as men who applied high self-efficacy to a particular purpose. Bandura emphasized that it was the combination of efficacy and particular purpose that enables moral exemplars to "submit to prolonged maltreatment rather than accede to what they regard as unjust or immoral" (pp. 29-30).

Bandura depicted purpose as something learned over time. Like Erikson, he believed that a rudimentary sense of purpose develops when healthy preschoolers internalize the standards of adult mentors (Bandura, 1977, p. 43; 1991). To facilitate this sense, Bandura encouraged parents to communicate standards explicitly and require compliance, using punishment if necessary. In his 1963 work with Walters, Bandura disparaged the "popularized belief . . . that the best way of producing prosocial behavior is through 'unconditional love,'" warning that parents must not reinforce all classes of behavior and "thus produce children whose behavior was directionless, asocial, and completely unpredictable" (pp. 224-25). Also like Erikson, Bandura believed that the standards of parents should eventually give way to standards derived from more comprehensive ideological systems. Bandura preferred systems grounded in structured religion rather than amorphous spirfualty because religion provides concrete exemplars (i.e., role models) of how to apply abstract principles to the crafting of one's particular purposes (Bandura, 2003, pp. 170-71).

Critique B. Our working model depicts humans as universally purposed for love and dominion work and some individuals as particularly purposed. By eschewing inward propulsion and keeping mum on the existence of a Creator, Bandura gave himself no theoretical or religious basis from which to assert a *universal* human purpose.

That said, there are several ways in which Bandura's perspective on *particular* purpose is obviously compatible with a Christian one. First, humans need to be grounded in standards that transcend us. Bandura warned that we must not be weathervanes; the apostle Paul warns that we must not be "tossed to and fro and blown about by every wind of doctrine" (Eph 4:14). Second, we learn these standards in our interactions with mentors who instruct us verbally, reinforce, punish, and model purposeful behavior in keeping with these standards. Third, purpose should benefit others. Although Bandura did not explicitly state that purpose involves love and dominion work, his examples of particularly purposed individuals, as well as his explicit linking of agency to "a vested interest in each other's welfare" (Bandura, 2001, p. 15), permit us to infer this.

A less obvious compatibility is Bandura's linkage of self-efficacy to the *realization* of purpose. With the parable of the talents (Mt 25:14-30), Jesus reveals that it is difficult to realize the dominion component of purpose (and perhaps the love component as well) without a healthy sense of efficacy. In this parable, two slaves doubled their master's money and increased his dominion and their own. A third slave hid the money in the ground. The master expressed anger at the third slave's fear to do even a psychologically safe thing (put the money in the bank) and transferred this slave's potential dominion to the first slave, who likely had the greatest sense of efficacy. Although the common application of this parable is that each of us should work to develop our *own* talents, a second application is that Christians familiar with the concept of self-efficacy can help others by striving to foster *their* self-efficacy. By identifying self-efficacy as an important contributor to the realization of purpose, Bandura complements a biblical perspective, detailing psychological processes not specifically addressed in Scripture.

Another less obvious compatibility is the way in which intrinsic and extrinsic contributors to purpose interact in the two perspectives. Christians hardwire humans with sophisticated cognitive capacities that *constitute* our purpose. Bandura hardwired us with many of the same capacities that permit us to *internalize* purpose. Functionally, the processes are almost the same in that both focus on essential cognitive structures being "activated" by a source that transcends the structures. Bandura's failure to identify God as the transcendent source of purpose notwithstanding, his view of purpose is quite compatible with a Christian one.

MORAL-ETHICAL TENDENCIES

Tenet C: Moral agency is learned, but nature tries to orient us toward good. Especially in his later years, Bandura placed a lot of emphasis on *moral* agency. He believed that moral agency is learned but that nature tries to orient us toward good. Nature does this by structuring us to discern moral precepts and evaluate ourselves negatively when we think of violating these precepts. Reflecting on how some psychologists like Milgram (1974) emphasized the capacity to be cruel or punitive in authoritarian situations (see chap. 5, note 30), Bandura (1991) counteremphasized the "equally striking evidence that most people steadfastly refuse to behave punitively, even in response to strong authoritarian commands, if the situation is personalized by having them see the victim or requiring them to inflict pain directly rather than remotely" (pp. 90-91). Personalization is important because our capacity for moral discernment is rooted in our capacity for empathy. Bandura (2015) wrote, "To perceive another as a sentient human being with the same basic needs as one's own arouses empathy and compassion for the plight of others through a sense of common humanity" (p. 84).

Although nature hardwires us for empathy, "the level and pattern of empathetic reactions" are largely determined by learning (Bandura, 2015, p. 92). Fortunately, most societies provide mentors who teach standards that prompt us to become aroused by others' distress. Plans to violate these standards then trigger negative self-appraisals that "serve as deterrents to transgressive acts" (Bandura, 1977, p. 43).

Unfortunately, the same cognitive structures that permit negative self-appraisals also permit us to *suppress* these appraisals. Bandura attributed humanity's bad behavior to our capacity to reconstrue bad acts as good. Reconstrual is the prerequisite to bad behavior because "people do not ordinarily engage in reprehensible conduct until they have justified to themselves the morality of their actions. What is culpable can be made righteous through cognitive reconstrual. In this process, detrimental conduct is made personally and socially acceptable by portraying it in the service of moral purposes. People then act on a moral imperative" (Bandura, 1991, pp. 72-72; see also 2015, p. 49).

As Bandura told Görlach in his 2013 interview for *The European*, "Our problem is good people doing bad things." Thus, the theoretical challenge is to explain "how is it that people can behave cruelly and still feel good about themselves." Bandura took up this challenge in his last book, *Moral Disengagement* (2015). In this book, he identified eight specific methods of disengagement:

- Moral justification (i.e., the end justifies the means)
- Euphemistic language (e.g., bystanders killed by a bomb are "collateral damage")
- Advantageous comparison (i.e., the lesser of the two evils)
- Displacement of responsibility
- Diffusion of responsibility
- Distortion/denial of harmful effects
- Dehumanization
- Attribution of blame (analogous to blaming the victim)

Bandura filled this book with case studies of the evils that humankind has perpetrated on our fellows. The book is disheartening, and without the introduction and the epilogue it would be easy to conclude that Bandura had changed his mind about the way humanity inclines. But Bandura bookended his treatise with reminders that SCT views self-sanctions—not reconstrual—as the norm. Before and after documenting a whole lot of bad, Bandura reiterated his belief that humans are structurally predisposed toward good.

Critique C. Our working model presents humans as sinful despite being structurally good, as does Bandura. Bandura hardwired humans for moral discernment as a function of our hardwired capacity for empathy. The former is accordant with the *substantive* view of the *imago Dei* and the latter with the *relational* view. Bandura's assertion that we have difficulty hurting someone we recognize as a similarly sentient being calls to mind Genesis 9:6, wherein God forbids the shedding of human blood on the basis of humans' shared creational structure. Of course, humans do shed blood and sin against our fellows in many ways described in both the Bible and Bandura's work (2015).

Bandura's perspective also accords with the Bible's attention to the importance of a good environment. His assertion that the activation/degree of empathy and the transmission of moral precepts come through the experience of good mentors is compatible with Scripture's emphasis on instruction and modeling, especially in the socialization of children and new believers.

Bandura's most important contribution to the understanding of moral behavior is his psychological explication of how humans reconstrue evil acts to make them acceptable to self. Bandura believed that cognitive restructuring almost always precedes evil acts. Although it would be difficult to prove that this is always true, there are many examples of cognitive restructuring in Scripture. With the help of the serpent,[8] Eve reconstrues fruit eating as not only morally acceptable but morally beneficial (Gen 3:6: "the tree was to be desired to make one wise"). Cain and Pilate engage in

---

[8]Supernatural influence on cognitive restructuring is also the theme of C. S. Lewis's popular *Screwtape Letters* (1942), wherein a senior demon (Screwtape) instructs a less experienced demon (Wormwood) in how to cognitively guide a young Christian to "Our Father Below" (p. 2).

displacement of responsibility (Gen 4:9; Mt 27:24). Saul and David rationalize that their ends justify their means (1 Sam 13; 2 Sam 11).

A theological deficit in Bandura's model is his failure to depict sin as inherent in any way. Some readers were no doubt troubled by Erikson's rejection of Calvin's reified version of original sin, but Erikson at least specified inherent drives (e.g., will) that can manifest as emergent sin. As a learning theorist who eschewed intrinsic motivation, Bandura had no theoretical basis to explain why structurally good humans would reconstrue bad as good in the first place, save a bad environment.

This makes Bandura's perspective incomplete with respect to the working model developed in part one, *even as* it calls to mind the presentation of sin in Genesis 3. In this passage, we begin with humans who are sinless. The humans find themselves in a bad environment (a serpent urging them to reconstrue bad as good), and they sin—no *explicitly specified* inherently bad motivation linking environmental factors to action required. Like the account in Genesis 3, Bandura's account leaves us struggling to articulate an inherent impetus for sin.

Bandura also neglected to explicitly identify God as the source of the moral precepts that transcend us, even as he valued formal religion for offering both ideology and concrete role models that show us how to live. Because Bandura was so guarded about his own religious beliefs (or the lack thereof), it is difficult to access the compatibility of some aspects of his model with our own. These aspects notwithstanding, his presentation of contemporary humans as sinful *despite* being structurally good is compatible with Christian theology. Likewise, Bandura's delineation of the cognitive processes influencing moral-ethical behavior (e.g., empathy, cognitive reconstrual) is helpful for Christians seeking to foster moral-ethical behavior in ourselves and others.

AGENCY/ACCOUNTABILITY

Tenet D1: Behavior is determined, but a partially free self is one of the determinants. As stated earlier, Bandura is known for triadic reciprocal determinism. In this model, three sets of determinants—personal, behavioral, and environmental—each influence the other two (Bandura, 1997,

2015). *Personal* determinants are held together by the self-system that exerts partial control over one's behavior. Because of the self-system,

> the choice of actions from among alternatives is not completely and in-
> voluntarily determined by environmental events. Rather, the making of
> choices is aided by reflective thought, through which self-influence is
> largely exercised. People exert some influence over what they do by the
> alternatives they consider; how they foresee and weigh the visualized out-
> comes, including their self-evaluative reactions; and how they appraise
> their abilities to execute the options they consider. (Bandura, 1997, p. 7)

Because the self-system influences behavior, "some measure of freedom is possible" (Bandura, 1997, p. 7), even though our behavior is determined.

This seeming contradiction requires some unpacking. Bandura (1997) was trying to do two things at once. First, he was rejecting Skinner's model wherein organisms are "only pawns of external forces" (p. 8). Therefore, he equipped humans with a self-system to *free* us from *total environmental determinism*, making us "at least partial architects of our own destiny" (p. 8). Second, he was shifting some of the determinism Skinner accorded to the environment to the self-system, so that behavior is now determined by *two* sets of determinants rather than just one. (For example, in Skinner's model, I play video games instead of studying for my test, because gaming is reinforcing. In Bandura's model, I play video games because gaming is reinforcing *and* because I have learned that I will likely not pass the test anyway. This *combination* of game-related reinforcement and low self-efficacy determines my continued gaming.)

Bandura (1997) was explicit that "self-influences operate deterministi-cally on behavior in the same way environmental forces do" (p. 7). This means that Bandura, like Skinner, had no use for concepts like autonomy and free will. For both theorists, these descriptors required the capacity to behave unconstrained by *any* determinants. Interestingly, both theorists appealed to theology in their deconstruction of free will, but in different ways. Skinner argued that Christians could believe in environmental de-terminism because we already believe in theological determinism (chap. 7, Critique D). Bandura argued that even though some Christians teach free will, theological accounts of the first humans *repudiate* this claim. Bandura (2015) wrote,

> In ancient theology, human nature was ordained by original divine design. Having been divinely granted the power of free will, individuals were free to choose how to behave in the likeness of absolute agency. Free will is an enigmatic, autonomous force that is self-negating in function. If individuals have the power of free choice, why do they choose wrong while under evil influences? An autonomous free will that succumbs to pernicious influence is a contradiction in terms. Over the years, many lively debates have been devoted to this misnomer. (p. 16)

Tenet D2: Humans are partially accountable and should be trained to take greater responsibility for self and others. To the degree that humans are free, we are also accountable. Accountability was another primary focus for Bandura in his later years. His last book, *Moral Disengagement* (2015), is an explicit call for those with greater freedom to behave better, and for the general public to hold them accountable when they do not. In the prefatory chapter, Bandura voiced concern with certain neuroscientific approaches that focus only on "first-order" (i.e., lower-level) neural networks and avoid taking a stance on accountability. Bandura countered, "A deterministic thesis that humans have no conscious control over what they do, in fact, is a position on moral accountability—it is one of moral nonaccountability" (p. 43). Bandura then emphasized the necessity of grounding neuroscience research in SCT, because "in a cognitive and affective neuroscience that recognizes second-order control exercised through moral self-sanctions people can be held partly accountable for what they do" (p. 47).

Toward this end, Bandura (2015) used the eight methods of moral disengagement listed in Tenet C as a framework for exposing institutions and industries that he viewed as behaving immorally. These include the entertainment industry for its love of violence, the finance world, the gun industry and the NRA, the tobacco industry,[9] terrorists and counterterrorists,

---

[9]To appreciate Bandura's (2015) thoroughness in ascribing blame, see his list of 15 contributors to tobacco-related immorality, such as chemists, farmers, movie actors, stockholders, the US Department of Agriculture, and trade representatives who threaten sanctions to countries that try to limit the import of US cigarettes (pp. 100-101).

proponents of the death penalty, institutions that cover up sexual abuse, and those who exploit the environment. In his discussion of the latter, Bandura expressed particular frustration with "some radical Christians" who draw on Scripture to justify this exploitation (p. 373). His hope was that "a public that is well versed in the various modes of moral disengagement can see through self-exonerative practices, making it harder for wrongdoers to apply them successfully" (p. 445).

Bandura also advocated *responsibility-taking* and viewed the failure to take responsibility for others (when one could) as a moral failing. To increase responsibility-taking in moral situations, Bandura (1991, p. 53) discussed techniques for training children in moral conduct as soon as children can engage in discussions about the feelings of others. He said mentors should strive to communicate moral precepts through direct instruction, modeling, and social reinforcement. He recognized the utility of sanctions and punishment but believed that aversive discipline techniques do not work well by themselves. Rather, they must be combined with techniques that promote empathy and negative self-evaluation so that malefactors are self-motivated to keep future bad behavior in check.

Bandura practiced what he preached, collaborating on many projects to increase self-efficacy in developing countries. As described in the biography section, many of these projects promoted the self-efficacy of women and girls, increasing their school matriculation and facilitating their physical well-being (e.g., birth control, prevention of HIV[10]).

Critique D. Our working model depicts humans as agentic, accountable for self, and responsible for others—in varying degrees. Bandura's depiction of humans as a determined species with partial freedom, partial agency, partial accountability, and partial responsibility is compatible with this model. Bandura's humans are what my colleagues Paul Moes and Don Tellinghuisen (2014) have termed "responsible limited agents."

Determinism/freedom/agency. TRD reconciles human agency with limitations on this agency in a way that accords with most people's lived experience. In contrast to the rhetorically consistent/inflammatory claims of

---

[10]In some African countries, sex with a virgin (sometimes a baby or child) is believed to cure HIV/ AIDS (Leclerc-Madlala, 2002).

Skinner, or the rhetorically inconsistent[11]/eschatological claims of the apostle Paul, Bandura offers a model of temporal agency that we can directly apply to improve the behavior of ourselves and others. His attention to environmental determinants helps us reckon the power of the situation. His attention to the self-system helps us reckon the power of the person and then actively facilitate the person's agency. This pragmatic approach is *functionally* compatible with Scripture's depiction of humans as limited by various forces and its directives to act with agency in spite of these limitations.

Accountability. In contrast to the other theorists, Bandura (2015) provided us an explicit statement on accountability, declaring "people can be held partly accountable for what they do" (p. 47). Toward this end, his last book is a "Woe to you" account that rivals the candor of Jesus. Like Jesus during his time on earth, Bandura seemed more interested in *calling out* social systems and *calling for* social change than in denigrating specific individuals.[12] (If Bandura had traveled with Jesus, I expect that *Moral Disengagement* would have included chapters on the scribes, the Pharisees, and the temple moneychangers.)

Bandura's declaration of partial accountability relies on humans' capacity to reflect on our behavior and make choices. It is in keeping with Scripture's instructions to engage in self-examination (Ps 4:4; Lam 3:40; 2 Cor 3:5; Gal 6:4; 1 Jn 3:18-22) and depiction of adults as knowing how to refuse evil and choose good (Deut 30:15; Josh 24:15; Is 7:15). Bandura's recommendation that those in authority supplement sanctions with techniques that help their charges *want* to avoid harming others is in keeping with the biblical model of moral maturity wherein standards rooted in love are superior to those based on fear of punishment.

Responsibility. Bandura's approach to responsibility was to facilitate self-efficacy. Scripture does not use Bandura's terminology, but some narratives seem to support his claim that the willingness and capacity to take

---

[11]Example, we are free in Christ; we are slaves of righteousness (see chap. 7, Critique D).

[12]Bandura calls out individuals with less vitriol. This is evident in his discourse on a US soldier who behaved immorally at the Abu-Ghraib prison in Iraq. As Bandura told Görlach (2013), "Under proper conditions almost anyone can behave in a cruel way. Look at the girl [who] . . . became the face of Abu-Ghraib. . . . I would say: Her nature was gentle. But within that context she was doing bad things."

responsibility for others is rooted in self-efficacy. For example, Joseph likely had high self-efficacy. His father treated him like a prince, and he imagined himself a monarch even as a youth. While this was off-putting to his family, Joseph's highly agentic food rationing saved Egypt from starvation (Gen 41). In contrast, Moses was born into slavery, sent down the river, and may have had a speech impediment. When God directed Moses to rescue the Israelites, every one of Moses' five protests suggests low self-efficacy (Ex 3–4). Moses did lead the people out of Egypt, but he was prone to overly dramatic manifestations of control, including murder (Ex 2:11-12), striking a rock he was instructed to speak to (Num 20:8-12), and hurling/breaking the first set of stone tablets (Ex 32:19).

Bandura's efforts to increase the self-efficacy of women were particularly laudatory. Self-efficacy *exceeding cultural norms* is the primary way that women get positively recognized in the Bible. A poignant example is the Gentile woman in Mark 7:24-30 who sought to have her daughter delivered of an evil spirit. Jesus' first response is troubling: "It is not fair to take the children's food and throw it to the dogs." But the woman persists, saying, "Sir, even the dogs under the table eat the children's crumbs." Jesus then rewards the woman's seeming self-efficacy by delivering her daughter of the demon. Another example is Mary the mother of Jesus. While Mary is often held up as an example of submission to God, she was also a force to be reckoned with. In John 2, she compels Jesus to begin his ministry *over* his declaration that "my hour has not yet come" (Jn 2:4). These examples, as well those of Rahab, Jael, Ruth, Hannah, Esther, the Proverbs 31 woman, the persistent widow (Lk 18), and Mary of Bethany bring us full circle to Bandura's (2001) assertion that "the capacity to exercise control over the nature and quality of one's life is the essence of humanness" (p. 1).

WHAT CHRISTIANS CAN LEARN FROM BANDURA

The differences between Bandura's perspective and a Christian perspective on personhood are primarily a function of omission. As a learning theorist who refrained from acknowledging (or denying) a Creator, Bandura left himself no source of universal purpose, transcendent moral standards, or inherent moral-ethical tendencies. If we bracket these omissions about origins (like Bandura himself did), Christians can learn a lot from Bandura.

One thing we can learn is how important it is to *expect* that we will be *effective* in doing good. Christians place a lot of emphasis on recognizing and desiring good; Bandura helps us understand the role of perceived agency in actually doing good. He attributes the perseverance of moral exemplars such as Gandhi, Mandela, King, and More to their strong purpose combined with high self-efficacy. He explicitly contrasts the *benefits* of viewing God as a supportive partner requiring action with the *risks* of passively waiting on God to solve one's problems. Imitating Bandura's facilitation of self-efficacy in women would be a particularly good goal for contemporary Christians, given our history of discouraging female agency.

Also important is Bandura's demonstration of how readily we reconstrue bad as good when it is in our self-interest to do so. Although awareness of the eight methods of moral disengagement is beneficial for anyone, it is particularly valuable for Christians. This is because Christians sometimes appeal too quickly to Matthew 5:11—to treat even appropriate challenges to our reasoning as validation that we are right. (*You disagree? Then I'm blessed to be reviled and persecuted for the sake of Christ.*) Instead, we should be like King David, appreciating how difficult it is to discern our hidden errors (Ps 19:12), or the prophet Jeremiah, acknowledging that all hearts deceive (Jer 17:9), or the psychologist Bandura, recognizing that all people reconstrue.

More generally, Bandura's focused but comprehensive model offers Christians another concrete framework within which to evaluate theological conundrums such as determinism versus free will and prevention versus punishment. As a learning theory focused on conscious cognition, triadic reciprocal determinism offers not only hope that we can improve but also specific techniques for doing so (e.g., role modeling, empathy elicitation). Of the five psychological theories in this book, TRD is arguably the most efficient model for promoting social change in accordance with a Christian view of the person.

CHAPTER NINE

Evolutionary Psychology

IN THIS CHAPTER I critique a *specific* evolutionary paradigm called evolutionary psychology (EP). Approximating the format used for the single theorists, this chapter has three sections.

In the first section, I provide a history of evolutionary thought. My goal here is to help readers understand EP and distinguish it from other evolutionary perspectives within biology and psychology (e.g., sociobiology, evolutionary developmental psychology [EDP]). Evolutionary perspectives share many basic principles but are also distinctive in ways that have important implications for the understanding of personhood.

In the second section, I discuss belief in evolution and belief in God. Because some people think that a Christian *cannot* believe in evolution, it is important to establish that even though EP has little use for God, some evolutionary theorists are publicly proclaimed people of faith. It should also be stated that people of faith hold a variety of views on both micro (within species) and macro (across species) evolution. This chapter focuses on the former. For readers interested in various Christian perspectives on both types of evolution as well as the age of the earth and monogenism (the belief that all humans descended from a single couple), I recommend the BioLogos website (biologos.org) and the book *Origins* by Deborah and Loren Haarsma (2011).[1]

In the third section, I present EP's perspectives on essence, purpose, moral-ethical tendencies, and agency/accountability (this book's four organizing themes).

---

[1]The Haarsmas also have an (almost verbatim) 2007 edition marketed to a Reformed audience.

A HISTORY OF EVOLUTIONARY THOUGHT

To understand the specific evolutionary paradigm being critiqued in this chapter, we must distinguish it from the evolutionary perspectives that preceded it and emerged in response to it. In my review of the paradigms that preceded EP, I lean heavily on the summary provided by Buss (2004).[2]

By the late 1700s/early 1800s, there was considerable talk about the transformation or evolution of life forms. Notable among the talkers was Jean-Baptiste Lamarck (1744–1829). Lamarck proposed that animals must struggle to survive, and that this struggle causes their nerves to secrete a fluid that enlarges the organs involved in the struggle (e.g., a giraffe struggling to reach the leaves at the top of the tree grows a longer neck). Lamarck's highly speculative theory gained little traction, but early geologists and biologists were very aware of different kinds of fossils in different geological layers, similarities in embryological development across species, and the fact that many facets of animal morphology seem particularly suited to the environment the animals inhabited (facets now called *adaptations*). By the mid-1800s there was a general sense of progression of life forms in the geological record, but science lacked a compelling theory to explain the pattern of evidence.

Darwin and natural selection. In 1858, Charles Darwin (1809–1882) and Alfred Russel Wallace (1823–1913) jointly proposed a theory of evolution which Darwin further articulated in his 1859 publication *On the Origin of Species by Means of Natural Selection, or the Preservation of Favoured Races in the Struggle for Life*. As the name suggests, Darwin's primary goal was to determine how new species emerge. Darwin was also interested in why species disappear and why organisms seem so well suited to their local environments. He addressed all of these questions with his theory of *natural selection*, which is based on three principles:

1. Genetic variation within a population affords the possibility of different traits (e.g., 50% of the birds on an island have a sharp beak; 50% a rounded beak).

---

[2]Content not specifically cited in the historical section of the chapter should be credited to Buss (2004). For additional historical context, see Larson (2004).

2. Organisms that possess traits that contribute to survival in general, or reproduction specifically, are more likely to live long enough to reproduce (e.g., in a dry season, when the only food available is hard nuts, birds with a sharp nut-cracking beak are more likely to survive and reproduce than birds with a rounded beak).

3. Over time, an increasing percentage of the population will be descended from organisms that possessed the traits that fostered survival and reproduction in their particular environment (e.g., after several dry seasons, all rounded beaks have died out; the island population that used to be 50% long-beaked is now 100% long-beaked).

Although many aspects of animal morphology made sense to Darwin, he also noticed aspects of animals' bodies that would seem to interfere with survival. A prime example is peacock plumage, which is unwieldy and attracts the attention of predators.[3] To explain anomalies like peacock plumage, Darwin proposed a second theory: the theory of *sexual selection*. In this theory, adaptations arise not because they contribute to survival but because they contribute to mating. In short, peahens prefer peacocks with beautiful plumage. Although natural and sexual selection are now encompassed under the same general construct (*differential reproductive success* attributable to heritable differences in design), Darwin's distinction highlights the fact that adaptations come in two types: those that contribute directly to survival and those that increase one's chances of mating.

Darwin's book met resistance from both the scientific community and the general populace. One scientific concern was that Darwin lacked a coherent theory of inheritance. Additionally, it was difficult to imagine how the early stages of an adaptation (e.g., a partial eye) could provide any advantage to an organism.

More controversial, were Darwin's claims that natural selection was sufficient to account for new species and that all species were linked in a

---

[3]Rumor has it that Darwin was so troubled by peacock plumage that he once said, "The sight of a feather in a peacock's tail, whenever I gaze at it makes me sick!" (Cronon, 1991, p. 113, as quoted by Buss, 2004, p. 7).

grand tree of descent. Many people objected because they viewed species as immutable (i.e., unchanging, created suddenly in their present form). Moreover, they interpreted the claim that humanity had emerged slowly (see Darwin's *Descent of Man*, 1871) to mean that humanity was unplanned. Darwin's views challenged beliefs that an all-knowing deity was governing nature and that humanity occupied a special place above the rest of creation (Larson, 2004).

Mendel, genetics, and the modern synthesis. Darwin was unable to provide a coherent view of inheritance because he viewed all aspects of inheritance as a *blending* of the contributions of two parents (sort of like mixing white and red paint to make pink). Although an Augustinian Friar Gregor Mendel (1822–1884) was contemporaneously demonstrating that inheritance was not blended but "particulate" in pea plants, his discoveries were not well known. It was not until the 1930s and 1940s that the work of Darwin and the work of Mendel were united in what biologists now call the "modern synthesis." This joining of Darwinian natural selection with Mendelian genetics placed Darwinian evolutionary theory on a firmer scientific footing.

Ethology. Meanwhile, the discipline of psychology was moving *away* from biological explanations for behavior. Although psychologists who published in the late 1800s (Sigmund Freud, William James) were significantly influenced by Darwin and placed a great deal of emphasis on instincts, the 1930s and 1940s were the heyday of behaviorism (see chap. 7). Even though Darwin envisioned his theory of natural selection as applicable to both behavior and cognition, there was little move toward either, until the ethology movement of the 1950s. Like behaviorists, ethologists focused primarily on observable behavior without getting "into the heads" of animals, but Buss (2004) has noted the "glimmerings" of EP "in the early writings of Lorenz" (p. 13; on Lorenz, see chap. 6 in this book).

Inclusive fitness and sociobiology. Back in the discipline of biology, a graduate student named William Hamilton was busy expanding Darwin's theory of natural selection to include the favoring of characteristics that caused an organism's genes to be passed on not only through direct offspring but also through the offspring of kin. Hamilton's approach involved a sort of personification of the gene as an entity that wanted to be represented in the next generation. (Because approximately 50% of my sister's genes are copies of my own, helping her survive and reproduce is another way of ensuring that copies of some of my genes are represented in the next generation.) In a 1964 paper, Hamilton termed this broader view of natural selection *inclusive fitness theory.*

In addition to revolutionizing evolutionary biology, inclusive fitness theory set the stage for EP's application of the theory of natural selection to *cognition.* While selection for type of beak required no higher-level cognition on the part of Darwin's birds, providing aid to others requires the helper to make decisions about who to help, how much to help, and so on. Hamilton's influence was expanded in 1966 by George Williams, who (in easier-to-read prose) applied inclusive fitness theory to the theoretical problem of altruism. Evolutionary biologists had long wondered how altruism could have evolved when helping others would seem to incur costs to self. Williams and Hamilton argued that the likelihood of helping was, in part, a function of genetic relatedness. Subsequent work has revealed that humans are most likely to help offspring and full siblings who share 50% of our genes; then grandchildren, nieces, nephews, and half-siblings who share 25% of our genes; then first cousins who share 12.5%, and so on (Bernstein et al., 1994). The work of both Hamilton and Williams was then nuanced and applied to other social behaviors by Robert Trivers (1971, 1972, 1974).

This emphasis on social behaviors set the stage for a paradigm called *sociobiology*—formally introduced in an extensive book by E. O. Wilson in 1975. Although Buss (2004) does not view Wilson's book as containing any "fundamentally new theoretical contributions to evolutionary theory," it caused "a scientific and public uproar that rivaled the outrage caused by Charles Darwin in 1959," and gave an emerging field a name (p. 18). The book did *not*, however, encompass enough psychology to represent everyone who had begun applying Darwinian principles to humans. Wilson's book included only one chapter on humans and afforded limited attention to the mind. With biologists and sociobiologists providing a mechanism to understand selection, and anthropologists and sociologists providing rich descriptions of culture, some group still needed to focus on "the missing middle: the psychological mechanisms that come between theories of the selection pressures on the one hand and the fully realized sociocultural behavior on the other" (Cosmides et al., 1992, p. 6). Enter evolutionary psychology.

Evolutionary psychology. In the 1980s, a group of six scholars[4] began to use the term *evolutionary psychology.* Most of the credit for the theoretical chapters and edited handbooks that put EP on the map[5] goes to three of these scholars: John Tooby, Leda Cosmides, and David Buss. With respect to their name and distinctive niche, Tooby and Cosmides (2005) said,

> We sometimes read that evolutionary psychology is simply sociobiology, with the name changed to avoid the bad political press that sociobiology has received. Although it is amusing (given the record) to be accused of ducking controversy, these claims are historically and substantively wrong. . . . Evolutionary psychologists are generally admirers and defenders of sociobiology . . . [but the] new field focused on psychology— on characterizing the adaptations comprising the psychological architecture—whereas sociobiology had not. Sociobiology had focused mostly on selectionist theories, with no consideration of the computational level and little interest in mapping psychological mechanisms. Both the subject matter of evolutionary psychology and the theoretical commitments were simply different from that of sociobiology. (p. 15)

Put another way, EP takes a functional approach to the understanding of personhood. This means that limited biological knowledge is required on the part of researchers or readers, and the basic premises of EP can be succinctly stated. In brief, EP holds the following:

---

[4]"In the 1980s, Martin Daly, Margo Wilson, Don Symons, John Tooby, Leda Cosmides, and David Buss had many discussions about what to call this new field" (Tooby & Cosmides, 2005, p. 15). Alternatively, Cosmides and Tooby (2004) credited these six plus Steven Pinker and Gerd Gigerenzer (p. 93). Pinker (1997) credited only two, speaking of the "new approach christened 'evolutionary psychology' by the anthropologist John Tooby and the psychologist Leda Cosmides" (p. 23).

[5]Tooby and Cosmides put EP on a literal map in 1994, founding the Center for Evolutionary Psychology at the University of California Santa Barbara.

1. Humans and our immediate ancestors have been around for millions of years.

2. We spent most of this time as hunter-gatherers and faced many survival-related problems.

3. The reason we did not go extinct is that we developed adaptations. *Psychological* adaptations are cognitive or behavioral tendencies that

   a. have been reified[6] as "structures" of the mind;
   b. evolved during our extended time as hunter-gatherers;
   c. function to address a specific and recurring problem faced by hunter-gatherers; and
   d. are programmed to develop reliably across members of the species (or if sex-specific, across males or females).

4. Humans have a lot of these adaptations and together they constitute our *universal human nature* (i.e., the hardwired characteristics all humans share as opposed to individual differences).

According to Tooby and Cosmides (2005), "The long-term scientific goal toward which evolutionary psychologists are working is the mapping of our universal human nature" (p. 5). This work can be divided into three phases. First, evolutionary psychologists will identify the tendencies that humans share and decide whether these tendencies would have contributed to survival millions of years ago. If yes, they will classify these tendencies as adaptations. Second, they will specify the neural bases of these adaptations to create "circuit logic" or a map of adaptations. Third, they will use this map to predict and explain everything contemporary humans do. Edward Hagen (2005) wrote, "Fully realized, EP would constitute a functional understanding of the neural circuits underlying our every thought, emotion and action" (p. 171).

Although EP is (to the best of my reading) still operating in stage one, those associated with EP assert that it has revolutionized psychology. Per Buss (2005):

---

[6]By *reified* I mean that EP speaks of mind structures in the same way that Noam Chomsky spoke of a Language Acquisition "Device." Language is an emergent capacity involving many areas of the brain, but it is helpful to think of there being a "device" in our mind unconsciously directing us to pay attention to stress patterns, grammar rules, and so on.

Hundreds of psychological and behavioral phenomena have been documented empirically, findings that would never have been discovered without the guiding framework of evolutionary psychology. Evolutionary psychology has proved its worth many times over in its theoretical and empirical harvest. If a viable alternative to evolutionary psychology exists for understanding the origins and nature of the human mind, it has not been revealed to the scientific community. . . . Evolutionary psychology represents a true scientific revolution, a profound paradigm shift in the field of psychology. (pp. xxiii-xxiv)

However, critics of EP (e.g., Joubert, 2012; Taylor, 2014) are equally emphatic that EP has failed as a science. Richardson (2007) characterized EP as a maladapted psychology because it presumes to explain the structure of the mind by appealing to "evidence" that evolutionary biologists would deem insufficient to explain the structure of an orchid. Buller (2005) criticized EP's ad hoc explanations. (By this he means that the "science" of EP consists of documenting a human tendency and then thinking backward to figure out how this tendency would have been adaptive in the prehistoric world. While this makes for interesting theory, it is *not* an application of the scientific method, which requires the testing of a *forward* hypothesis, ideally in an experiment.) For its "reliance on 'reverse engineering' the mind," Buller dubbed EP "the emperor's new paradigm,"[7] meaning that EP pretends to have a paradigm, while others see nothing there (p. 282).

Evolutionary developmental psychology. EP is a very specific paradigm, even within the discipline of psychology. About 20 years after the emergence of EP, David Bjorklund and Anthony Pellegrini introduced a perspective they refer to as *evolutionary developmental psychology* (EDP). In their flagship publications (2000, 2002) they argued that EP has largely ignored the fact that selection pressures differ as a function of development (i.e., the characteristics that contribute to survival in a child are different from the ones that contribute to survival in an adult). In response, they

---

[7]Buller alludes to the popular children's story "The Emperor's New Clothes," in which an emperor is so unwilling to admit that he cannot see the fine "clothes" putatively being constructed by some rogue tailors that he processes through the streets naked.

encouraged developmentalists to consider how foundational principles of child development can be enhanced by reflecting on these principles from an evolutionary vantage. Principles put forth as particularly amenable to this type of study include epigenesis, the role of nature in the development of language, sex differences, and the importance of play.

Bjorklund and Pellegrini also argued that some of the foundational principles of EP are simply wrong. For example, EP asserts that humans are no longer evolving. Rather, we are static products of genetic pre-programming that was selected for prehistorically and may not even be adaptive in the contemporary world. In contrast, EDP views a child's brain as much more malleable and responsive to environmental input. Accordingly, EDP is much less deterministic than EP.

To my reckoning, EDP is not so much a distinctive paradigm as just mainstream developmental psychology.[8] The discipline of developmental psychology is a study of how humans change over time. Most developmentalists focus on changes occurring within individuals but present these changes as directed, in part, by universal genetic pre-programming (e.g., critical periods, boundaries that nature sets on the influence of the environment). Developmentalists who believe that this preprogramming is present because it is adaptive for our species and was naturally selected for over time operate under the general rubric of EDP—even if they do not know or use this specific label or make specific references to evolutionary processes in their lectures or scholarship. Because EDP is not especially controversial, it has not been afforded its own critique in this book.

BELIEF IN EVOLUTION AND BELIEF IN GOD

In my introductions of Erikson, Bowlby, Skinner, and Bandura, I tried to include information about the theorist's faith commitment, or lack thereof. This is more difficult with EP because so many representatives speak for the perspective and its intellectual precursors. Some of these representatives explicitly deny a Creator; others leave room for God.

---

[8]This may be a testimony to EDP's pervasive influence, or it may mean that EDP is just not that distinctive.

Darwin struggled with belief in God. Initially, he believed that creation evidenced a Creator, but he had difficulty reconciling faith with suffering.[9] He eventually decided it was easier to view parasites—which seem to have no function but to destroy other creatures—as an accident of nature rather than divine design. At different times Darwin identified as a theist[10] and an agnostic, but expressly not an atheist.[11]

Contemporary treatments of evolution and God often reference an essay by the late paleontologist Stephen Jay Gould. In this essay, Gould chastised those who claim that evolution can be used to argue either against or for God. Crediting a schoolteacher who taught him what inferences could and could not be drawn from scientific evidence, Gould (1992) insisted that

> science simply cannot (by its legitimate methods) adjudicate the issue of God's possible superintendence of nature. We neither affirm nor deny it; we simply can't comment on it as scientists. If some of our crowd have made untoward statements claiming that Darwinism disproves God, then I will find Mrs. McInerney and have their knuckles rapped for it (as long as she can equally treat those members of our crowd who have argued that Darwinism must be God's method of action).

Because respected evolutionary theorists included both atheists and people of faith, Gould continued by stating, "Either half my colleagues are enormously stupid, or else the science of Darwinism is fully compatible with conventional religious beliefs—and equally compatible with atheism."

---

[9]"But I may say that the impossibility of conceiving that this grand and wondrous universe, with our conscious selves, arose through chance, seems to me the chief argument for the existence of God: but whether this is an argument of real value, I have never been able to decide. I am aware that if we admit a first cause, the mind still craves to know whence it came, and how it arose. Nor can I overlook the difficulty from the immense amount of suffering through the world" (Darwin, 1887, p. 276).

[10]"When thus reflecting, I feel compelled to look to a First Cause having an intelligent mind in some degree analogous to that of a man; and I deserve to be called a Theist. This conclusion was strong in my mind about the time, as far as I can remember, when I wrote the *Origin of Species*, and it is since that time that it has very gradually, with much fluctuations, become weaker" (Darwin, 1887, p. 282).

[11]"I may state that my judgment often fluctuates. . . . In my most extreme fluctuations, I have never been an Atheist in the sense of denying the existence of a God. I think that generally (and more and more as I grow older), but not always, that an Agnostic would be the more correct description of my state of mind" (Darwin, 1887, p. 274).

Lending support to the half who believe that evolution is compatible with religious belief are many famous Christian scholars and leaders, including B. B. Warfield, Karl Barth, C. S. Lewis, Billy Graham, John Stott, Pope Benedict XVI, Pope Francis, N. T. Wright, Philip Yancey, John Ortberg, Tim Keller, and John Walton. (Sample quotes from the first six are provided by Kramer [2018].) Of particular note is Francis Collins, current director of the National Institutes of Health and founder of the BioLogos Foundation. There are also the 25 Christians who contributed chapters to a book titled *How I Changed My Mind About Evolution: Evangelicals Reflect on Faith and Science* (Applegate & Stump, 2016). One of the chapters in the book is written by psychologist Justin Barrett, who does not identify with EP but describes himself as "sympathetic to bringing evolutionary perspectives into cognitive and developmental psych" (personal communication, August 6, 2018; see also Barrett with King,[12] 2021, p. 1).

Speaking for atheists is ethologist Richard Dawkins, an elegant writer of popular science and an overt attacker of faith. In contrast to most academic scientists, Dawkins has gone out of his way to appropriate religious concepts to ridicule people of faith (1996)[13] and to insist that organisms that look like they were crafted by an "architect" were not (2006).[14] Not all atheists are happy to have Dawkins speak for them. As Michael Ruse (2003) wrote in a review of Dawkins's 2003 book, Dawkins's "attention has swung from writing about science for a popular audience to waging an all-out attack on Christianity" (p. 555). This open hostility has caused the "religiously unaffiliated" (e.g., Stove, 1995) and even some "public atheists" (e.g., Sparrow, 2015) to protest that Dawkins is actually a *mis*representative of scholars who espouse evolution and atheism. (I agree with these

---

[12]Barrett with King (2021) demonstrate how a broad *evolutionary perspective* (not the specific paradigm dubbed EP that I am focusing on) can help humans thrive. As such, their book is a nice complement to the present chapter.

[13]The title of Dawkins's 1996 book, *The Blind Watchmaker*, is a play on clergyman William Paley's (1837) argument that a person cannot find a watch without knowing it was made by a watchmaker. Dawkins says, "Natural selection . . . has no purpose in mind. It has no mind and no mind's eye. It does not plan for the future. It has no vision, no foresight, no sight at all. If it can be said to play the role of watchmaker in nature, it is the *blind* watchmaker" (p. 5). Similarly, a chapter on common ancestry is titled "The One True Tree of Life," which is presumably an allusion to Gen 2.

[14]When likening the 46 chromosomes in every human cell to 46 volumes of an architect's plan in every room of a building, Dawkins (2006) says, "Incidentally, there is of course no 'architect'" (p. 23).

critiques, but I introduce him here because his work figures into my critique of the EP perspectives on purpose and moral-ethical tendencies.)

Many within EP seem to have high regard for Dawkins and vice versa.[15] Like Dawkins, some have explicitly disavowed a Creator, taking unnecessary jabs at people of faith. Tooby and Cosmides (2006) said that natural selection "causes functional organization to emerge *naturally*, that is, without the intervention of an intelligent 'designer' or supernatural forces" (p. 178). Daly and Wilson derided both those who believe that humans bear the image of divinity (2002, p. 72) and "religiously-motivated creation myths" (1988, p. 297). Jesse Bering (2013) described himself as "godless" in an interview with Big Think.[16] Elsewhere he asserted that "the theory of natural selection should have vanquished God (or at least a God concerned with human affairs)" (2010, p. 91).

In contrast, Buss has left (a little) room for God by giving lip service to the religion/science divide espoused by Gould. In his textbook on EP, Buss explained that the major premise of creationism (a supreme being created everything) does not generate testable hypotheses. "Creationism," wrote Buss (2004), "is a matter of religion and belief, not a matter of science. It cannot be proved false, but it has not proven useful as a predictive or explanatory theory" (p. 38).

Buss (2004) then declared the theory of evolution by natural selection to be "the only known scientific theory that has the power to account for the origins and structure of complex adaptive mechanisms . . . that comprise human nature" (p. 38). This declaration is unfortunate because it implies greater scientific rigor than EP can rightfully claim. While Buss is correct that there is no way to test whether there is a God *directing* the processes that shaped human nature, the general approach by which *both* evolutionary psychologists and creationists seek evidence of these processes—and hold firmly to them, regardless of the data obtained—is more similar than not. By this I mean that both groups

- begin with a theoretical human in a theoretical environment;
- consider a problem faced in that environment;

---

[15]Buss dedicated his 2004 textbook to 15 scholars, one of whom is Dawkins. Dawkins provided the afterword to Buss's 2005 handbook.

[16]Bering (2013) also self-identified as an evolutionary psychologist.

- explain how humans responded to this problem; and

- look for descriptive evidence of this response in modern humans.

Although the two groups do treat potentially disconfirming data a bit differently (with EP more closely approximating the scientific method),[17] both groups ultimately hold fast to their core convictions about the processes that shaped human nature.

To his credit, Buss did refrain from what the Haarsmas (2011, p. 180) have termed evolution*ism* (defined as "attempts to use the theory of evolution to support atheistic claims that there is no Creator and purpose in human existence"). However, no theory based on untestable claims about prehistoric humans should be presented as a fully scientific account of human nature. Buss knows this, and later clarified that EP research proceeds from the assumption that evolutionary theory is correct, "but the research does not test that assumption directly" (Buss, 2004, p. 42). Epistemological modesty is also evidenced by Hagen (2005), who, in Buss's *Handbook of Evolutionary Psychology*, warned against the grounding of politics in scientifically untestable assumptions about human nature. Hagen stressed that "there are few solid facts and no proven theories about our behavior, thoughts and feelings" (p. 166).

THE FOUR THEMES

To write this section, I began with sources introducing the foundational principles of EP, particularly sources connected to John Tooby, Leda Cosmides, and David Buss. I incorporated works by additional evolutionary psychologists or EP promoters[18] when I came across titles that suggested

---

[17]Those associated with EP do modify depictions of human nature on the basis of descriptive data obtained with contemporary humans. In fact, they are sometimes criticized for too *readily* changing their depictions. This tendency has been discussed and defended by Mayr (1983), who wrote that "Gould and Lewontin ridicule the research strategy: 'If one adaptive argument fails, try another one.' Yet the strategy to try another hypothesis when the first one fails is a traditional methodology in all branches of science" (p. 326). In contrast, creationists typically refuse to modify their core convictions about human nature, which makes some (but not all) eschew scientific evidence.

[18]By "EP promoter" I mean someone who has an explicit publication-association with EP. For example, experimental cognitive psychologist Steven Pinker wrote the foreword to Buss's 2005 handbook of EP. Therein, Pinker discussed his frustration that psychology lacked explanation and said, "When I discovered evolutionary psychology in the 1980s through

specific address of the four themes.[19] This resulted in a summary of EP's core ideas and a nonsystematic sampling of various applications in keeping with the EP perspective, articulated as eight tenets.

A1. The central characteristic of personhood is a collection of mental "mechanisms" for solving adaptive problems in the ancestral world; these mechanisms constitute our universal human nature (essence).

A2. Really, there are two universal human natures—male and female (essence).

B1. Humans have been designed by natural selection, without existential purpose (purpose).

B2. Humans' primary social motivations are status and group membership (purpose).

C. Tendencies toward both good and bad were adaptive to the earliest humans; these tendencies are now part of the universal human nature (moral-ethical tendencies).

D1. A genetically determined mind is not synonymous with genetically determined behavior, but neither do we have free will (agency/accountability).

D2. A *sense* of accountability and responsibility are part of the universal human nature (agency/accountability).

D3. EP's contribution to a moral-ethical society is to help us understand the nature we cannot readily overcome (agency/accountability).

ESSENCE

Tenet A: The central characteristic of personhood is a collection of mental "mechanisms" for solving adaptive problems in the ancestral world; these mechanisms constitute our universal human nature. Two concepts foundational to EP are adaptations and adaptive problems. Defined precisely, an *adaptation* is a reliably developing characteristic of an organism that solves an adaptive problem (Tooby & Cosmides, 1992). An

---

the work of Donald Symons, Leda Cosmides, and John Tooby, I realized my wait was over. Evolutionary psychology was the organizing framework—the source of 'explanatory adequacy' or a 'theory of the computation'—that the science of psychology was missing" (pp. xiii-xiv).

[19]An obvious problem with this approach is that the authors who address these themes (and provide the most colorful quotes) may not always speak from, or for, the *core* of EP.

adaptive problem is any enduring impediment to survival or reproduction (Larsen & Buss, 2014).

Adaptations. Defined more comprehensively, a human adaptation is a
helpful characteristic that is genetically programmed into the development of all normal humans. Because genetic abnormalities occur, and
because extreme environments can stunt development, no scientifically
verifiable characteristic is 100% universal in a species, but all genetically
normal humans begin life programmed to develop two eyes, emotions,
language, and so on. EP refers to such characteristics as "universal" despite the rare exceptions.

The kinds of adaptations emphasized by EP are those constituted by
specific patterns of neural circuitry. In addition to having roots in evolutionary biology and ethology, EP arose out of the computational sciences, which provided evidence that logical operations could be carried
out by a machine "without the need for an animate interpretative intelligence to carry out the steps" (Tooby & Cosmides, 2005, p. 9). Likening
the circuitry of the brain to the hardware of a computer, EP views
the mind as "a set of information processing procedures (cognitive
programs) that are embodied in the neural circuitry of the brain" (Cosmides & Tooby, 1997, p. 71). These organic computer programs are variously called modules, structures, or "mental organs" (Tooby & Cosmides,
1990, p. 27).

It is unclear how many modules humans have. In its endeavor to unseat
the "standard" model of the mind as a largely undifferentiated, general-
purpose machine with just a few specialized modules (e.g., Chomsky's Language Acquisition Device), EP extends the logic of Chomsky to much of the
mind, ascribing to humans a lot of modules—"perhaps hundreds"—each an
"expert in one area of interaction with the world" (Pinker, 1997, p. 21). These
modules are integrated functionally and hierarchically, meaning that there
is a primary task with levels of subtasks. For example, a module that detects
moving shadows could be a component of an attention module, which is in
turn a component of an "avoid predators" module.

Modules are also species-specific, complex, and characterized by fairly
uniform architecture. This uniformity is easy to see in the architecture of

physical structures like the eye. EP asserts that the same principle applies to the architecture of the mind. All members of a species share genes that consistently code for certain neural patterns in the same way. In organisms with a mind, consistent coding yields not only structural but also psychological "universals." In EP, it is "these psychological universals that constitute human nature" (Tooby & Cosmides, 1990, p. 19).

Adaptive problems and our Stone Age minds. A more comprehensive definition of an adaptive problem emphasizes the word *enduring*. Within EP, the term *adaptive problem* refers only to impediments to survival and reproduction faced by a species in an *environment of evolutionary adaptedness* (EEA), a term coined by Bowlby. When I introduced it in chapter six, I defined it concisely as the environment experienced by most members of the species. For this chapter a more complex definition is needed.

In EP, the term EEA can refer to a specific set of conditions defined by place and epoch that were stable enough to permit an adaptation to arise. Different adaptations have different EEAs (e.g., the EEA that gave rise to the structure of the eye likely preceded the EEA that gave rise to male participation in caregiving). The term EEA can also apply to a composite of selection pressures *across* place and time referred to more generally as *the ancestral world* (Cosmides & Tooby, 1997). Although EP tends to place particular emphasis on the epoch known as the Pleistocene (approximately 2.6 million years ago until 11,700 years ago), the main point is that the human EEA is characterized by a different set of problems than those faced by most of us in the modern world. Applied to a composite of selection processes, the term EEA is more of a reference to prehistory in general than to a particular environment. The human EEA included dangers like malnutrition, predators, and social hierarchies in which males of low standing were denied access to a mate. It did not include nuclear radiation and modern assault weapons. Although the latter are certainly impediments to survival, they are too recent for humans to have "solved" with an adaptation.

The claim that humans have evolved adaptations *only* to problems experienced in the ancestral world has at least three important implications for the EP view of the person:

1. Humans are not currently evolving (Tooby & Cosimides, 1990).[20] Per Steven Pinker (1997): "The modern human condition is not conducive to real evolution. . . . We infest the whole habitable and not-so-habitable earth, migrate at will, and zig-zag from lifestyle to lifestyle. This makes us a nebulous, moving target for natural selection" (p. 205).[21]

2. Adaptations are often incongruent with conscious strivings. Concerning the "Darwinian imperative to survive and reproduce," Pinker (1997) concluded that "as far as day-to-day behavior is concerned, there is no such imperative. People watch pornography when they could be seeking a mate, forgo food to buy heroin, sell their blood to buy movie tickets, . . . postpone childbearing to climb the corporate ladder" (p. 207).

3. Some adaptations are now *maladaptive*. The most obvious mismatches concern taste preferences. Cravings for sugar, fat, and salt are currently doing more to curtail survival than to facilitate it in many industrialized countries.

In sum, humans now live in the modern world, but "our modern skulls house a Stone Age mind" (Cosmides & Tooby, 1997, p. 85).[22]

Individual differences and byproducts. While the goal of EP is to map the universal human nature (i.e., all our adaptations), evolutionary psychologists recognize that they must also explain the components of personhood that do not meet the criteria for an adaptation. (Recall: an adaptation must develop reliably in all humans *and* solve an adaptive problem.)

---

[20]With this assertion, proponents of EP distinguish themselves from Darwinian social scientists who believe that adaptation happens daily, and from functionalists who view adaptation as analogous to learning (Pinker, 1997, p. 206). They also distinguish EP from EDP. Representing EDP, Bjorklund and Pellegrini (2002) argued, "There is no question in our minds, for instance, that cultural changes over the past 10,000 years have drastically affected the way humans behave and develop" (p. 8). This assertion is also discordant with the theistic perspective on evolution proposed by Haight (2002), who encouraged Christians to view ourselves as participants in the divine creativity that extends over measureless eons of time (p. 46).

[21]Whether Pinker still holds the official EP stance is uncertain. In a later book, Pinker (2011) wrote, "Nothing rules out the possibility that human populations have undergone some degree of biological evolution in recent millennia or even centuries, long after races, ethnic groups, and nations diverged" (pp. 613-14).

[22]In their acknowledgments, Cosmides and Tooby credit William Allman for contributing this colorful quote.

Components of personhood that *do not* develop reliably in all humans are termed *individual differences*. Within EP, individual differences are most commonly attributed to the environment. While nature supplies all humans with a universal architecture, nurture has some say in the furnishings.[23] Variations are most often conceptualized as degrees of adaptations (e.g., high jealousy, low jealousy) or differences in activation threshold (e.g., easily triggered or not). Environments are depicted as current or early sensitizing (Tooby & Cosmides, 1990).

Components of personhood that *do* develop reliably, but do not seem to have evolved in response to a specific adaptive problem, are conceived of as *byproducts* of adaptations. Byproducts may or may not manifest evidence of design and are "carried along with characteristics that do have functional design because they happen to be coupled with those adaptations" (Buss et al., 1998, p. 537). For example, the utility of the nose in holding up one's spectacles is an incidental byproduct of the nose, which is an adaptation for smelling (Larson & Buss, 2014, p. 530). Byproducts are easy to conceptualize if we confine our examples to anatomy (as EP textbooks often to do). There is less agreement on what qualifies as a psychological byproduct. Buss requires a very close coupling between an adaptation and its byproducts.[24] Cosmides and Tooby were (at least in

---

[23]Exposure to environmental differences is the most common explanation for individual differences, but not the only one. EP also attributes individual differences to mutations that have not yet been eliminated from the gene pool. When mutations are not eliminated, it is assumed that the phenotypic properties for which they code have either a neutral or a conditionally positive impact on inclusive fitness. By *conditionally positive* I mean that the traits are positive in *some* conditions. Three conditions cited by Larsen and Buss (2014) include individual differences that are maintained by (a) contingencies among traits (e.g., aggression is more likely to be selected for in large rather than small men); (b) frequency-dependent selection (e.g. cheaters may have an easier time surviving and reproducing if they are the minority in a population that is mostly trustworthy and trusting); and (c) variations in the optimum level of a trait over time and space (e.g., ADHD may help one notice an approaching predator and hinder one from meeting an approaching deadline).

[24]"Byproduct has been used by different people to mean somewhat different things. The bottom line is that a hypothesis that something is a byproduct requires specifying in detail the adaptations of which it is a byproduct" (David Buss, personal communication, December 15, 2015). A candidate that meets this stringent criterion is humans' proclivity to gossip about celebrities. Barkow (1992, p. 628) believes we have been selected to be keenly interested in the activities of those with whom we are in relationship, whose behavior would be likely to impact our inclusive fitness (e.g., the sexual activities of a potential mate, rival, or relative). Gossip about media stars could not possibly be an adaptation because there was no mass media in the Pleistocene, but

1997) less concerned about close coupling and declared that the human capacity to solve *new* problems is a byproduct of circuits designed to solve the problems of the ancestral world, *without* linking this capacity to any specific adaptions (p. 79).[25] This looser coupling affords a theoretical mechanism for continued human survival in a changing world.

Again, some implications are spelled out by Pinker (1997). In a chapter titled "The Meaning of Life," Pinker explained that "man does not live by bread alone." Rather, we have a combinatorial mind that permits us to engage in a lot of biologically frivolous activities like art, literature, music, wit, religion, and philosophy. "They are the mind's best work, what makes life worth living" (p. 521). But all these activities are byproducts of adaptations.[26] They are unique to humans but do not define us. Per Tooby and Cosmides (2005), the EP human is defined as "collections of mechanisms designed to solve the adaptive problems posed by the ancestral world" (p. 11).

Tenet A2: Really, there are two universal human natures—male and female. In EP, "an organism can be described as a self-reproducing machine" (Tooby & Cosmides, 2006, p. 178). In organisms that live a long time, reproduction works best when it provides as much genetic diversity as possible without disrupting the universal architecture. One source of diversity is alleles (or "rival" genes) that code for functionally inconsequential traits like eye color (the "victor" of the blue versus brown rivalry has no impact on the eye's function). A second source of diversity is morphs. Morphs are variations on a universal design that differ from each other in functionally coordinated ways and, together, promote the survival of the species. For example, in the insect world, variations on a universal design often divide insects into

---

mass media likely mimics the psychophysical cues that would have triggered information-gathering modules under Pleistocene conditions.

[25] In contrast, Joyce (2006) views learning as an adaptation, not a byproduct. Joyce writes, "Though evolutionary psychology allows that a great deal of observable human behavior may be evolutionarily 'accidental' (in the sense that it is the result of innate mechanisms thrown into a novel environment), it also allows that humans are 'supposed' to be behaviorally malleable in many respects—that the very plasticity of many psychological mechanisms is an adaptation" (p. 6).

[26] Art may be a byproduct of modules related to status seeking. Music may be related to pitch development associated with language. "Religion and philosophy are in part the application of mental tools to problems they were not designed to solve" (Pinker, 1997, p. 525).

"castes" (soldiers, workers, and queens). Similarly, males and females constitute morphs, such that "an individual has the necessary psychological traits either of a female or a male, but not a mixture of the two (except in pathological individuals)" (Tooby & Cosmides, 1990, p. 41).

In humans, male and female are the only definitively accepted morphs, and EP devotes a great deal of attention to documenting their differences. EP does this to demonstrate that contemporary sex differences reflect different adaptive problems experienced by males and females in the ancestral world, lending credence to the construct of adaptations in general. In contemporary hunter-gatherer societies, males do the majority of the hunting and females do the majority of the gathering. If we assume the same division of labor during the Pleistocene, males would have benefited from a keen sense of cardinal direction (*we need to travel southeast to return this meat to our clan*), and females would have benefited from coding landmarks (*there are berries on the bush near the rock resembling a mastodon*). If these differences in navigation contributed to fitness and were selected for, we should see differences in the navigational strategies of contemporary males and females. And we do. When contemporary males and females are walked on a roundabout path through an unfamiliar wooded area, males have an easier time than females returning to the starting point using "the most direct route possible" (Buss, 2004, p. 86). In contrast, when shown a visual array of 27 randomly scattered objects (fork, cat, lamp, umbrella, etc.), females are better able to recall the object next to the lamp.[27]

But cognitive differences tend to be small compared to differences in the mating/reproductive domain. According to Trivers (1985, p. 301), the primary reason for sex differences is the amount of effort each sex must invest in producing surviving offspring. Across species, the sex that invests more (usually the female, but not always)[28] is choosier about a mate, and the sex that invests less is more competitive with same-sex counterparts for

---

[27]Silverman's work on gender-specific navigational skills has been reviewed by Buss (2004, pp. 86-87).

[28]Species in which males must invest more include the poisonous arrow frog, the pipefish seahorse, and the Mormon cricket.

access to the choosier sex. In humans, both sexes invest instrumentally and economically in their offspring, but it was only Pleistocene females who invested physiologically in pregnancy, childbirth, and lactation. Thus, EP asserts that females have more adaptations related to the acquisition and retention of resources necessary to care for offspring. Support for this hypothesis is drawn from empirical studies indicating that females are much more likely than males to turn down sexual propositions from strangers (Clark & Hatfield, 1989). Females are also *somewhat* more attuned than males to their partner's socioeconomic status and earning power (Buss & Barnes, 1986; Townsend & Levy, 1990) and report that they would be less troubled by a partner's sexual infidelity than emotional infidelity.[29]

Alternatively, males have more adaptations related to the securing of procreative opportunities. While virtually any fertile female can find a male to impregnate her, a male's chances of securing a consenting sexual partner are closely linked to social dominance. Because females are sexually attracted to males who exhibit dominant behavior (even when they don't actually like them; Sadalla et al., 1987), males often engage in displays of resources and physical prowess like fighting other males, athletic competitions, and accentuating their size.[30] Males (especially low-dominance males) also need to make the most of every opportunity by targeting fertile females. Thus, males are attracted to signs of female fertility signaled by clear eyes and skin, healthy hair, high energy, and a waist-to-hip ratio (WHR) of 0.70.[31] One of the best predictors of fertility is a female's age.

---

[29] Buss and colleagues (1992) found that only 17% of female college students would view a partner's sexual infidelity as more distressing than his emotional infidelity, whereas 60% of male college students reported this. However, a study by Harris (2002) with men and women who actually experienced infidelity suggests less dissimilar responses.

[30] Pinker (1997) has noted that "the word for 'leader' in most foraging societies is 'big man,'" and that "men everywhere exaggerate the size of their head (with hats, helmets, headdresses and crowns), their shoulders (with pads, boards, epaulettes, and feathers), and, in some societies, their penises (with impressive codpieces and sheaths, sometimes a yard long)" (pp. 495-96).

[31] The ratio is calculated as waist measurement divided by hip measurement. A healthy adult female WHR ranges from 0.67 to 0.80. Women with higher WHRs have more difficulty conceiving and have higher rates of various ailments, including diabetes, heart diseases, and stroke. Whereas men's preferences for a particular body *size* vary across cultures, their preference for a WHR of approximately 0.70 is fairly universal in food-rich, nonforaging societies. The WHR indicator was proposed by Singh (1993). Health indicators and crosscultural research on the WHR have been reviewed by Buss (2004, pp. 145-50).

Males over the age of 20 are attracted to signs of youth (rounder face, fuller lips) and report that they prefer younger females. In contrast, teenage males report that their ideal partner would be several years older (Kenrick et al., 1996), presumably because teenage females reach reproductive maturity before teenage males.

Even when males and females manifest the same tendencies, they tend to do so in somewhat sex-specific ways. Buss (1981) found that dominant college students of both sexes endorsed items such as "I took charge of things at the committee meeting." But males also expressed dominance through acts of personal ascension that elevated their own status or power (e.g., "I told others to perform menial tasks instead of doing them myself"). In contrast, females were more likely to express dominance in communal ways (e.g., "I settled a dispute among members of the group"). Given the persistence of so many sex-specific Pleistocene protocols in contemporary humans, Gaulin and McBurney (2004) declared that "there are two human natures: male and female" (p. 141).

Critique A. Our working model of essence depicts humans as embodied creatures with the capacity for reason, relationships, and dominion. We derived these capacities from the doctrine of the *imago Dei.*

The EP perspective on human essence is descriptively compatible but theologically incompatible with all three views of the *imago Dei.* As delineated in part one, a *substantive* view of the *imago Dei* defines us by our rational, contemplative power of thought. EP emphasizes our unconscious, noncontemplative, and irrational thought. Moreover, EP characterizes much of our rational thought as a *byproduct* of the adaptations by which we are defined, rather than an essential element. A *relational* view of the *imago Dei* defines us by our capacity to have inherently valuable relationships with God and others. While Christianity teaches that relationships are inherently valuable even when they instrumentally *cost* us, EP fails to acknowledge God and reduces relationships to their instrumental benefits. In EP, the primary value of relationships is that they increase inclusive fitness (the survival of myself or copies of my genes in others). A *functional* view of the *imago Dei* defines us by our exercise of dominion, which includes both earth-keeping and cultural development. As with relationships, EP reduces earth-keeping and cultural development to their instrumental adaptations; we find certain ecological environments (and artwork depicting these environments) aesthetically pleasing because these environments were associated with food, protection, and medicine during the Pleistocene (Daly & Wilson, 1994; Silverman & Choi, 2005).

EP is much more accordant with a Christian emphasis on embodiment. EP not only defines us by neural circuitry but also places more emphasis on sex and procreation than the other four developmental theories combined. Concerning sex, EP's delineation of males and females as morphs (variations on a universal design that differ from each other in functionally coordinated ways) calls to mind even the rhetorical structure of Genesis 1:27:

> So God created humankind in his image,
>> in the image of God he created them;
>> male and female he created them.

Most Christian understand Genesis 1:27 to establish some functionally coordinated design features in the sexes even before the fall, but disagree about whether these features revolved around dominance. EP can be linked to *both* of the commonly held theological explanations for differences identified in chapter two.

In keeping with historic Christianity, complementarianism emphasizes males' greater suitability for leadership as the most important difference between the sexes. Formerly, proponents of this view appealed to 1 Corinthians 11:7 (see chap. 2, note 3) and "obvious" facts of nature to claim that males are better suited for leadership because they are better imagers of God. But this appeal has become increasingly difficult to make as females have become more educated and leadership capacity has become less dependent on brute strength. Scientific investigations of sex differences have revealed many leadership advantages in females (e.g., better language skills, emotional discernment, physical health). Likewise, many male proclivities seem antithetical to the *imago Dei* (e.g., higher rates of violence, crime, drunkenness, learning disabilities).[32] Perhaps in response to this

---

[32]For a succinct summary of sex differences favoring males and females, see Gunnoe (2003, pp. 287-88).

difficulty, some prominent proponents of complementarianism (who do not speak for all who espouse complementarianism) have declared that *all* sex-linked behavior—even the male proclivity for rape and the female proclivity for depression—will *not* be viewed negatively. Rather, God *intended* these "so-called weaknesses" to "call forth and highlight" the other sex's strengths (Piper & Grudem, 1991, p. 49).[33] This sanctification of sex-linked dysfunction is in keeping with EP's approach to sex differences as both "intended" (by natural selection) and intractable, and EP's supposition that maladaptive traits that have persisted in the human gene pool must serve some adaptive function, at least in some situations (see the third point in note 23 above).

In contrast, Christians who promote gender egalitarianism view sex-linked dysfunction as a consequence of the fall. To review from chapter two, Van Leeuwen (2002) focused on males' tendency to turn dominion into domination, and females' tendency to do whatever it takes to preserve relationships with males, even when these relationships are unhealthy (p. 47). Van Leeuwen's observations are compatible with EP's focus on males as more concerned with dominance and competition, and more violent and promiscuous than females. They are also compatible with findings that females are attracted to dominant males even when they don't like them, and more willing than males to stay with a partner who has been sexually unfaithful, if the partner is invested in other ways. Van Leeuwen's assertion that Christians should work to restore the gender relations intended at creation is compatible with Pinker's (2011) observation that the world is becoming somewhat more peaceful as women have assumed positions of leadership (pp. 525-29). Both Van Leeuwen and Pinker see more egalitarian gender relationships as an antidote to the "natural" conditions of the sexes. However, Pinker views egalitarianism as a new condition, whereas Van Leeuwen views it as a return to our creational condition.

If we limit our comparison to simple *description*, the EP depiction of personhood actually has considerable overlap with a Christian one. Both approaches posit a hardwired universal design that makes humans

---

[33]It is possible that Grudem now regrets this sanctification of gender-based dysfunction. Grudem has recently decided that women *can* leave an abusive marriage (Randall, 2019).

intelligent, relational "masters" of the physical environment, and very interested in procreation. Both emphasize two common variants on a universal design, with coordinated characteristics.[34] The problem with EP's presentation is that it lacks magnanimity. In Christian theology, humans are made in the image of God and are given bodies to register God's presence in the world. In EP, humans are first and foremost self-reproducing machines.

PURPOSE

Tenet B1: Humans have been designed by natural selection, without existential purpose. According to EP, all species were designed by natural selection. In this section I provide commentary on how EP uses the word *designed*, the pragmatics of natural selection, and the implications of claiming that all species are designed by natural selection with respect to purpose.

In 1802 a British clergyman named William Paley offered the now well-known watchmaker analogy. Paley proposed that a person walking through a desolate area would make different assumptions about the origin of a stone versus a watch. While one could make few assumptions about the origin of a stone, certain conclusions about the watch are inevitable: it was designed by a watchmaker for its apparent purpose. Paley's book (reprinted in 1837) inspired the vocational interests of the young Charles Darwin,[35] and 200 years later Paley's analogy is still influential. The controversial ethologist Richard Dawkins commandeered the analogy for the title of his book *The Blind Watchmaker*, and Young Earth Creationists promote *Creation Moments*, two-minute radio broadcasts featuring "scientific evidence that points to proof of a world designed by our Creator, not by evolutionary chance" (creationmoments.com/radio).

The rhetorical problem with appealing to design to discourage belief in evolution is that proponents of evolution appeal to the exact same

---

[34]As in Christianity, some within EP are beginning to attend to non-cisgender categories of personhood. For example, it has been proposed that transgendered men in hunter-gatherer societies are a valuable asset because they help with child-rearing. See VanderLaan et al. (2013).

[35]"The old argument from design in Nature, as given by Paley, which formerly seemed to me so conclusive, fails, now that the law of natural selection has been discovered" (Darwin, 1887, p. 278).

phenomenon—design—as evidence for natural selection. Per Tooby and Cosmides (1997): "Adaptations are problem solving machines, and they can be identified using the same standards of evidence that one would use to recognize a human made machine: design evidence" (p. 88). Similarly, Pinker (2005) has asserted that vision, language, emotion, and cognitive faculties "are complex, useful, and nonrandomly organized, which means that they must be a product of the only physical process capable of generating complex, useful, non-random organization, namely natural selection" (p. xiv). By designating natural selection as the *process* by which humans were designed, EP avoids the need to designate an agentic designer.

EP also affords itself an evolutionary process that is conceptually easy to understand. Evolutionary *biologists* are faced with the difficult theoretical task of "building up" higher-order species from lower ones with very simple genetic profiles. In contrast, EP begins with "large reservoirs of genetic variability" (Tooby & Cosmides, 1992, p. 79) and then *pares down* genetic variability to a universal nature. A helpful analogy of this paring has been provided by Trivers (one of the evolutionary biologists who helped set the stage for EP). To paraphrase Trivers (1985, p. 21), imagine we are going to design the word *cat* by choosing letters, three at a time, out of a bin that has 100 copies of each letter of the alphabet. The probability of choosing all three in one draw would be approximately 1 in 3,000 (very unlikely). But now imagine that each time we draw, we sort the letters, returning the targeted letters to the bin and discarding the other letters. Additionally, imagine that each time we draw either C-A or A-T or C-A-T in sequence, we staple them together before returning them to the bin. With each successive draw, our chances of drawing C-A-T will rise, until there is a universal draw (i.e., we get C-A-T every time).

Trivers's analogy is *helpful* in at least two regards. First, it demonstrates how adaptations could evolve, but only in carriers who possessed all the genes "for" that adaptation (which is all EP explicitly claims; Buss, 2004, p. 39). Second, it highlights the interplay between random events and natural laws. In Trivers's word analogy, the draw is random, but the sorting process is rule-driven. Likewise, in natural selection, mutations are random, but the sorting process is rule-driven: only mutations that facilitate fitness are retained. This interplay is worth mentioning because many Christians who eschew evolution criticize those who espouse evolution for proposing things that "couldn't just happen." If we are fair, we must acknowledge that evolutionary theorists do a better job playing by scientific rules than those who advocate massive-scale creation out of nothing (which evolutionary theorists argue *really, really* couldn't just happen). Trivers's analogy is *misleading* (from an EP vantage) in that it implies an agent with an a priori end goal who established the sorting process by which to accomplish this goal. Not only is there no explicit agent in EP, there is no a priori goal.[36]

Much of the EP discourse on purpose has focused on convincing readers that humans are not only *not* progressing toward a particular goal (e.g., human thriving), but some of our Stone Age adaptations are actually working against this. Pinker (1997) stressed that there is nothing within an evolving or evolved human, or within the process of natural selection, that compels the human toward a particular teleological end (pp. 205-8). Pinker made this point to distinguish the EP view from the Darwinian view that engendered an "illusion of teleology" (p. 206) in that the organism seemed to be striving for fitness. Similarly, Tooby and Cosmides (2005) sought to distinguish the EP view from E. O. Wilson's sociobiological view,[37] writing that

> one of the several reasons why evolutionary psychology is distinct from human sociobiology and other similar approaches lies in its rejection of fitness maximization as an explanation for behavior. . . . Although organisms sometimes appear to be pursuing fitness on behalf of their genes, in reality they are executing the evolved circuit logic built into their neural programs, whether this corresponds to current fitness maximization or not. (p. 14)

---

[36]There are, however, subgoals (my word) in the sense that each adaptation is an organic program that, unless thwarted, will run to its end (Daly, 1991, p. 719). Because some sets of genes "cooperate" and get selected as a package deal, organisms have an "integrated purposiveness," even though some adaptations are no longer adaptive for the contemporary context and, as such, do not maximize an organism's fitness or direct humans to a *global* teleological end.

[37]According to Wilson (1978), "The species lacks any goal external to its own biological nature" (p. 3).

Some EP authors have also gone out of their way to disavow purpose as something ascribed by God. Daly and (Margo) Wilson (2002) emphasized luck and happenstance in the evolutionary process. Their argument is that because the population of humans 50,000–100,000 years ago was so small, the role of luck in human survival is "uncontroversial (except perhaps among those who believe that this particular upright ape is the image of divinity and the point of creation)" (p. 72). An even more explicit attack on God was made by Bering. In an essay titled *The Nonexistent Purpose of People* (2010), Bering deemed the belief that humans were created by God for a purpose "almost certainly a fairy tale" (p. 290).

Tenet B2: Humans' primary social motivations are status and group membership. Although the EP human has no purpose, the EP human has a lot of motivations. To understand the EP perspective on motivation, we must distinguish between conscious human experience and the "gene's eye view," a paradigm credited to Williams, Hamilton, and Trivers and made infamous by Dawkins in his popular book *The Selfish Gene*. Many human behaviors make it *appear* as though genes are conscious entities striving to reproduce themselves in either direct descendants or the descendants of their copies. (Again, because my sister carries copies of approximately 50% of my genes, aid to her and my niece increases the longevity of my genes' copies).

Of course, genes are *not* conscious beings with minds to strive to do anything. Genes are just segments of DNA. But genes that have replicated enough times to constitute the universal human nature are special in that they code for adaptations that help their bearers survive long enough to reproduce. (Again, recall Darwin's birds with two kinds of beaks. The genes coding for the pointed beak did not have minds that made them want to reproduce. Rather, genes coding for pointed beaks were selected for, whereas genes coding for rounded beaks could not be selected because all the birds with round beaks died in the drought.)

So, what kinds of genes would code for psychological modules that help their bearers reproduce? Obviously, genes that code for modules *directly* related to survival and reproduction (e.g., enjoyment of sex) are good candidates. But survival and reproduction are not humans' foremost social motivations. On a day-to-day basis, Pleistocene humans probably directed more psychological energy to sustaining the social conditions that assured the *opportunity* to survive and reproduce than to actually copulating 24/7. Per Hogan[38] (1983): "(a) people always live in groups, and (b) every group is organized in terms of a status hierarchy. This suggests that the two most important problems in life concern attaining status and popularity" (p. 56). Because selection is most likely to have favored modules for solving our most important problems, it follows that the EP person's primary social motivations would be status and acceptance by the group.

Of these, status is viewed as the more important of the two because status gives one "priority of access to resources in competitive situations" (Cummins, 2005, p. 677). Many psychological studies have shown that humans are very sensitive to status, permitting EP to argue that humans have evolved many modules related to status. In a review article, Cummins (2005) concluded that social dominance is one of the earliest-emerging and most stable personality traits. Even as toddlers, we prefer to imitate high-status rather than low-status individuals. By adulthood we are very adept at recognizing status. Kalma (1991) found that people were able to predict their own status within a new group before anyone had ever said a single word. Status is also tightly linked to our neuroendocrinology in a recip-rocal relationship. Whether researchers compare winners and losers in a competition, devoted fans who observe the competition, spouses in hier-archical marriages, or persons of different self-perceived socioeconomic status, those on top have the preferred physiological profile (lower stress hormones, lower blood pressure, better sleep, better body fat distribution, etc.).[39] This evidence has led Buss (2004) to declare that "if there were ever a reasonable candidate for a universal human motive, status striving would be at or near the top of the list" (pp. 344-45).

Humans also seem to have many modules related to group mem-bership, which (as we know from American Express commercials) has

---

[38]Robert Hogan's socioanalytic theory of personality has been influenced by evolutionary theory, but Hogan has disassociated himself from EP. Reacting specifically to the modularity of the mind that is claimed by EP, Hogan (2011) wrote, "My views of evolutionary theory tend to depart from the conventional wisdom as set forth by John Tooby and Leda Cosmides."
[39]For a review of these studies and their citations, see Cummins (2005, p. 677).

its privileges. Membership gives one access to food, information, care, protection, and potential mates. Although group membership doesn't *guarantee* access in competitive situations, even a person of low group status is likely to have more access to resources than someone who has no group at all. As with status modules, evidence for the primacy of membership modules comes from both social psychology (resource sharing and external threats promote group bonding) and neuropsychology (social rejection is mediated by the same circuitry that mediates physical pain).[40] Adaptations associated with group membership include modules for reciprocity, alliance formation, love, anxiety over negative social evaluations, and the propensity to reject those who inflict costs on the group—through aggression, cowardice, unjustified cheating, stealing of mates, and so on. Of these, the strongest is likely the propensity for reciprocity (Cosmides & Tooby, 1997).[41]

Critique B. Christianity teaches that humans were designed by God and purposed for love and dominion work. EP teaches that humans were designed by natural selection and have no purpose. Both the explicit disavowal of purpose and the eschewing of God by many within EP make the EP perspective on purpose incompatible with a Christian one.

Some Christians also take issue with EP's emphasis on natural selection, while others espouse natural selection as a process used by God to guide the development of the species. By way of analogy, if Paley learned that the watch he assumed was made by hand was actually made by machine, he would still believe in a watchmaker. Christians who believe that God used natural selection are sometimes divided into two broad subgroups: *evolutionary creationists*, who accept evolution as the primary model for the creation of the world, and *progressive creationists*, who emphasize a combination of natural selection and miraculous intervention (Haarsma & Haarsma, 2007/2011, chap. 8). So it is not the appeal to natural selection as a process that makes EP's view of purpose

---

[40]This research has been reviewed in chap. 8 of Larsen and Buss (2014).

[41]"Social exchange appears to be an ancient, pervasive, and central part of human social life. The universality of a behavioral phenotype is not a sufficient condition for claiming that it was produced by a cognitive adaptation, but it is suggestive. As a behavioral phenotype, social exchange is as ubiquitous as the human heartbeat" (Cosmides & Tooby, 1997, p. 94).

incompatible with our working model of purpose; it is EP's ascription of "total design power" to this process.

There is greater intersection between EP and Christian theology on the topic of motivation. As I argued in part one, if humans were purposed for love and dominion work, we should be very motivated to engage in these activities. To make this argument, I appealed to the doctrine of the *imago Dei*. From a *relational* view of the *imago Dei*, it follows that humans should care a great deal about relationships. In the EP view, we do—and we have evolved many adaptations to manage the quality of these relationships. From a *functional* view of the *imago Dei*, it follows that we should care a great deal about dominion. Again, we do; social status is very much related to dominion. The theological problem with EP is that neither our relationship-related nor our dominion-related activities have anything to do with imaging God. Done as God intends, relationships and dominion work have *both* inherent and instrumental value. Done as EP intends, even love is reduced to its instrumental functions (Buss, 2006, p. 66).

EP also shares overlap with Genesis 3. In this account, the serpent offers Eve the status of God and she bites. This exchange lends credence to the EP assertion that humans' primary social motivation is status. If status was this appealing in Eden, how much more so in a warped world? Prefall humans had the opportunity to enjoy relationships, dominion work, and procreation commensurate with their created nature. Postfall humans are still wired for the same activities, but accomplishing these things can be fraught with difficulty. Because status makes all these essential activities more accessible, EP may be correct that status seeking is our primary postfall social motivation.

This shift from abundant living to self-preservation has been described by John Chryssavgis (1992) in his presentation on the Orthodox perspective on original sin:

> For Orthodox theology and spirituality, the "Fall" of humanity is the renunciation of the possibility of participating in true life, in personal and loving communion. The biblical account of the Fall refers to the initial choice of autonomy and self-sufficiency, as opposed to dependence upon and subsistence in God, the origin of life and love. This implies alienation from God

and from oneself, fragmentation of the world and of human nature. The various needs of self-preservation become an end in themselves, and the Fall is ultimately *from the level of life to that of survival.* (p. 197)

As with EP's presentation of essence, EP's presentation of humans' essential activities as ends in themselves makes the EP perspective on human motivation descriptively compatible with a Christian one, but only in a reductive way.

MORAL-ETHICAL TENDENCIES

Tenet C: Tendencies toward both good and bad were adaptive to the earliest humans; these tendencies are now part of the universal human nature. In this section I will address how good and bad are defined in EP, the specific good and bad tendencies emphasized by EP, and why it is difficult to identify a primary directional tendency in the EP depiction of the person.

What is meant by good and bad. The EP approach to morality is to identify good and bad tendencies in contemporary humans and then work backward to explain how these tendencies would have increased fitness in the ancestral world. By *tendencies* I mean behaviors as well as sentiments that influence behaviors (e.g., feeling inclined to help someone, experiencing guilt when we cause harm). By *good* and *bad* I mean evaluations corresponding to most people's *felt* moral convictions, not necessarily something that transcends humans (such as God-given or natural law). This distinction was explicitly made by sociobiologist E. O. Wilson (1998), who contrasted "transcendentalists, who think that moral guidelines exist outside the human mind, and empiricists, who think them contrivances of the mind." Wilson then explicitly sided with the latter.

Some within EP share Wilson's view that morality is a critical component of human nature but exists only within the human mind. According to Daly and (Margo) Wilson (2008):

When we consult our sense of what is right or just . . . we are consulting moral/emotional/cognitive mechanisms of the human mind. These mental mechanisms must surely have been shaped, like any other organized

species-typical attributes of body and mind, by a history or selection. . . .
Morality is the device of an animal of exceptional cognitive complexity, pur-
suing its own interests in an exceptionally complex social universe. (p. 254)

Others within EP have been more circumspect. Cosmides and Tooby
(2004) asserted that humanity's contrived moral intuitions (i.e., what *is*) tell
us nothing about what *ought* to be—but stopped short of specifying whether
an independent *ought* exists.[42] Given this pair's subsequent disavowal of an
"intelligent designer" (Tooby & Cosmides, 2006), we can assume that they
do not link morality to God but they may believe in natural law. Pinker also
hints at belief in natural law. In a discussion of ethics, he stated that humans
assign "moral value to behavior through the behavior's *inherent nature* [em-
phasis added] or its consequences" (1997, p. 55).

Specific good and bad tendencies emphasized by EP. In EP, humans have
many adaptations that incline us toward good. EP places particular emphasis on cooperation, reciprocity, and altruism. Cooperation and reciprocity are easy to explain from a Darwinian perspective. Two hunters can
bring down a large animal to eat more easily than one can; a hunter's meat
exchanged for a gatherer's berries improves the fitness of both. Altruism
(broadly defined as behavior that *increases* the fitness of neighbors but
decreases the fitness of self) is more difficult to explain. Altruism toward
kin is typically linked to Hamilton's theory of inclusive fitness. (Recall:
inclusive fitness benefits not just my genes but also copies of my genes.)
Altruism toward nonkin is typically presented as a byproduct of cooperation, reciprocity, or kin altruism. These practices would have been critical
to survival during the Pleistocene.

Adaptations for good behavior are accompanied by adaptations for
good sentiments. These sentiments are viewed as enabling reciprocity.
Liking is a sentiment that initiates and helps maintain cooperative partnerships; gratitude calibrates our desire to reciprocate to the costs/benefits of

---

[42]"Natural selection favors designs on the basis of how well they promote their own reproduction,
not on how well they promote ethical behavior. . . . Human nature is comprised of programs
that were selected for merely because they outreproduced alternative programs in the past. There
is nothing in this process to ensure the production of decision rules or moral sentiments that
track the desiderata of an ethically justifiable moral system" (Cosmides & Tooby, 2004, pp. 91-92).

the original act; conscience keeps our selfish tendencies in check (helping us maintain the reputation of a trustworthy partner); guilt prompts us to make amends before exploited partnerships are irreconcilably severed (Trivers, 1971; Pinker, 1997).

Some scholars include religiosity as an adaptation that promotes good behavior. Proponents of the *religion-as-adaptation* position stress that religiosity promotes fitness by fostering hope and meaning, increasing group cohesion and the sharing of resources, and justifying and legitimizing morality. This does not mean that all promoters of this position believe in God. Rather, they argue that even misplaced attributions can promote existential reflection and moral behavior. Other scholars see religion as a byproduct of a hyperactive agency-detector. For a thorough discussion of the religion-as-adaptation versus religion-as-byproduct debate, see Atran and Norenzayan (2004) and the 25 responses from peer commentators.[43]

The same process that designed structures for good (natural selection) also hardwired structures that incline us toward bad—particularly when resources are scarce. Because access to resources and mates was so closely linked to status during the Pleistocene, EP argues that natural selection would have favored not only strategies for dominance (often violent) but also strategies to subvert the dominant (often antisocial, but not always). As explained by Cummins (1998), "If you are big enough to take what you want by force, you are sure to dominate available resources—unless your subordinates are smart enough to deceive you. If you are subordinate, you must use other strategies—deception, guile, appeasement, bartering, coalition formation, friendship, kinship—to get what you need to survive" (p. 37). Given that males are, on average, bigger than females, it is not surprising that attempts to attain and maintain status via violence are much more prevalent in males.[44] In contrast, antisocial tactics that have subversive value are evident in both males and females by about age four.

---

[43] Atran and Norenzayan (2004) promote the byproduct position. They and their supporters argue that religion does all the good things claimed by those who view religion as an adaption, but other cultural phenomena and ideologies can also accomplish these things (admittedly less effectively), and there is no unique adaptive problem that is solved by religion.

[44] A concise EP perspective on violence has been provided by Gaulin and McBurney (2004, pp. 138-42). See also *Homicide* (2008) and many other publications by Daly and Wilson.

Primary directional tendency. In the prior four chapters, I attempted to discern the primary directional tendency promoted by the featured theorist (e.g., I proposed that Bandura views humans as more inclined toward good than bad). Discerning the directional tendency (if any) of the EP person is difficult for several reasons.

First, one way that EP distinguishes itself from other evolutionary approaches within psychology is that it emphasizes *mental modularity*. Accordingly, many EP writings are presentations of individual adaptations rather than holistic syntheses of human nature.

Second, several EP-related writings on moral tendencies have been reactive rather than proactive. This is because theories of social evolution are often perceived as endorsing selfishness.[45] This perception is at least partially attributable to the publication of *The Selfish Gene* by ethologist Richard Dawkins. Capitalizing on a metaphor that works well to describe gene activity, Dawkins (2006) said, "Let us try to teach generosity and altruism because we are born selfish" (p. ix, quoting the 1976 edition). Later, Dawkins (2006) stated that he regretted this statement (p. ix) and added, "Personification of genes really ought not to be a problem, because no sane person thinks DNA molecules have conscious personalities, and no sensible reader would impute such a delusion to an author" (p. x).

One defense against selfishness came from Daly and Wilson (1994), who explained, "'Selfish gene' theory is an account of the process that created human nature . . . but it is not itself a description of human nature." Rather: "People and other animals do all sorts of things that do not 'bring some benefit to copies of their genes,' for although fitness maximization is the criterion of adaptive design over evolutionary time, it is not isomorphic with any creature's purposes in ecological time" (p. 44). Daly and Wilson (2002) also argued that the "moral circle" to whom humans are offering empathy and benefit is becoming more and more inclusive over time.

---

[45]Pinker (1997, p. 45) quoted distinguished primate researcher Sarah Blaffer Hrdy as saying "I question whether sociobiology should be taught at the high school level, or even the undergraduate level. . . . The whole message of sociobiology is oriented toward the success of the individual. It's Machiavellian, and unless a student has a moral framework already in place, we could be producing social monsters by teaching this. It really fits in very nicely with the yuppie, 'me-first,' ethos."

A second defense against selfishness was offered by anthropologist Edward Hagen (2005), who wrote,

> EP critics fear that if psychological adaptations are a product of selfish genes, then we must all be essentially selfish. Yet, *every* adaptation in the body evolved by natural selection, that is, by selfish genes that outcompeted (replaced) alternative alleles at some point in the past. The genes coding for your hair gradually replaced less effective versions of those genes in the past and are, therefore, *selfish*. Despite this, no one worried that selfish genes have produced selfish hair. Critics only worry when a process widely accepted to have produced the body's specialized structure is claimed to have also produced the brain's specialized structure. But describing most psychological adaptations as selfish is as nonsensical as it is for hair. (p. 150)

Hagen then said, "There is a narrow but important set of psychological adaptations whose properties do correspond to our folk notion of selfishness. . . . [But we possess] adaptations for both competition and cooperation, adaptations based on genes that were equally selfish" (pp. 150-51).

A third reason that it is difficult to discern the primary directional tendency of the EP person is that authors are not always consistent in their claims. This is particularly the case when EP is proffered to a popular audience, as Pinker does. In his 1997 book, *How the Mind Works*, Pinker characterized humans as "more savage than noble" (p. 51).[46] In the prologue to his 2011 book, *The Better Angels of Our Nature: Why Violence Has Declined*, Pinker says, "Humans are not innately good (just as they are not innately evil)" (p. xxv). Rather, we come equipped with motives that orient us toward and away from violence as a function of environmental conditions. While this more neutral characterization could indicate that Pinker has revised his opinion on humankind, Pinker's animated prose in other parts of the 2011 book suggest that his prior inclination still holds. For example, in the chapter on humanity's five "inner demons,"[47] Pinker says, "So let me begin by

---

[46]Full quote: "Recorded history from the Bible to the present is a story of murder, rape, and war, and honest ethnography shows that foraging peoples, like the rest of us, are more savage than noble" (Pinker, 1997, pp. 50-51).

[47]The five demons are predatory or instrumental violence, dominance, revenge, sadism, and ideology that justifies violence. The four angels are empathy, self-control, moral sense, and reason. Pinker (2001, p. xxiii) credits the phrase *better angels of our nature* to Abraham Lincoln. It was used in Lincoln's first inaugural speech.

convincing you that most of us—including you, dear reader—are wired for violence" (p. 483). In his discussion of the fourth "angel"—our moral sense—he asks, "How can we make sense of this crazy angel—the part of human nature that would seem to have the strongest claim to be the source of our goodness, but that in practice can be more diabolical than our worst inner demon?" (p. 622). Like Bandura (chap. 8, Tenet C), Pinker recognizes that humans often apply our moral sense to the justification of violence. But unlike Bandura, who inclines humanity toward good despite this misapplication, Pinker proposed that "the net contribution of the human moral sense to human well-being may well be negative" (p. 622).

The EP party line is that humans have value-neutral inclinations toward behaviors that many psychologists would categorize as good and bad. (But lurking behind the party line is a darker figure that EP sometimes attempts to disguise with various rhetorical treatments.)

Critique C. The EP model of moral-ethical tendencies *differs* from a Christian one in at least three important ways. The first difference concerns structure. One of the most provocative areas of overlap between Christianity and EP is that both require a reach back into prehistory. In contrast to the other four theorists, from whom we can glean substantial psychological insight irrespective of their view on origins, both the Christian perspective and the EP perspective require faith that (a) the earliest humans were quite different from contemporary ones and (b) what happened long ago is the primary basis for understanding current moral tendencies. Because the two perspectives differ in their account of prehistory, they structure us differently. Even though there is intrafaith disagreement on how and when humans arrived on the scene, Christians believe that humans were structured by God, with God-intended, God-like capacities. Per our working model, humans are *structurally good.* Christians also believe that humans are inherently prone to sin (but are unable to agree on the physical process whereby evil got inside us). In contrast, EP depicts humans as *designed* (by natural selection) to be structurally good *and structurally bad.*

The second difference concerns the attitude toward explicit training. Christians actively promote training in moral-ethical tendencies, appealing to verses like Proverbs 22:6 ("Train children in the right way, / and when old, they will not stray"). EP allows for plasticity in the development of psychological structures but tends to avoid terms like *learning* or *training*. If humans are currently behaving better than we did during the Pleistocene, it is because our brains are preprogrammed to behave differently under different conditions (Pinker, 1997).

The third difference involves the nature of good and evil. Whereas Christians believe that good and evil transcend humankind, some within EP insist that good and evil are only contrivances of the mind.

The two perspectives *overlap* in at least four ways. First, both perspectives appreciate that moral tendencies are rooted in our embodiment. Second, both emphasize the centrality of the moral sense *and* recognize that the moral sense often does not function as it should. Pinker's designation of the moral sense as a "crazy angel" is compatible with the theological teaching that sin has warped every aspect of our being. It is also compatible with the Bible's depiction of humans as adept at deceiving ourselves about what is right (see Prov 21:2). Third, both perspectives recognize status seeking as a motivational basis for evil, and salient environmental factors as a trigger for this motivation. In the Genesis 3 account, it is humans' grasp at God-like status, triggered by the serpent's suggestion that God was keeping humankind down, that constitutes the first action sin.

A fourth similarity is that both perspectives emphasize human universals more than individual differences. In theology, an emphasis on universals is appropriate because theology aims to explicate the relationship between God and corporate humankind, not everything there is to know about individuals. In contrast, EP aims to describe humans comprehensively. (Recall Hagen's [2005] assertion that "fully realized, EP would constitute a functional understanding of the neural circuits underlying our every thought, emotion and action" [p. 171]). EP's almost-exclusive emphasis on universals leaves many readers wanting better explanations for the heterogeneity in humans' moral-ethical tendencies than EP is presently able to give.[48]

These areas of functional overlap notwithstanding, different design plans, different attitudes toward training, and different views of transcendent morality make the EP view of moral-ethical tendencies foundationally incompatible with a Christian one.

AGENCY/ACCOUNTABILITY

Tenet D1: A genetically determined mind is not synonymous with genetically determined behavior, but neither do we have free will. Psychology teaches that humans have a semi-structured mind that causes us to interact with the world in predictable ways. Contemporary students of psychology learn this in their introductory courses, but this presentation was controversial 50 years ago when sociobiology burst onto the scene. Per Joyce (2006): "The early opponents of sociobiology were so eager to discredit the program that they kept chanting 'genetic determinism!' until this accusation lodged in the popular consciousness" (p. 8).[49]

With roots in sociobiology, some of the EP discourse on determinism has continued to focus on defending EP against the misconception of genetic determinism. In the "controversial issues" chapter of Buss's handbook, Hagen (2005) stressed that "EP comes down squarely in favor of the primacy of nature" (p. 160) but learning also plays a role. Nature hardwires psychological systems "to collect information about their environments and alter their properties in an adaptive fashion" (p. 161). The fact that nature determines us to be flexible in accordance with the environment means that our *behavior* is not genetically determined even if our psychological mechanisms are. Put another way, nurture causes behavioral variability at the behest of nature and within boundaries set by nature.

---

[48] Although EP has devoted a little attention to the development of individual differences (see note 23), even its proponents have acknowledged that individual differences are "the most challenging level of analysis" for EP (Larsen & Buss, 2014, p. 248).

[49] According to Pinker (1997), popular conception feared these three things: (a) if the mind has an innate structure, different categories of people (gender, race) could have *different* structures, which could be used to justify discrimination; (b) if tendencies toward bad behaviors (e.g., aggression, rape, war) are innate, attempts at reform are futile; and (c) if behavior is caused by genes, people cannot be held responsible for their behavior (pp. 46-47).

That said, greater delineation of the mind's structure does contribute to psychology's ever-increasing capacity to predict patterns of behavior resulting from the interdependence of nature and nurture. We are not genetically determined, but neither do we have free will. As Pinker (1997) explains, it is the job of science to take previously unexplained behavior and subject it to natural laws; thus, "science is guaranteed to appear to eat away at the will, *regardless* of what it finds, because the scientific mode of explanation cannot accommodate the mysterious notion of uncaused causation that underlies the will" (p. 54).

Promoters of EP have responded differently to this scientific eating away of the will. Daly and Wilson (2008) unabashedly compartmentalize, saying, "As practicing scientists, we embrace determinism; in our other roles as human protagonists, we simply switch to the contrary and seemingly incompatible world view" (p. 269). Bering (2010) accords humans *degrees* of free will fully within the science game. Appealing to EDP (which specifies more behavioral flexibility than EP), Bering holds that "one person may indeed be freer than another to be 'good' than 'evil' given their inherited individual differences (such as in temperament and general intelligence) in combination with their prior experiences. In reality, we're only as free as our genes are pliable in the slosh of our developmental milieus (see Bjorklund & Pelligrini, 2001)" (p. 90).

Tenet D2: A sense of accountability and responsibility are part of the universal human nature. Promoters of EP approach accountability and responsibility the same way they approach all commonly manifested human tendencies. They document the prevalence of the tendency, figure out how the tendency would have been adaptive in the ancestral world, and then name and frame the tendency to emphasize its adaptive function.

EP addresses accountability but rarely uses the term. This is because accountability requires a transcendent moral agent or standard for humans to be accountable *to*, which promoters of EP either explicitly disavow or speak obliquely about. The only EP reference to accountability that I located was in an article about children. Bering (2010) stated that children's social transgressions are generally treated with tolerance, "but by adolescence, individuals are held accountable for their failure to conform to the moral prescriptions of the group and are subsequently punished" (p. 431). Instead of accountability, EP emphasizes humans' *moral sense.* Our own moral sense prompts us to behave in ways that help us maintain reputation as a trustworthy affiliate and to make amends when a relationship has been compromised (Pinker, 1997, pp. 404-5). The moral sense of others prompts them to punish us when we fail to comply with group standards.

Likewise, EP rarely uses the term *responsibility*, instead focusing on the direct caregiving of offspring or altruism. The former is adaptive in that it promotes the survival of one's own offspring. The latter is in keeping with inclusive fitness theory applied by Hamilton, Williams, and Trivers in the 1960s and 1970s (see the history section). Per inclusive fitness theory, our human ancestors assumed responsibility for the care of others because caring for kin increased their inclusive fitness. Inclinations toward responsibility and altruism now persist as byproducts of the adaptations for kin-care.

Put concisely, promoters of EP are interested in humans' moral sense of accountability and behavioral care of others. They describe these tendencies but do not locate them in any moral philosophy.

Tenet D3: EP's contribution to a moral-ethical society is to help us understand the nature we cannot readily overcome. Cosmides and Tooby (2004) understand that "the nature of human nature is relevant to anyone wishing to create a more just and humane workplace and society" (p. 91). Promoters of EP want a more just and humane society. The problem is that their theoretical framework makes it difficult to offer more than simple description of the way things are.

A good example of the descriptive-only approach has been provided by Bering (2005) in an essay demonstrating humans' predilection to believe in supernatural agency. Although Bering wears atheism on his sleeve (see Bering, 2010), he recognizes that belief in God facilitates responsible behavior that increases fitness by helping people retain group membership. He advises that "the idea of supernatural agency should not be exorcised from human minds by scientists with sociopolitical agendas, but carefully studied as a way of understanding what it means to be human" (p. 413).

Bering's descriptive-only approach is more intellectually coherent than the compartmentalization approach encouraged by Daly and Wilson (see Tenet D1) and by Pinker (1997). For Pinker, ethics and science are "two self-contained systems played out among the same entities in the world, just as poker and bridge are different games played with the same fifty-two card deck" (p. 55). To promote both ethics and science, Pinker advises that a person knows where they stand on the former before engaging in the latter.

A third approach is to promote EP as an endeavor that can facilitate moral-ethical behavior, and then fail to offer any concrete techniques for facilitating this behavior, or—worse yet—encourage readers to *accept* their moral-ethical failings. EP is often framed as a new way of understanding human nature (Cosmides & Tooby, 2004; Daly & Wilson, 2008, p. 297; Pinker, 2011, pp. xxii-xxiii). Sometimes this new understanding is proposed as a first step toward overcoming our destructive tendencies (Buss, 2004, p. 20; Pinker, 2011).[50] But other times readers are encouraged to accept their destructive tendencies and work within them. For example, Cosmides and Tooby (2004) wrote an article on business ethics promoting "the art of designing policies that achieve ethical goals by taking advantage of the moves that our human nature is already prepared to make" (p. 122). This sounds like a good plan, void of context. It sounds less good when the proposed plan directly follows a *disparagement* of those who view ethical behavior as "a Manichean struggle, in which 'willpower' is deployed to counteract the low and degrading forces of our evolved human nature" (p. 122). Continuing their disparagement, these authors said, "We think this is a losing strategy. Our minds are indeed equipped with over-ride programs—willpower, if you will (Baron-Cohen, Robertson, and Moriarty, 1994; Frith, 1992). But if override is necessary, the battle is already half lost" (p. 122). Implicit disparagement of active struggle can also be seen in Pinker's (2011) book on violence. In the prologue (pp. xxii-iii) Pinker emphasizes that he will present violence simply

---

[50]"An ability to hold our instincts up to the light, rather than naïvely accepting their products in our consciousness as the way things are, is the first step in discounting them when they lead to harmful ends" (Pinker, 2011, p. 529).

as a collection of statistical trends, *not* as "a heroic struggle of justice against evil, nor an unstoppable force for progress that is carrying us toward an omega point of perfect peace."

To the point, all three of these approaches settle for explaining the "is," without contributing any programmatic strategies for facilitating the "ought." This is because EP has no theoretical base from which to launch an "ought" offensive. This lack of ethical grounding is of grave concern to Hagan (2005), who envisaged dire consequences should a "fully realized" EP replace all the ideologies that have heretofore supported programs of responsibility (e.g., free will, supernatural agency, telos, mind-body dualism, blank slate in need of socialization). Hagen warned that "EP challenges the foundations of crucial enlightenment values, values we undermine at our peril. Perhaps the mix of secular and religious values on which the priceless institutions of democracy rest are like a tablecloth that can be quickly yanked out, leaving everything standing on some solid, though as yet unknown, base. But I wouldn't bet on it" (p. 171).

Hagan (2005) also expressed concern that EP will provide the "power to mold our humanity to a disquieting degree" (p. 171). Because EP proffers no *proactive* program, I spent a long time pondering how EP was trying to mold us, and to what end. Eventually I decided that Hagen was not using the term *mold* in an active sense (which would perhaps ascribe too much malicious intent), but rather highlighting the unintentional transformation of society that EP is likely to foster by its *neglect* of intentional molding. Like behaviorism, EP is reductive. Like attachment theory, EP is deterministic. But Skinner and Bowlby made very tangible contributions to the prevention and treatment of human maladies. While it is possible that a positive programmatic approach from EP is forthcoming, mainstream EP has heretofore been content to simply yank out the tablecloth.

Critique D. Our working model depicts humans as agentic, accountable, and responsible in varying degrees. EP's reductive treatment of these characteristics is compatible in some ways and incompatible in more important ways.

Agency. The two perspectives on agency are compatible in that both place a great deal of emphasis on the determining nature bequeathed to us by our ancestors, especially the malevolent manifestations of this nature. Although the biblical concept of nature is not synonymous with a scientific one (see chap. 3), the Bible is clear that our physical inclinations are incredibly difficult to resist. In Romans 7 the apostle Paul writes of the war going on between his inmost self and his body, which he characterizes as a slave to sin. He explicitly laments, "I can will what is right, but I cannot do it" (Rom 7:18).

A major difference is revealed in the two perspectives' responses to the malevolent manifestations of our nature. EP depicts all aspects of our nature as something we should work to accept, explicitly discounting an eventual "omega point of perfect peace" (Pinker, 2011, p. xxiii). Christianity teaches that good can and will overcome evil because Christ is the Alpha and the Omega (Rev 22:13). As partners in this overcoming, Christians are to view ourselves as having sufficient agency to strive for self-control (Titus 2:5; 2 Pet 1:6), shun evil and pursue good (1 Cor 6:18; 2 Tim 2:22), and "fight the good fight" (1 Tim 6:12). According to Ephesians 6:12, the fight against evil is ultimately a spiritual battle. But even if we limit our critique to the temporal, EP fosters a much more complacent stance toward evil than Christians should abide.

Accountability and responsibility. Concerning accountability and responsibility, the two perspectives are compatible in that both present humans as accountable for self and responsible for others. Both also recognize a developmental component to accountability, designating adults more accountable than children.

A major difference is revealed in explanations for *why* humans are accountable and responsible. EP appeals to the instrumental functions of accountability and responsibility in an evolution based on happenstance. Christianity posits a noble, intentional reason for accountability and responsibility: humans were created by God in the image of God. Per the *substantive* view of this doctrine, we have the capacity to make moral judgments and behave accordingly. Per the *relational* view, relationships with others must be carefully tended because they have value that transcends their instrumental functions. Per the *functional* emphasis, we were purposed to represent God in caregiving.

EP's failure to articulate a transcendent reason for behaving accountably and responsibly makes it foundationally incompatible with Christian theology. As with agency, EP's stance on accountability and responsibility is purely naturalistic. Again, EP assumes this stance because it lacks any moral/philosophical grounding that would permit it to do otherwise.

WHAT CHRISTIANS CAN LEARN FROM EVOLUTIONARY PSYCHOLOGY

The EP depiction of personhood is descriptively compatible with a Christian one in many regards. Both perspectives present a being who is capable of reason, relational, able to overcome the physical environment, embodied, sexed, gendered, procreative, inherently inclined toward both good and bad, accountable for self, and responsible for others.

Unfortunately, this descriptive accord is countered by a striking discord with theological beliefs that are central to the Christian faith. In EP, the *imago Dei* is explicitly disavowed or functionally reduced to adaptations facilitating inclusive fitness (or byproducts). Our design is attributed to an intention-less process, and thus void of even temporal purpose. Our brains are vestiges of the Stone Age, providing us no prescriptive path to flourishing. Our best hope of raising accountable and responsible children is to teach them to compartmentalize their science and ethics, or to keep them duped, believing in a deity that does not exist.

So, what can Christians learn from EP? Given the liabilities just listed, we might be tempted to say "not much." But that would be a knee-jerk reaction. As with Skinner, I feel that I have not so much learned *from* EP (i.e., I have not adopted the specific paradigm) but rather learned *because* EP challenged me to think harder on a variety of issues.

The greatest contribution EP makes to our understanding of personhood is its presentation of humans as not only embodied but "embrained." Obviously, the brain is part of the body, but EP pushes us to consider the degree to which we are influenced by hardwired response patterns in our mental circuitry. Multiple times in this book, I have stated that Christians have not yet articulated a scientifically plausible explanation for how evil became inherent in structurally good beings. Naturally selected mental modules offers us another concrete way to think about inherent evil. Although a more precise acquisition process needs to be worked out, I find it much easier to fathom new wiring attributable to learned experience—adaptive in a changing environment and selected for over generations—than a sudden deprivation of preternatural gifts or infusion of reified blight.

EP's extensive documentation of sex differences also lends credence to Christians' theological stance that humans were created gendered. EP's presumption of a normative link between sex and gender, coupled with the recognition that noncisgender development is also hardwired, is accordant with Johnson's (2017) theologically—*and* scientifically—informed perspective on gender (see chap. 2).

Finally, EP challenges Christians to think hard about ways of knowing and what evidence constitutes a good argument. There were several times during the writing of this chapter when I was struck by the similarity of the way adherents of Christianity and adherents of EP ascertain truth. Both perspectives rest on faith that the earliest humans were quite different from contemporary ones and that what happened long ago is the basis for understanding contemporary personhood. Members of both groups appeal to complex design in the contemporary world as proof that their account of prehistory is the right one. Members of both groups scorn the other for not seeing the "obvious" truth. Given these similarities in epistemology, it would seem that a more charitable, intellectually humble treatment of the other would be appropriate from both sides.

CHAPTER TEN

Learning from Developmental Theory

THIS BOOK WAS MOTIVATED by my desire for Christians to learn from developmental theory, assimilating wisdom that is compatible with Christian thought even as we reject claims that explicitly contradict it. The last five chapters each concluded with a section titled "What Christians Can Learn from . . ." These conclusions were theorist-specific. In this chapter, I briefly revisit the four organizing themes, synthesizing the most important contributions *across* theorists.

ESSENCE

In chapter two, I characterized humans as embodied creatures with emergent God-like capacities. Christians believe that we have these capacities because we were created in the image and likeness of God. Theological writings articulate temporal manifestations of image and likeness but often present these manifestations as static or "adultist" in orientation (Johnson, 2017, p. 200). They acknowledge that we are presently a poor approximation of what we will be in eternity, but rarely focus on how temporal manifestations vary across individuals and the lifespan.

Christians need developmental psychology to understand how the *imago Dei* develops *in this life*. In contrast to theologian Millard Erickson (2001), who presented the substantive aspects of the *imago Dei* as the basis for the relational and functional aspects (pp. 170-78), developmental psychologists present relationships as the foundational aspect. Erik Erikson and Bowlby rooted the conscience (substantive aspect) in the relational, and Bandura rooted agency (functional aspect) in the relational. Greater attention to the relational aspect as foundational can help Christians *foster* the development of *imago Dei* characteristics rather than just describe them.

Developmental psychology also helps us understand our creation in God's *likeness*. In keeping with the scholarship of Garr (2003) and others, I proposed that we understand likeness as the capacity to continue God's creative work, perpetually registering the presence of God in the world. Contemporary theorists who have extended Bowlby's work to the God-human relationship have explicated specific psychological processes whereby children view parents as representing God's presence in form and function. Erikson identified stage seven, generativity versus stagnation, as the time when healthy adults turn their attention to establishing and mentoring the next generation. Erikson (1974) eventually defined generativity as a broad but intentional participation "in the establishment, the guidance, and the enrichment of the living generation and the world it inherits" (p. 123). With their discourse on maturation-specific and activity-specific manifestations of the image and likeness of God, developmental theorists ground theological writings on image and likeness in concrete exemplars.

Developmental theory can also help Christians with more circumscribed concerns. For example, knowledge of typical development can help us prudently position ourselves in the cultural war over sex and gender. Concerning gender identity, EP's declaration of sex-specific mental modules helps us appreciate what it means to perceive the world in a gendered way. Concerning gender roles, Erikson (1969) provides a model for how egalitarian-minded Christians can document gender differences with integrity. Bucking the conventional wisdom that promoting gender equity requires scholars to downplay gender differences, Erikson documented differences *and* called for more female involvement in the shaping of ecological and humanitarian social policy (pp. 292-93). Skinner also envisioned greater parity across the genders, but his dismissal of all things essential makes it difficult to learn much about essence from his perspective.

PURPOSE

In chapter two, I proposed that humans were *universally* purposed for love and dominion work. While all of the theorists depict humans as engaging in these activities, only Erikson made purpose inherent by delineating a teleological-like progression with specific stages focused on these activities. Erikson also described the psychological processes contributing to the embrace of *particular* purposes in particular contexts and identified the stage (adolescence) in which psychologically healthy people begin this in earnest.

Bandura also contributed to a Christian understanding of purpose, even though he did not view purpose as inherent. Bandura's most important contribution is his emphasis on learned self-efficacy as a prerequisite for perseverance in purposes that promote the common good. Most Christians understand the need to be intentional in teaching that humans are purposed for love and dominion work. Bandura helps us appreciate the need to be intentional in constructing the psychological scaffolding necessary to effectively *engage* in love and dominion work.

We learn less about purpose from Skinner, Bowlby, and EP. Skinner categorized purpose as an explanatory fiction. Bowlby (1969) subverted all instinctual behavior to survival, warning that we must not get "trapped in theories of a teleological kind" (p. 124). EP depicts humans as designed by the process of natural selection, explicitly disavowing an agentic designer in favor of happenstance. EP divests the process of natural selection of *even* the "illusion of teleology" (Pinker, 1997, p. 206). These claims directly contradict a Christian perspective on purpose and should not be assimilated.

MORAL-ETHICAL TENDENCIES

In chapter three, I provided evidence that the Bible depicts all humans, not just Christians, as tending toward both good and bad. Tendencies toward good arise out of our good creational structure. The physical process whereby evil "got inside" us is unclear. Inclinations toward both good and evil are also attributable to learning.

Psychological structures and primary directional tendency. Four of the developmental theories contribute to a Christian understanding of moral-ethical tendencies by equipping humans with psychological structures. Some of these structures are more scientifically plausible than others, but each offers another mechanism to talk about inherent morality.

Erikson equipped humans with a radiant core first illuminated by the mother and ultimately illuminated by God. A radiant core is more theological than scientific (indeed, the concept was derived from Scripture), but Erikson's identification of our primary caregiver as our first temporal source of good is scientific. Erikson said that humans must know enough good in their infant environment to develop trust and hope (the infant version of faith). Erikson also specified the development of a conscience based on rules and obedience. Countering those who depict humans as fundamentally rebellious, Erikson asserted that we are, by nature, "authority acceptors" (1964, p. 142), and that during the preschool years the child "now hears, as it were, God's voice without seeing God" (1980, p. 84). Erikson's ground plan also includes the capacity for an ethical sense based on ideals, but the development of ethics is not universal.

Bowlby equipped humans with a conscience by retaining Freud's superego. Like Erikson, he rooted the conscience in the quality of the parent-child relationship, explaining that parents must be sensitive and responsive so that the child has an "audience worth pleasing" (Ainsworth & Bowlby, 1991, p. 338). This focus on early sensitivity is valuable for Christians because Scripture says so little about the emotional tenor of the child's earliest relationships, leading some Christians to value obedience over emotional orientation, even during infancy (Carton, 2008).

Bandura (1978) equipped humans with a "self-system" composed of "cognitive structures and subfunctions for perceiving, evaluating, and regulating behavior" (p. 344). Important subfunctions include empathy, forethought, self-reflection, and self-regulation. Together, the subfunctions predispose us to discern moral precepts and evaluate ourselves negatively when we violate these precepts.

When considering the contributions of Erikson, Bowlby, and Bandura, it is important to state that *none* of these theorists *structured* humans for bad. Rather, each viewed our tendencies toward bad as arising from the same structures that incline us toward good. Erikson specifically stated that goodness and sin arise out of the same basic processes preprogrammed into humans from creation/conception. In the developing child, sin emerges contemporaneously with will, the virtue associated with stage two. Erikson (1969) shored up his view of sin as emergent rather than structural by explicitly rejecting the "Calvinist sense" of original sin (p. 252). Bowlby focused on clinical dysfunction rather than sin but rooted his explanation for a muted conscience in caregivers' failure to foster the child's "natural behavioral disposition to comply with the wishes of the principle attachment figure" (Ainsworth & Bowlby, 1991, p. 338). Like Erikson, Bowlby (1951) went out of his way to juxtapose his theory of mental disturbance with theories "which stress constitutional and inherited factors, sometimes to the point of Calvinist predestination" (p. 13). Bandura believed that the self-system so inclined us toward good that we had to *reconstrue bad as good* in order to persist in bad.

In contrast, EP equips humans with *separate* neural structures, some inclining us toward good and some toward bad. By specifically hardwiring adaptations for bad, EP fails to recognize the qualitative distinction between *structural* good and *emergent* bad suggested in the Genesis origins narratives. However, if we do not require an instantaneous infusion of evil corresponding with the first act of human disobedience (as some Protestant depictions of the fall seem to do), adaptations for bad, selected over successive generations, provide a plausible scientific mechanism for how evil got inside us. Created/structural tendencies toward good, combined with learned/selected structural tendencies toward evil, are an interesting way to think about humans' inherent moral-ethical tendencies.

The only theorist to fail to equip us with moral-ethical "structures" was Skinner, who eschewed all specialized mental structures.

Learned tendencies. Four of the developmental theories also addressed humans' *learned* tendencies toward good and evil. Erikson, Bowlby, and Bandura all emphasized the need to combine parental warmth with the clear communication of standards. Bandura confirmed the utility of punishment *combined with* techniques that promote empathy and negative self-evaluation so that malefactors eventually become self-motivated to limit bad behavior. All three theorists believed that the internalization of parental standards *fostered* moral-ethical behavior. Erikson and Bandura wrote that parental standards should eventually be replaced with standards derived from more comprehensive ideological systems, and both had a positive view of religion as a source of such standards.

Skinner also recognized the value of ideological systems that help us articulate moral precepts, but he differed from Erikson, Bowlby, and Bandura in that he disavowed the internalization of standards as a *cause* of moral behavior. Skinner located all causal impetus outside the person, in histories of reinforcement. (We feel "right" after behaving in ways we know to be reinforcing, and "guilty" after behaving in ways we know to be punishable [Skinner, 1976a, pp. 69-70].) While Skinner's refusal to imbue humans with even *learned* causal inclinations is problematic for most Christians, I appreciate his presentation of the environment as a powerful influence on moral-ethical behavior. I also appreciate his holistic view of human nature (in contrast to some dualists' view of sin as a personified agent living inside a bodily shell).[1]

The only theory placing almost no emphasis on learned moral-ethical tendencies is EP. That is because EP emphasizes the environment of evolutionary adaptedness (EEA) as the context in which moral adaptations were selected, and views the current environment as having limited impact on moral inclinations. In contrast to the other four theories, it is difficult to apply EP to the *fostering* of moral-ethical tendencies.

AGENCY/ACCOUNTABILITY

In chapter four, I provided evidence that Scripture depicts humankind as powerful agents, accountable for ourselves and responsible for others. I also provided evidence that there are degrees of agency, and thus degrees of accountability and responsibility. Agency is limited by inherent and environmental constraints as well as the sovereignty of God. Articulating the relationship between agency and the determinants that limit agency is a major challenge for both theologians and psychologists. Developmental psychologists contribute to a Christian understanding of this relationship

---

[1]For an easy-to-read introduction to faith-based perspectives on monism and dualism, I recommend Moes and Tellinghuisen (2014), chaps. 3 and 4.

by offering a variety of concrete paradigms within which to consider the tension. Some offer specific techniques for increasing temporal agency.

Erikson (1975, p. 19) held that humans must reckon various determinants (e.g., irreversibly given attributes, our finiteness before God) with "the fact that one's own life is one's own responsibility" (1980, p. 104). As for "free will," we need to believe we have it in order to be psychologically healthy and behave responsibly as individuals and societies. Although I'm not entirely comfortable with Erikson's ready dismissal of the question of free will, I find his explicit psychological directive to *believe you have it, even if you don't* easier to assimilate than many theological presentations.[2] As previously stated, Jonathan Edwards reduced free will to a delusion (chap. 7, Critique D; see also John Calvin's exposition, chap. 4, note 3). Other Christians all but dismiss eschatological and temporal determinants to bolster a theology *centered* on free will. Unencumbered by the need to advance a specific theological tradition, Erikson offers Christians from *all* traditions an approach we can *apply* to help humankind temporally thrive.

Bandura also emphasized the psychological value of perceived agency, referring to social cognitive theory as "an agentic perspective." Bandura (1997) gave the environment more influence than the self but recognized that the environment could be intentionally constructed to build up self-efficacy as "the key factor of human agency" (p. 3). For example, Bandura collaborated to produce television serials where protagonists assumed responsibility for their own thriving, prompting viewers in developing countries to do the same.

Bandura's learning theory drew on some of the basic principles of learning identified by Skinner. Although Skinner's predilection for consistent rhetoric required him to depict humans as fully determined by our environment, Skinner also viewed humans as highly agentic. He saw constructed environments as the mechanism for science to shape a better future for all humankind. Particularly intriguing to me is the nursery at

---

[2]Erikson's dismissal is a bit like the compartmentalization for which I faulted EP. A difference concerns the attitude that each takes toward compartmentalization. Erikson encourages a pragmatic approach to human thriving as he acknowledges his inability to reconcile competing ideas. In contrast, EP explicitly encourages compartmentalization.

Walden Two, where three-year-olds are systematically taught to delay gratification with sugarcoated lollipops. Skinner's (1976a) declaration that "man can now control his own destiny" (p. 277) is heretical, but as someone who purports to be salt and light to the world, I find his fervor to improve the temporal world both inspiring and humbling.

Not surprisingly, the theorists who ascribe humans the most agency are the ones most explicitly concerned with accountability and responsibility. With his specification of an *inherent* moral sense in preschool and an ethical sense in adulthood (for some), Erikson helps us understand what individuals in various developmental stages should be held accountable and responsible for. As we mature, we should operate less out of an obedience mindset and more out of love of neighbor. We gain a better appreciation of *nurture's* contributions to accountability and responsibility from Skinner and Bandura. Both learning theorists called out structural factors that contribute to behavioral sin, and Bandura explicated many of the specific cognitive processes involved. This structural and psychological understanding engendered in them a rehabilitative stance toward perpetrators of sin. Skinner (1972) explicitly argued that a punishment orientation is rooted in the view of humans as free and thus responsible. He said that we must reexamine this orientation when "a scientific analysis reveals unsuspected controlling relations between behavior and environment" (p. 20). Although punishment is a prominent theme in the Old Testament, Jesus promotes a paradigmatic shift in the New Testament. Learning theories offer some concrete methods of realizing this shift.

Proponents of our other two theories, attachment and EP, are less manifestly concerned with agency, accountability, and responsibility. Bowlby is more concerned with clinical dysfunction. EP stresses that we ought not be too concerned by aspects of our nature that we cannot change. This might suggest that there is little to learn about agency/accountability from these two theories, but this is not the case. Both Bowlby and EP push us to consider whether functional agency and accountability might be limited by neural circuitry, hardwired to help us survive. EP proposes *universal* circuitry that putatively determines agency and accountability. Bowlby helps us understand how nature-intended circuitry can be miswired in an *individual* that does not experience a (species-typical) supportive environment during infancy.

Because attachment theory is one of the best explanations for extreme dysfunction resulting from specific deprivation, it is arguably the most useful developmental theory for Christians who take a missional approach to both preventing psychological dysfunction and preparing people for the kingdom of God. As explained in chapter six, depriving a child of a healthy early attachment relationship can hardwire a variety of adverse characteristics including muted conscience, emotional and behavioral sabotage of self and family, and the inability to feel/accept God's love. Knowledge of the importance of healthy early attachment should compel Christians to make its facilitation a top social priority, even when this can only be accomplished by placing parentless children with adoptive parents who do not share our faith, or voting for policies that provide poor families the necessary resources to meet young children's comprehensive needs. On the back end, knowledge of attachment theory can help communities who have taken in attachment-disturbed children understand why these children may be unresponsive to concerted parental attempts to socialize accountability and responsibility—and love these children despite their limited capacity for these essential human characteristics.

CONCLUSION

God reveals truth through both Scripture and nature (Rom 1:20). A Christian view of the person should be scaffolded by broad biblical principles and filled in with psychological knowledge that is compatible with these principles. Psychology can also help us discern more and less insightful interpretations of Scripture across historical epochs and traditions and appreciate how these interpretations play out in community life.

Of the developmental theorists in this book, Erikson and Bandura are generally the most helpful for filling in specific details about personhood. Many of their claims are very compatible with Christian perspectives on the temporal aspects of personhood. Wrestling with Skinner and Bowlby helps us understand intragroup dissension within Christian theology. (*What does it mean to say that sin is inherent? Do we have free will? Are there some who functionally can't be "made new" in this life?*) Detailed knowledge of the specific evolutionary perspective called EP is necessary to help Christians distinguish evolutionary perspectives that identify God as orchestrating evolution (or leave room for God) from those that explicitly disavow God and subjugate us to a Stone Age mind. Most developmental textbooks devote minimal if any attention to these critical distinctions in evolutionary perspectives. This obligates professors and therapists to serve as trusted experts for students and clients who may have been taught that a person cannot be a Christian and believe in evolution, especially for those on the verge of abandoning faith because of this perceived forced choice.

Christians are directed to love God with every aspect of our being. To love God with our minds, developmental psychologists must delve into both Christian theology and developmental theory, integrating and assimilating the truth that each offers us.

References

Ahearn, B. (2010, February 3). The radical in radical behaviorism. *Psychology Today.* www.psychologytoday.com/us/blog/radical-behaviorist/201002/the-radical-in-radical-behaviorism

Ainsworth, M. D. S., & Bowlby, J. (1991). 1989 APA award recipient address: An ethological approach to personality development. *American Psychologist, 46*(4), 333-41.

Applegate, K., & Stump, J. B. (Eds.). (2016). *How I changed my mind about evolution: Evangelicals reflect on faith and science.* IVP Academic.

Atran, S., & Norenzayan, A. (2004). Religion's evolutionary landscape: Counterintuition, commitment, compassion, communion. *Behavioral and Brain Sciences, 27*(6), 713-70.

Augustine. (1958). *City of God* (G. G. Walsh, D. B. Zema, G. Monahan, & D. J. Honan, Trans.). New York: Image.

Bandura, A. (n.d.). *Spirituality.* Albert Bandura. www.albertbandura.com/albert-bandura-spirituality.html

Bandura, A. (1973). *Aggression: A social learning analysis.* Prentice Hall.

Bandura, A. (1977). *Social learning theory.* Prentice Hall.

Bandura, A. (1978). The self-system in reciprocal determinism. *American Psychologist, 33*(4), 344-58.

Bandura, A. (1982). The psychology of chance encounters and life paths. *American Psychologist, 37*(7), 747-55.

Bandura, A. (1986). *Social foundations of thought and action: A social cognitive theory.* Prentice Hall.

Bandura, A. (1991). Social cognitive theory of moral thought and action. In W. M. Kurtines & J. L. Gewirtz (Eds.), *Handbook of moral behavior and development* (pp. 45-103). Erlbaum.

Bandura, A. (1994). Self-efficacy. In V. S. Ramachaudren (Ed.), *Encyclopedia of human behavior* (Vol. 4, pp. 71-81). Academic Press. www.uky.edu/~eushe2/Bandura/BanEncy

Bandura, A. (1995). Exercise of personal and collective efficacy in changing societies. In A. Bandura (Ed.), *Self-efficacy in changing societies* (pp. 1-45). Cambridge University Press.

Bandura, A. (1997). *Self-efficacy: The exercise of control.* W. H. Freeman.

Bandura, A. (1999). Social cognitive theory: An agentic perspective. *Asian Journal of Social Psychology, 2,* 21-41.

Bandura, A. (2001). Social cognitive theory: An agentic perspective. *Annual Review of Psychology, 52,* 1-26. www.uky.edu/~eushe2/Bandura/Bandura2001ARPr.pdf

Bandura, A. (2003). On the psychosocial impact and mechanisms of spiritual modeling. *International Journal for the Psychology of Religion, 13*(3), 167-73.

Bandura, A. (2006). Autobiography. In M. G. Lindzey & W. M. Runyan (Eds.), *A history of psychology in autobiography* (Vol. 9, pp. 42-75). American Psychological Association. http://professoralbertbandura.com/pdfs/Albert-Bandura-Autobiography.pdf

Bandura, A. (2015). *Moral disengagement: How people do harm and live with themselves.* Worth Publishers.

Bandura, A., & Walters, R. H. (1963). *Social learning and personality development.* Holt, Rinehart and Winston.

Barkow, J. H. (1992). Beneath new culture is old psychology: Gossip and social stratification. In J. H. Barkow, L. Cosmides, & J. Tooby (Eds.), *The adapted mind* (pp. 627-37). Oxford University Press.

Baumeister, R. F. (2009, February 15). Just exactly what is determinism? *Psychology Today.* www.psychologytoday.com/blog/cultural-animal/200902/just-exactly-what-is-determinism-0

BBC Radio 4 (2014, November 7). *The Libet experiment: Is free will just an illusion?* [Video]. YouTube. https://youtu.be/OjCt-L0Ph5o

Belsky, J. (2019). *Experiencing the lifespan.* New York: Worth.

Berger, K. S. (2017). *The developing person through the lifespan.* New York: Worth.

Bering, J. M. (2005). The evolutionary history of an illusion: Religious causal beliefs in children and adults. In B. J. Ellis & D. F. Bjorklund (Eds.), *Origins of the social mind: Evolutionary psychology and child development* (pp. 411-37). Guilford.

Bering, J. (2010). The nonexistent purpose of people. *The Psychologist, 23*(4), 290-93.

Bering, J. (2013, April 20). How I became a godless gay evolutionary psychologist. *Big Think.* https://bigthink.com/in-their-own-words/how-i-became-a-godless-gay-evolutionary-psychologist

Bernstein, E., Crandell, C., & Kitayama, S. (1994). Some neo-Darwinian decision rules for altruism: Weighing cures for inclusive fitness as a function of the biological importance of the decision. *Journal of Personality and Social Psychology, 67*, 773-89.

Bjork, D. W. (1997). *B. F. Skinner: A life.* HarperCollins.

Bjorklund, D. F., & Pelligrini, A. D. (2000). Child development and evolutionary psychology. *Child Development, 71*(6), 1687-1708.

Bjorklund, D. F., & Pelligrini, A. D. (2002). *The origins of human nature: Evolutionary developmental psychology.* Oxford University Press.

Børreson, K. E. (Ed.) (1991). *Image of God and gender models in Judaeo-Christian tradition.* Fortress Press.

Bowlby, J. (1947). Forty-four juvenile thieves: Their characters and home lives. *International Journal of Psychoanalysis, 25*(19-53), 107-27. (Original work presented 1944 and published 1946).

Bowlby, J. (1951). *Maternal care and mental health* (Vol. 2). World Health Organization.

Bowlby, J. (1958). The nature of the child's tie to his mother. *International Journal of Psychoanalysis, 39*(5), 350-73.

Bowlby, J. (1960). Grief and mourning in infancy and early childhood. *The Psychoanalytic Study of the Child, 15,* 9-52.

Bowlby, J. (1969). *Attachment and loss: Vol. 1. Attachment.* Basic Books. (Reprinted by Penguin Books, 1971; 2nd ed. 1982).

Bowlby, J. (1973). *Attachment and loss: Vol. 2. Separation: Anxiety and anger.* Basic Books.

Bowlby, J. (1979). *The making and breaking of affectional bonds.* Tavistock Publications.

Bowlby, J. (1980). *Attachment and loss: Vol. 3. Loss: Sadness and depression.* Basic Books.

Bowlby, J. (1988). Developmental psychiatry comes of age. *The American Journal of Psychiatry, 145*(1), 1-10.

Bretherton, I. (1991). The roots and growing points of attachment theory. In C. M. Parkes, J. Stevenson-Hinde, & P. Marris (Eds.), *Attachment across the life cycle.* [Kindle]. London: Routledge. https://doi.org/10.4324/9780203132470

Brown, L. B. (2007). *Original Sin.* www.whyislam.org/common-ground/original-sin/

Brown, W. S., Murphy, N., & Malony H. N. (Eds.). (1998). *Whatever happened to the soul? Scientific and theological portraits of human nature.* Augsburg Fortress.

Brueggemann, W. (1982). *Genesis.* John Knox Press.

Bufford, R. K. (1981). *The human reflex: Behavioral psychology in biblical perspective.* Harper & Row.

Buller, D. J. (2005). Evolutionary psychology: The emperor's new paradigm. *Trends in Cognitive Sciences, 9*(6), 277-83. https://doi.org/10.1016/j.tics.2005.04.003

Burston, D. (2007). *Erik Erikson and the American psyche: Ego, ethics, and evolution.* Jason Aronson.

Buss, D. (1981). Sex differences in the evaluation and performance of dominant acts. *Journal of Personality and Social Psychology, 40*(1), 147-54.

Buss, D. (2004). *Evolutionary psychology: The new science of the mind.* Allyn and Bacon.

Buss, D. (2005). Introduction: The emergence of evolutionary psychology. In D. Buss (Ed.), *The handbook of evolutionary psychology* (pp. xxiii-xxv). John Wiley & Sons.

Buss, D. (2006). The evolution of love. In R. J. Sternberg & K. Weise (Eds.), *The new psychology of love* (pp. 65-86). Yale University Press.

Buss, D. M., & Barnes, M. (1986). Preferences in mate selection. *Journal of Personality and Social Psychology, 50,* 559-70.

Buss, D. M., Haselton, M. G., Shackelford, T. K., Bleske, A. L., & Wakefield, J. C. (1998). Adaptations, exaptations, and spandrels. *American Psychologist, 53*(5), 533-48.

Buss, D. M., Larsen, R. J., Weston, D., & Semmelroth, J. (1992). Sex differences in jealousy: Evolution, physiology, and psychology. *Psychological Science, 3,* 251-55.

Carton, B. (1998, February 17). Striking behavior. *Wall Street Journal,* A1, A8.

Catholic Church. (1997). *Catechism of the Catholic Church* (2nd ed.). www .scborromeo2.org/catechism-of-the-catholic-church

Cherry, K. (2016). B. F. Skinner biography (1904–1990). *Verywell Mind.* www .verywell.com/b-f-skinner-biography-1904-1990-2795543

Cherry, K. (2017). How social learning theory works: A closer look at how people learn through observation. *Verywell Mind.* www.verywellmind.com/social-learning -theory-2795074

Cherry, K. (2019, July 29). 10 influential psychologists: A look at eminent thinkers in psychology. *Verywell Mind.* www.verywellmind.com/most-influential -psychologists-2795264

Chirban, J. T. (2014, September 1). B. F. Skinner's struggle with God: The journal of a truth seeker. *Psychology Today.* www.psychologytoday.com/blog/alive-inside /201409/b-f-skinner-s-struggle-god

Chryssavgis, J. (1992). Original sin—an Orthodox perspective. Appendix to N. Ormerod, *Grace and disgrace: A theology of self-esteem, society, and history* (pp. 197-206). E. J. Dwyer.

Clark, R. D., & Hatfield, E. (1989). Gender differences in receptivity to sexual offers. *Journal of Personality and Human Sexuality, 2*(1), 39-55.

Cohen, S. Marc. (2016). Aristotle's metaphysics. In E. N. Zalta (Ed.), *The Stanford encyclopedia of philosophy* (Winter 2016 ed.). Stanford University. https://plato .stanford.edu/archives/win2016/entries/aristotle-metaphysics

Concord Media (2014, July 1). *A two year old goes to hospital (Robertson Films)* [Video]. YouTube. https://youtu.be/sl4Q-_Bxc_U

Cooper, J. W. (1989). *Body, soul, and life everlasting: Biblical anthropology and the monism-dualism debate.* Eerdmans.

Cosmides, L., & Tooby, J. (1997). The modular nature of human intelligence. In A. B. Scheibel & J. W. Schopf (Eds.), *The Origin and Evolution of Intelligence* (pp. 71-101). Jones and Bartlett Learning.

Cosmides, L., & Tooby, J. (2004). Knowing thyself: The evolutionary psychology of moral reasoning and moral sentiments. In R. E. Freeman and P. Werhane (Eds.), *Business, Science, and Ethics* (pp. 91-127). Society for Business Ethics.

Cosmides, L., Tooby, J., & Barkow, J. H. (1992). Introduction: Evolutionary psychology and conceptual integration. In J. H. Barkow, L. Cosmides, & J. Tooby (Eds.), *The adapted mind: Evolutionary psychology and the generation of culture* (pp. 3-15). Oxford University Press.

Couenhoven, J. (2005). St. Augustine's doctrine of original sin. *Augustinian Studies, 36*(2), 359-96.

Cover, R. C. (1992). Sin, sinners: Old Testament. In D. N. Freedman (Ed.), *The Anchor Bible dictionary* (Vol. 6, pp. 31-40). Yale University Press.

Cummins, D. D. (1998). Social norms and other minds: The evolutionary roots of higher cognition. In D. D. Cummins & C. Allen (Eds.) *The evolution of mind* (pp. 30–50). Oxford University Press.

Cragg, K. (1984). *Muhammad and the Christian: A Question of Response.* Orbis.

Cummins, D. (2005). Dominance, status, and social hierarchies. In D. Buss (Ed.), *The handbook of evolutionary psychology* (pp. 676-96). John Wiley and Sons.

Daly, M. (1991). Natural selection doesn't have goals, but it's the reason organisms do. *Behavioral and Brain Sciences, 14*(2), 219-20.

Daly, M., & Wilson, M. (1988). *Homicide.* Taylor & Francis.

Daly, M., & Wilson, M. (1994). Comment on "Can selfishness save the environment?" *Human Ecology Review, 1,* 42-45.

Daly, M., & Wilson, M. (2002). Progress and evolution. In C. L. Anderson & J. W. Looney (Eds.), *Making progress: Essays in progress and public policy* (pp. 67-77). Lexington Books.

Darwin, C. (1859). *On the origins of species.* John Murray.

Darwin, C., & Murray, J. (1871). *The descent of man: And selection in relation to sex.* London: John Murray, Albemarle Street.

Darwin, P. (1887). *The life and letters of Charles Darwin* (Vol. 1). D. Appleton.

Dawkins, R. (1996). *The blind watchmaker.* Norton.

Dawkins, R. (2003). *A devil's chaplain: Reflections on hope, lies, science, and love.* Houghton Mifflin Harcourt.

Dawkins, R. (2006). *The selfish gene* (30th anniversary ed.). Oxford University Press.

Demorest, A. (2005). *Psychology's grand theorists: How personal experience shaped professional ideas.* Lawrence Erlbaum.

Denzinger, H. (1957). *The sources of Catholic dogma* (R. J. Deferrari, Trans.). Herder.

Drury, S. S., Gleason, M. M., Theal, K., Smyke, A. T., Nelson, C. A., Fox, N. A., & Zeneah, C. H. (2012). Genetic sensitivity to the caregiving context: The influence of 5httlpr and BDNF val66met on indiscriminate social behavior. *Physiological Behavior, 106*(5), 728-35. https://doi.org/10.1016/j.physbeh.2011.11.014

Dunn, J. D. G. (1988). *Romans 1–8.* Word Books.

Erickson, M. J. (2001). *Introducing Christian doctrine* (2nd ed.). Baker Book House.

Erikson, E. H. (1962). *Young man Luther.* Norton.

Erikson, E. H. (1963a). *Childhood and society.* Norton.

Erikson, E. H. (1963b). The Golden Rule and the Cycle of Life. In R. W. White (Ed.), *The Study of Lives* (pp. 410-28). Aldine Atherton.

Erikson, E. H. (1964). *Insight and responsibility: Lectures on the ethical implications of psychoanalytic insight.* Norton.

Erikson, E. H. (1966). The concept of identity in race relations: Notes and queries. *Daedalus, 95*(1), 145-71. www.jstor.org/stable/20026970

Erikson, E. H. (1968). *Identity, youth and crisis.* Norton.

Erikson, E. H. (1969). *Gandhi's truth: On the origins of militant nonviolence.* Norton.

Erikson, E. H. (1974). *Dimensions of a new identity.* Norton.

Erikson, E. H. (1975). *Life history and the historical moment: Diverse presentations.* Norton.

Erikson, E. H. (1980). *Identity and the life cycle.* Norton. (Original work published 1959)

Erikson, E. H. (1996). The Galilean sayings and the sense of "I." *Psychoanalysis and Contemporary Thought, 19*(2), 291-337.

Erikson, E. H., & Erikson, J. M. (1997) *The life cycle completed* (extended version). Norton.

Erikson, E. H., Erikson, J. M., & Kivnick, H. Q. (1989). *Vital involvement in old age.* Norton.

Evans, R. I. (1968). *B. F. Skinner: The man and his ideas.* E. P. Dutton.

Evans, R. I. (1989). *Albert Bandura: The man and his ideas—a dialogue.* Praeger.

Everhard, M. (2016, March 18). Freedom of the will: synopsis. *Jonathan Edwards Studies*. https://edwardsstudies.com/2016/03/18/freedom-of-the-will-synopsis/

Foster, C. (2006, September/October). Confidence man. *Stanford Magazine*. https://alumni.stanford.edu/get/page/magazine/article/?article_id=33332

Fowler, J. W. (1981). *Stages of faith: The psychology of human development and the quest for meaning*. Harper & Row.

Freddoso, A. J. (Trans.). (n.d.). *New English translation of St. Thomas Aquinas's Summa Theologiae: Part 1*. www3.nd.edu/~afreddos/summa-translation/Part%20I/st1-ques93.pdf

Garcia, J., & Koelling, R. A. (1966). Relation of cue to consequence in avoidance learning. *Psychonomic Science, 4,* 123-24.

Garr, W. R. (2003). *In his own image and likeness: Humanity, divinity, and monotheism*. Brill.

Gaulin, S. J. C., & McBurney, D. H. (2004). *Evolutionary psychology* (2nd ed.). Pearson.

Gender Spectrum. (n.d.). *Understanding gender*. www.genderspectrum.org/quick-links/understanding-gender

Gendzel, G. (2010). Resisting McCarthyism: To sign or not sign California's loyalty oath [Review essay]. *California Legal History, 5,* 349-58. http://scholarworks.sjsu.edu/cgi/viewcontent.cgi?article=1004&context=hist_pub

Gl0balElite. (2009, June 18). *B. F. Skinner—operant conditioning and free will* [Video]. YouTube. https://youtu.be/yhvaSEJtOV8

Goode, E. (2021, July 29). Albert Bandura, leading psychologist of aggression, dies at 95. *The New York Times*. www.nytimes.com/2021/07/29/science/albert-bandura-dead.html

Görlach, A. (2013). Morality and the self: Interview with A. Bandura. *The European*. www.theeuropean-magazine.com/946-bandura-albert/947-morality-and-the-self

Gorter, B. A., Helder, E. J., Oh, Y. I, & Gunnoe, M. L. (2017). Are disinhibited social behaviors among internationally adopted children mediated by attachment environment or by children's difficulties with inhibitory control? *Adoption Quarterly, 20*(4), 291-308.

Gould, S. J. (1992). Impeaching a self-appointed judge. *Scientific American, 267*(1), 118-21.

Granqvist, P., & Dickie, J. R. (2006). Attachment and spiritual development in childhood and adolescence. In E. C. Roehlkepartain, P. E. King, L. Wagener, & P. L. Benson (Eds.), *The handbook of spiritual development in childhood and adolescence* (pp. 197-210). Sage.

Grosskurth, P. (1986). *Melanie Klein: Her world and her work*. Alfred A. Knopf.

Gunnoe, M. L. (2003). Two models of Christian marriage: Scripture, social science, and the question of hierarchy vs. partnership. In S. W. VanderStoep (Ed.), *Science of the soul: Christian perspectives on psychological research* (pp. 269-302). University Press of America.

Haarsma, D. B., & Haarsma, L. D. (2007). *Origins: A Reformed look at creation, design, and evolution.* Faith Alive.

Haarsma, D. B., & Haarsma, L. D. (2011). *Origins: Christian perspectives on creation, design, and evolution.* Faith Alive.

Hagen, E. H. (2005). Controversial issues in evolutionary psychology. In D. Buss (Ed.), *The handbook of evolutionary psychology* (pp. 145-73). John Wiley & Sons.

Haggbloom, S. J., Warnick, R., Warnick, J. E., Jones, V. K., Yarbrough, G. L., Russell, T. M., Borecky, C. M., McGahhey, R., Powell, J. L., III, Beavers, J., & Monte, E. (2002). The 100 most eminent psychologists of the 20th century. *Review of General Psychology 6*(2), 139-52. http://creativity.ipras.ru/texts/top100.pdf

Haight, J. F. (2002). *God after Darwin.* Westview Press.

Hall, E. (1972, November). Will success spoil B. F. Skinner? *Psychology Today.* (Printed conversation adapted from filmed interviews available from CRM Films Division, Del Mar, California, 92014.)

Hall, T. W., & Maltby, L. E. (2014). Attachment-based psychotherapy and Christianity. In E. D. Bland and B. D. Strawn (Eds.), *Christianity and psychoanalysis: A new conversation.* IVP Academic.

Hamilton, W. D. (1964). The genetical evolution of social behavior I and II. *Journal of Theoretical Biology, 7,* 1-52.

Hardon, J. A. (1999). Preternatural gifts. In *Modern Catholic dictionary.* Eternal Life. www.catholicculture.org/culture/library/dictionary/index.cfm?id=35763

Harris, C. R. (2002). Sexual and romantic jealousy in heterosexual and homosexual adults. *Psychological Science, 13*(1), 7-12.

Heidelberg Catechism. (1563). Christian Reformed Church. www.crcna.org/sites/default/files/HeidelbergCatechism.pdf

Hoare, C. H. (2002). *Erikson on development in adulthood: New insights from the unpublished papers.* Oxford University Press.

Hoekema, A. A. (1986). *Created in God's image.* Eerdmans.

Hogan, R. (1983). A socioanalytic theory of personality. In M. Page and R. Dienstbier (Eds.), *Nebraska symposium on motivation, 1982* (pp. 55-89). University of Nebraska Press.

Hogan, R. (2011, October 13). Self-deception and evolutionary theory. *Hogan Assessments.* www.hoganassessments.com/self-deception-and-evolutionary-theory

Holmes, J. (1993). *John Bowlby and attachment theory*. Routledge.

Hopko, T. (2016). Sin. In *The Orthodox Faith: Vol. 1. Doctrine and Scripture*. SVS Press. https://oca.org/orthodoxy/the-orthodox-faith/doctrine-scripture/the-symbol-of-faith/sin

Jacobs, J., & Eisenstein, J. D. (1906). Sin. In *Jewish encyclopedia*. www.jewishencyclopedia.com/articles/13761-sin

Joachim, R. L. (1984). *Relationship between four temperament types and nineteen spiritual gifts*. Dissertations. 470. https://digitalcommons.andrews.edu/dissertations/470

Johnson, E. L. (2017). *God & soul care: The therapeutic resources of Christian faith*. InterVarsity Press.

Joubert, C. (2012). Evolutionary psychology: Why it fails as a science and is dangerous. *Answers Research Journal, 5*, 231-32. https://answersresearchjournal.org/evolutionary-psychology-dangerous/

Joyce, R. (2006). *Evolution of morality*. MIT Press.

Kagan, J. (1984). *The nature of the child*. Basic Books.

Kalma, A. (1991). Hierarchisation and dominance assessment at first glance. *European Journal of Psychology, 21*(2), 165-81.

Kenrick, D. T., Gabrielidis, C., Keefe, R. C., & Cornelius, J. S. (1996). Adolescents' age preferences for dating partners: Support for an evolutionary model of life-history strategies. *Child Development, 67*(4), 1499-511. https://doi.org/10.2307/1131714

Kidd, C., Palmeri, H., & Aslin, R.N. (2013). Rational snacking: Young children's decision-making on the marshmallow task is moderated by beliefs about environmental reliability. *Cognition, 126*(1), 109-14. https://doi.org/10.1016/j.cognition.2012.08.004

Kohlberg, L. (1976). Moral stages and moralization: The cognitive-development approach. In T. Likona (Ed.), *Moral development and behavior*. Holt, Rinehart and Winston.

Korn, J., Davis, R., & Davis, S. (1991). Historians' and chairpersons' judgments of eminence among psychologists. *American Psychologist, 46*, 789-92.

Kramer, B. (2018, August 8). *Famous Christians who believed evolution is compatible with Christian faith*. BioLogos. https://biologos.org/articles/famous-christians-who-believed-evolution-is-compatible-with-christian-faith/

Larsen, R. J., & Buss, D. M. (2014). *Personality psychology: Domains of knowledge about human nature* (5th ed.). McGraw Hill Educational.

Larson, E. J. (2004). Evolution: The remarkable history of a scientific theory. New York: Modern Library.

Leclerc-Madlala, S. (2002). On the virgin cleansing myth: Gendered bodies, AIDS and ethnomedicine. *African Journal of AIDS Research, 1*(2), 87-95. https://doi.org/10.2989/16085906.2002.9626548

Lewis, C. S. (1942). *The Screwtape letters*. London: Geoffrey Bles.

Libet, B. (1985). Unconscious cerebral initiative and the role of conscious will in voluntary action. *Behavioral and Brain Sciences, 8*(4), 529-39.

Libet, B. (1999). Do we have free will? *Journal of Consciousness Studies, 6*(8-9), 47-57.

Lindbeck, G. A. (1973). Erikson's young man Luther: A historical and theological appraisal. *Soundings, 56*(2), 210-27.

Luther, M. (1958). *Luther's works: Vol. 1. Genesis chapters 1–5* (J. Pelikan, Ed.). Concordia Publishing House.

MacKay, D. M. (1986). Brain research and human responsibility. In S. L. Jones (Ed.), *Psychology and the Christian faith: An introductory reader* (pp. 34-50). Baker Book House.

Mann, M. H. (2006). *Perfecting grace: Holiness, human being, and the sciences*. T&T Clark International.

Martin, J. (2017). Carl Rogers' and B. F. Skinner's approaches to personal and societal improvement: A study in the psychological humanities. *Journal of Theoretical and Philosophical Psychology, 37*(4), pp. 214-29. https://doi.org/10.1037/teo0000072

Mayr, E. (1983). How to carry out an adaptationist program. *The American Naturalist, 121*, 324-34.

McKim, D. K. (Ed.). (2001). *Calvin's institutes: Abridged edition*. Westminster John Knox Press.

Milgram, S. (1974). *Obedience to authority*. Harper & Row.

Middleton, J. R. (2005). *The liberating image: The imago Dei in Genesis 1*. Brazos Press.

Middleton, J. R. (2006). A new heaven and a new earth: The case for a holistic reading of the biblical story of redemption. *Journal for Christian Theological Research, 11*, 73-97.

Mischel, W., Ayduk, O., Berman, M. G., Casey, B. J., Gotlib, I. H., Jonides, J., Kross, E., Teslovich, T., Wilson, N. L., Zayas, V., & Shoda, Y. (2010). 'Willpower' over the lifespan: Decomposing self-regulation. *Social Cognitive and Affective Neuroscience, 6*(2), 252-56. https://doi.org/10.1093/scan/nsq081

Moes, P., & Tellinghuisen, D. J. (2014). *Exploring psychology and Christian faith*. Baker Academic.

Mooney, C. G. (2010). *Theories of attachment: An introduction to Bowlby, Ainsworth, Gerber, Brazelton, Kennell & Klaus*. Redleaf Press.

Moore, J. (2001). On distinguishing methodological from radical behaviorism. *European Journal of Behavior Analysis, 2*(2), 221-44. https://doi.org/10.1080/15021149.2001.11434196

Morgan, C. L. (1894). *An introduction to comparative psychology*. London: Walter Scott, Ltd.

Mueller, J. T. (1976). *Commentary on the Epistle to the Romans by Martin Luther*. Kregel.

Myers, D. G., & DeWall, C. N. (2018). *Psychology in Modules* (12th ed). Worth Publishers.

Neusner, J., & Green, W. S. (Eds.). (1996). *Dictionary of Judaism in the biblical period: 450 BCE to 600 CE* (Vol. 2). Simon & Schuster.

On this day. (1994, May 13). *New York Times*. www.nytimes.com/learning/general /onthisday/bday/0615.html

Ormerod, N. (1992). *Grace and disgrace: A theology of self-esteem, society, and history*. E. J. Dwyer.

Oxford University Press. (n.d.). Behaviourism. In *Oxford English online dictionary*. Retrieved October 2, 2021 from https://en.oxforddictionaries.com/definition /behaviourism

NHS Foundation Trust. (n.d.). John Bowlby 1907–1990. https://tavistockandportman .nhs.uk/about-us/celebrating-100-years-tavistock-and-portman/john-bowlby -1907-1990/

Pajares, F. (2004). Albert Bandura: Biographical sketch. Albert Bandura. https:// albertbandura.com/bandura-bio-pajares/albert-bandura-bio-sketch.html

Paley, W. (1837). *Natural theology; or, evidences of the existence and attributes of the Deity*. Gould, Kendall and Lincoln. https://books.google.com/books?id=VURKAAAAYAAJ

Payne, F. E. (2003). Consciously exploring the unconscious: Hoping for some clarity! *Journal of Biblical Ethics in Medicine, 9*(1). https://bmei.org/consciously-exploring -the-unconscious-hoping-for-some-clarity/

Peterson, J. (2010). *Changing human nature: Ecology, ethics, genes and God*. Eerdmans.

Pinker, S. (1997). *How the mind works*. W. W. Norton.

Pinker, S. (2005). Foreword. In D. Buss (Ed.), *The handbook of evolutionary psychology* (pp. xi-xvi). John Wiley and Sons.

Pinker, S. (2011). *The better angels of our nature: Why violence has declined*. Viking.

Piper, J., & Grudem, W. (1991). *Recovering Biblical manhood and womanhood: A response to evangelical feminism*. Crossway Books.

Plantinga, C., Jr. (2002). *Engaging God's world: A Reformed vision of faith, learning, and living*. Eerdmans.

Randall, R. (2019, November 26). Wayne Grudem changes mind about divorce in cases of abuse. *Christianity Today*. www.christianitytoday.com/news/2019 /november/complementarian-wayne-grudem-ets-divorce-after-abuse.html

Polkinghorne, J. (1998). *Belief in God in an age of science*. New Haven, CT: Yale University Press.

Reeves, C. (2005). A duty to care: Reflections on the influence of Bowlby and Winnicott on the 1948 Children Act. In J. Issroff (Ed.), *Donald Winnicott and John Bowlby: Personal and professional perspectives* (pp. 179-207). Karnac Books.

Richardson, R. C. (2007). *Evolutionary psychology as maladapted psychology.* MIT Press.

Rizutto, A. M. (1980). The psychological foundations of belief in God. In C. Brusselmans (Ed.), *Toward moral and religious maturity* (pp. 115-35). Silver Burdett.

Ruse, M. (2003, November–December). Through a glass, darkly [Review of *A devil's chaplain: Reflections on hope, lies, science, and love,* by R. Dawkins]. *American Scientist, 91*(6), 554-56. www.jstor.org/stable/27858307

Rutter, M., Colvert, E., Kreppner, J., Beckett, C., Castle, J., Groothues, C., & Sonuga-Barke, E. (2007). Early adolescent outcomes for institutionally deprived and non-deprived adoptees. I: Disinhibited attachment. *Journal of Child Psychology and Psychiatry, 48*(1), 17-30.

Sadalla, E. K., Kendrik, D. T., & Vershure, B. (1987). Dominance and heterosexual attraction. *Journal of Personality and Social Psychology, 52*(4), 730-738.

Sanders, E. P. (1992). Sin, sinners: New Testament. In D. N. Freedman (Ed.), *The Anchor Bible dictionary* (Vol. 6, pp. 40-47). Yale University Press.

Schaeffer, F. A. (2010). *Genesis in time and space.* InterVarsity Press.

Schneewind, K. A. (1995). Impact of family processes on control beliefs. In A. Bandura (Ed.), *Self-efficacy in changing societies* (pp. 114-48). Cambridge University Press.

Schneider, S. M., & Morris, E. K. (1987). A history of the term radical behaviorism: From Watson to Skinner. *The Behavior-Analyst, 10*(1), 27-39.

Schwöbel, C. (2006). Recovering human dignity. In R. K. Soulen & L. Woodhead (Eds.), *God and human dignity* (pp. 44-58). Eerdmans.

Shapiro, F. (2008, July–August). Who wrote the sinner's prayer? Yale Alumni Magazine. https://yalealumnimagazine.com/articles/2143

Silverman, I., & Choi, J. (2005). Locating places. In D. Buss (Ed.), *The handbook of evolutionary psychology* (pp. 177-99). John Wiley & Sons.

Singh, D. (1993). Adaptive significance of waist-to-hip ratio and female physical attractiveness. *Journal of Personality and Social Psychology, 65,* 293-307.

Skinner, B. F. (1938). *The behavior of organisms: An experimental analysis.* Appleton-Century.

Skinner, B. F. (1953). *Science and human behavior.* Macmillan.

Skinner, B. F. (1956). A case history in scientific method. *American Psychologist, 11*(5), 221-33.

Skinner, B. F. (1957). *Verbal Behavior.* Appleton-Century-Crofts.

Skinner, B. F. (1964). Behaviorism at fifty. In W. T. Wann (Ed.), *Behaviorism and phenomenology: Contrasting bases for modern psychology* (pp. 79-109). University of Chicago Press.

Skinner, B. F. (1972). *Beyond freedom and dignity.* Alfred A. Knopf.

Skinner, B. F. (1976a). *About behaviorism.* Random House.

Skinner, B. F. (1976b). *Particulars of my life.* Alfred A. Knopf.

Skinner, B. F. (1976c). *Walden Two.* Macmillan.

Skinner, B. F. (1979). *The shaping of a behaviorist* (pp. 31-32). Knopf.

Skinner, B. F. (1983). *A matter of consequences: Part three of an autobiography.* Alfred A. Knopf.

Smith, D. L. (1994). *With willful intent: A theology of sin.* Victor Books.

Smith, M. S. (2010). *The priestly vision of Genesis 1.* Fortress Press.

Sparrow, J. (2015, November 29). We can save atheism from the new atheists like Richard Dawkins and Sam Harris. *The Guardian.* www.theguardian.com /commentisfree/2015/nov/30/we-can-save-atheism-from-the-new-atheists

Sroufe, A., & Waters, E. (1977). Attachment as an organizational construct. *Child Development, 48,* 1184-99.

Stove, D. (1995). *Darwinian fairytales.* Encounter Books.

Sullivan, J. E. (1963). *The image of God: The doctrine of St. Augustine and its influence.* Priority Press.

Tatum, B. D. (1997). *Why are all the Black kids sitting together in the cafeteria?* Basic Books.

Taylor, S. (2014, December 9). How valid is evolutionary psychology? *Psychology Today.* www.psychologytoday.com/us/blog/out-the-darkness/201412/how-valid -is-evolutionary-psychology

Thomas, R. M., Jr. (1997, August 8). Joan Erikson is dead at 95; shaped thought on life cycles. *New York Times.* www.nytimes.com/1997/08/08/us/joan-erikson-is-dead -at-95-shaped-thought-on-life-cycles.html

Timpe, Kevin "Sin in Christian Thought," *The Stanford Encyclopedia of Philosophy* (Summer 2021 Edition), Edward N. Zalta (ed.), https://plato.stanford.edu /archives/sum2021/entries/sin-christian/

Tooby, J., & Cosmides, L. (1990). On the universality of human nature and the uniqueness of the individual: The role of genetics and adaptation. *Journal of Personality, 58*(1), 17-67.

Tooby, J., & Cosmides, L. (1992). The psychological foundations of culture. In J. Barkow, L. Cosmides, & J. Tooby (Eds.), *The adapted mind: Evolutionary psychology and the generation of culture* (pp. 19-136). Oxford University Press.

Tooby, J., & Cosmides, L. (2005). Conceptual foundations of evolutionary psychology. In D. Buss (Ed.), *The handbook of evolutionary psychology* (pp. 5-67). John Wiley & Sons.

Tooby, J., & Cosmides, L. (2006). Toward mapping the evolved functional organization of mind and brain. In E. Sober (Ed.), *Conceptual Issues in Evolutionary Biology* (3rd ed., pp. 176-95). Bradford Books.

Townsend, J. M., & Levy, G. D. (1990). Effects of partners' physical attractiveness and socioeconomic status on sexuality and partner selection. *Archives of Sexual Behavior, 19,* 149-64.

Trivers, R. (1971). The evolution of reciprocal altruism. *Quarterly Review of Biology, 46,* 35-57.

Trivers, R. (1972). Parental investment and sexual selection. In B. Campbell (Ed.), *Sexual Selection and the Descent of Man: 1871–1971* (pp. 136-79). Aldine.

Trivers, R. (1974). Parent-offspring conflict. *American Zoologist, 14,* 249-64.

Trivers, R. (1985). *Social evolution.* Benjamin/Cummings.

van Dijken, S. (1994). *John Bowlby: His early life; A biographical journey into the roots of attachment theory.* Free Association Books.

van IJzendoorn, M. H., & Kroonenberg, P. M. (1988). Cross-cultural patterns of attachment: A meta-analysis of the strange situation. *Child Development, 59,* 147-56.

Van Leeuwen, M. S. (2002). *My brother's keeper: What the social sciences do (and don't) tell us about masculinity.* InterVarsity Press.

Van Vliet, J. (2009). *Children of God: The imago Dei in John Calvin and his context.* Vandenhoeck & Ruprecht.

VanderLaan, D., Ren, Z., & Vasey, P. (2013). Male androphilia in the ancestral environment: An ethnological analysis. *Human Nature, 24*(4), 375-401. https://doi.org/10.1007/s12110-013-9182-z

Venema, D. R., & McKnight, S. (2017). *Adam and the genome: Reading scripture after genetic science.* Brazos Press.

Wainwright, W. "Jonathan Edwards." In E. N. Zalta (Ed.), *The Stanford encyclopedia of philosophy* (Winter 2016 ed.). Stanford University. https://plato.stanford.edu/archives/win2016/entries/edwards/

Warners, D. P., & Heun, M. K. (Eds.). (2019). *Beyond stewardship: New approaches to creation care.* Calvin College Press.

Watson, J. B. (1913). Psychology as the behaviorist views it. *Psychological Review, 20*(2), 158-77.

Westminster Shorter Catechism (1647). www.apuritansmind.com/westminster-standards/shorter-catechism/

Williams, G. C. (1966). *Adaptation and natural selection: A critique of some current evolutionary thought.* Princeton University Press.

Wilson, E. O. (1975). *Sociobiology: The new synthesis.* Belknap Press.

Wilson, E. O. (1978). *On human nature.* Harvard University Press.

Wilson, E. O. (1998, April). The biological basis of morality. *The Atlantic.* www .theatlantic.com/magazine/archive/1998/04/the-biological-basis-of-morality /377087/

Winnicott, D. W. (1971). *Playing and reality.* New York: Basic Books.

Zimmerman, A. (1998). *Evolution and the sin in Eden: A new Christian synthesis.* University Press of America.

Zock, H. (1990). *A psychology of ultimate concern: Erik Erikson's contribution to the psychology of religion.* Rodipi.

General Index

Bold indicates a definition

Scripture Index

CAPS